Praise for
50 Psychology Classics

"At long last a chance for those outside the profession to discover that there is so much more to psychology than just Freud and Jung. *50 Psychology Classics* offers a unique opportunity to become acquainted with a dazzling array of the key works in psychological literature almost overnight."

Dr Raj Persaud
Gresham Professor for Public Understanding of Psychiatry

"This delightful book provides thoughtful and entertaining summaries of 50 of the most influential books in psychology. It's a 'must read' for students contemplating a career in psychology."

VS Ramachandran MD PhD, *Professor and Director,*
Center for Brain and Cognition, University of California, San Diego

"A brilliant synthesis. The author makes complex ideas accessible and practical, without dumbing down the material. I found myself over and over thinking, 'Oh, that's what that guy meant.'"

Douglas Stone, lecturer on law at Harvard Law School
and co-author of **Difficult Conversations**

"Butler-Bowdon writes with infectious enthusiasm... he is a true scholar of this type of literature."

USA Today

50 Psychology Classics

Who we are, how we think, what we do

Insight and inspiration from 50 key books

Tom Butler-Bowdon

NICHOLAS BREALEY
PUBLISHING

LONDON · BOSTON

First published by
Nicholas Brealey Publishing in 2007
Reprinted in 2007 (twice), 2008 (twice), 2009 (twice), 2010, 2011

3–5 Spafield Street   20 Park Plaza, Suite 1115A
Clerkenwell, London   Boston
EC1R 4QB, UK   MA 02116, USA
Tel: +44 (0)20 7239 0360   Tel: (888) BREALEY
Fax: +44 (0)20 7239 0370   Fax: (617) 523 3708

www.nicholasbrealey.com
www.butler-bowdon.com

© Tom Butler-Bowdon 2007
The right of Tom Butler-Bowdon to be identified as the author of this work
has been asserted in accordance with the Copyright, Designs and Patents Act
1988.

ISBN 978-1-85788-386-2

Library of Congress Cataloguing-in-Publication Data

Butler-Bowdon, Tom, 1967–
  50 psychology classics.
    p. cm.
  ISBN-13: 978-1-85788-386-2
  ISBN-10: 1-85788-386-1
  1. Psychological literature. I. Title. II. Title: Fifty psychology classics.

  BF76.8.B88 2007
  150--dc22

2006026586

British Library Cataloguing in Publication Data
A catalogue record for this book is available from the British Library.

Printed in Finland by Bookwell.

For Cherry

Alfred Adler   Gavin de Becker   Eric Berne

Robert Bolton   *Edward de Bono*   Nathaniel Branden

Isabel Briggs Myers   Louann Brizendine   *David D. Burns*

Robert Cialdini   Mihaly Csikszentmihalyi   **Albert Ellis**

Robert A. Harper   *Milton Erickson*   Erik Erikson

Hans Eysenck   **Susan Forward**   Viktor Frankl

Anna Freud   SIGMUND FREUD   *Howard Gardner*

Daniel Gilbert   *Malcolm Gladwell*   Daniel Goleman

John M. Gottman   **Harry Harlow**   *Thomas A. Harris*

Eric Hoffer   KAREN HORNEY   William James

Carl Jung   Alfred Kinsey   *Melanie Klein*

R. D. Laing   **Abraham Maslow**   Stanley Milgram

Anne Moir   David Jessel   IVAN PAVLOV

Fritz Perls   *Jean Piaget*   **Steven Pinker**

V. S. Ramachandran   **Carl Rogers**   *Oliver Sacks*

Barry Schwartz   **Martin Seligman**   Gail Sheehy

B. F. Skinner   Douglas Stone   Bruce Patton

Sheila Heen   WILLIAM STYRON   **Robert E. Thayer**

Contents

Acknowledgments

Each book in the *50 Classics* series has been a major effort, involving thousands of hours of research, reading, and writing. Beyond this core work, the series is made successful thanks to the team at Nicholas Brealey Publishing.

I'm very grateful for the editorial input of Nicholas Brealey and Sally Lansdell in NB's London office, which has made *50 Psychology Classics* a better book. Thanks also for the efforts with international rights to ensure that the book will be read by as many people as possible around the world.

Many thanks also to Patricia O'Hare and Chuck Dresner in the Boston office for their commitment to this book and to the *50 Classics* series, and for increasing its profile in the United States.

Finally, this book could obviously not have been written without the wealth of remarkable ideas and concepts expressed in the classic books covered. Thank you to all the living authors for your contributions to the field.

Introduction

In a journey that spans 50 books, hundreds of ideas, and over a century in time, *50 Psychology Classics* looks at some of the most intriguing questions relating to what motivates us, what makes us feel and act in certain ways, how our brains work, and how we create a sense of self. Deeper awareness in these areas can lead us to self-knowledge, a better understanding of human nature, improved relationships, and increased effectiveness—in short, to make a real difference to your life.

50 Psychology Classics explores writings from such iconic figures as Freud, Adler, Jung, Skinner, James, Piaget, and Pavlov, and also highlights the work of contemporary thinkers such as Gardner, Gilbert, Goleman, and Seligman. There is a commentary devoted to each book, revealing the key points and providing a context of the ideas, people, and movements surrounding it. The blend of old and new titles gives you an idea of writings that you should at least know about even if you are not going to read them, and newer, really practical titles that take account of the latest scientific findings.

The focus is on "psychology for nonpsychologists," books everyone can read and be enlightened by, or that were expressly written for a general audience. In addition to psychologists, the list includes titles by neurologists, psychiatrists, biologists, communications experts, and journalists, not to mention a dockworker, an expert in violence, and a novelist. As the secrets of human behavior are too important to be defined by a single discipline or point of view, we need to hear from such an eclectic collection of voices.

The book does not focus primarily on psychiatry, although works by psychiatrists such as Oliver Sacks, Erik Erikson, R. D. Laing, and Viktor Frankl are included, plus some by famous therapists including Carl Rogers, Fritz Perls, and Milton Erickson. *50 Psychology Classics* is less about fixes to problems than supplying general insights into why people think or act as they do.

Despite the inclusion of some titles relating to the unconscious mind, the emphasis is also not on depth psychology, or concepts of the psyche or soul. Some of the best popular writers in this area, including James Hillman (*The Soul's Code*), Thomas Moore (*Care of the Soul*), Carol Pearson (*The Hero Within*), and Joseph Campbell (*The Power of Myth*), have been covered in *50 Self-Help Classics* and *50 Spiritual Classics*, which explore books on the more transformational and spiritual sides of psychology.

The list of 50 psychology classics does not claim to be definitive, just to range over some of the major names and writings. Every collection of this type will be to some extent idiosyncratic, and no claims are made to cover the various fields and subfields in psychology comprehensively. Here we are seeking basic insights into some of the most intriguing psychological questions and concepts, and a greater knowledge of human nature.

The rise of a science

"Psychology is the science of mental life." William James

As the early memory researcher Hermann Ebbinghaus (1850–1909) wrote, "Psychology has a long past, but only a short history." He meant that people have been thinking about human thought, emotion, intelligence, and behavior for thousands of years, but as a discipline based on facts rather than speculation psychology is still in its infancy. Even though he made his statement a hundred years ago, psychology is still considered young.

It emerged from two other disciplines, physiology and philosophy. German Wilhelm Wundt (1832–1920) is seen as the father of psychology because he insisted it should be a separate discipline, more empirical than philosophy and more focused on the mind than physiology. In the 1870s he created the first experimental psychology laboratory, and wrote his huge work *Principles of Physiological Psychology*.

As Wundt is read today only by those with a specialized interest, he is not included in the list of classics. American philosopher William James (1842–1910), however, also considered a "founding father" of modern psychology, is still widely read. The brother of novelist Henry James, he trained in medicine and then transferred to philosophy, but like Wundt felt that the workings of the mind deserved to be a separate field of study. Building on a theory by German neuroanatomist Franz Gall that all thoughts and mental processes were biological, James helped to spread the remarkable idea that one's self—with all its hopes, loves, desires, and fears—was contained in the soft gray matter within the walls of the skull. Explanations of thoughts as the product of some deeper force such as the soul, he felt, were really the realm of metaphysics.

James may have helped define the parameters of psychology, but it was Sigmund Freud's writings that really made it a subject of interest to the general public. Freud was born 150 years ago, in 1856; his parents knew he was bright, but even they could not have imagined the impact his ideas would have on the world. On leaving school he was set to study law, but changed his mind at the last minute and enrolled in medicine. His work on brain anatomy and with patients suffering from "hysteria" led him to wonder about the influence of the unconscious mind on behavior, which sparked his interest in dreams.

Today, it is easy to take for granted how much the average person is familiar with psychological concepts such as the ego and the unconscious mind, but these and many others are all—for better or worse—Freud's legacy. Well over half the titles covered in *50 Psychology Classics* are by either

Freudians or post-Freudians, or mark themselves out by being anti-Freud. It is now fashionable to say that Freud's work is unscientific, and his writings literary creations rather than real psychology. Whether this is accurate or not, he remains far and away the most famous person in the field, and although psychoanalysis—the talking therapy he created to peep into a person's unconscious—is now much less practiced, the image of a Viennese doctor drawing out the deepest thoughts of his couch-lying patient is still the most popular image we have when we think of psychology.

As some neuroscientists have intimated, Freud may be due for a comeback. His emphasis on the major role of the unconscious in shaping behavior has not been proved wrong by brain imaging techniques and other research, and some of his other theories may yet be validated. Even if not, his position as psychology's most original thinker is not likely to change.

The reaction to Freud came most obviously in the form of behaviorism. Ivan Pavlov's famous experiments with dogs, which showed that animals were simply the sum of their conditioned responses to environmental stimuli, inspired behaviorism's leading exponent B. F. Skinner, who wrote that the idea of the autonomous person driven by an inner motive was a romantic myth. Instead of trying to find out what goes on inside a person's head ("mentalism"), to know why people act as they do, Skinner suggested, all we need to know is what circumstances caused them to act in a certain way. Our environments shape us into what we are, and we change the course of our actions according to what we learn is good for our survival. If we want to construct a better world, we need to create environments that make people act in more moral or productive ways. To Skinner this involved a technology of behavior that rewards certain actions and not others.

Emerging in the 1960s, cognitive psychology used the same rigorous scientific approach as behaviorism but returned to the question of how behavior is actually generated inside the head. Between the stimulation received from the environment and our response, certain processes had to occur inside the brain, and cognitive researchers revealed the human mind to be a great interpreting machine that made patterns and created sense of the world outside, forming maps of reality.

This work led cognitive therapists such as Aaron Beck, David D. Burns, and Albert Ellis to build treatment around the idea that our thoughts shape our emotions, not the other way around. By changing our thinking, we can alleviate depression or simply have greater control over our behavior. This form of psychotherapy has now largely taken the place that Freudian psychoanalysis once assumed in treating people's mental issues.

A more recent development in the cognitive field is "positive psychology," which has sought to reorient the discipline away from mental problems to the study of what makes people happy, optimistic, and productive. To some extent

3

this area was foreshadowed by pioneering humanistic psychologist Abraham Maslow, who wrote about the self-actualized or fulfilled person, and Carl Rogers, who once noted that he was pessimistic about the world, but optimistic about people.

In the last 30 years, both behavioral and cognitive psychology have been increasingly informed by advances in brain science. The behaviorists thought it wrong to merely surmise what happened inside the brain, but science is now allowing us to see inside and map the neural pathways and synapses that actually generate action. This research may end up revolutionizing how we see ourselves, almost certainly for the better, because while some people fear that the reduction of human beings to how the brain is wired will dehumanize us, in fact greater knowledge of the brain can only increase our appreciation of its workings.

Today's sciences of the brain are enabling us to return to William James's definition of psychology as the "science of mental life," except that this time we are able to advance knowledge based on what we know at the molecular level. Having evolved partly out of the field of physiology, psychology may be returning to its physical roots. The irony is that this attention to minute physicality is yielding answers to some of our deepest philosophical questions, such as the nature of consciousness, free will, the creation of memory, and the experience and control of emotion. It may even be that the "mind" and the "self" are simply illusions created by the extraordinary complexity of the brain's neural wiring and chemical reactions.

What is the future of psychology? Perhaps all we can be certain of is that it will become a science more and more based on knowledge of the brain.

A quick guide to the literature

Part of the reason psychology became a popular field of study is that its early titans, including James, Freud, Jung, and Adler, wrote books that ordinary people could understand. We can pick up one of their titles today and still be entranced. Despite the difficulty of some of the concepts, people have a deep hunger for knowledge on how the mind works, human motivation, and behavior, and in the last 15 years there has been something of a new golden age in popular psychology writing, with authors such as Daniel Goleman, Steven Pinker, Martin Seligman, and Mihaly Csikszentmihalyi fulfilling that need.

Below is a brief introduction to the titles covered in *50 Psychology Classics*. The books are divided into seven categories that, although unconventional, may help you to choose titles according to the themes that interest you most. At the rear of this book you will find an alternative list of "50 More Classics." Again, this is not a definitive list, but it may assist in any further reading you wish to do.

Behavior, biology, and genes:
A science of the brain
Louann Brizendine, *The Female Brain*
William James, *The Principles of Psychology*
Alfred Kinsey, *Sexual Behavior in the Human Female*
Anne Moir & David Jessel, *Brainsex*
Jean Piaget, *The Language and Thought of the Child*
Steven Pinker, *The Blank Slate*
V. S. Ramachandran, *Phantoms in the Brain*
Oliver Sacks, *The Man Who Mistook His Wife for a Hat*

For William James, psychology was a *natural* science based on the workings of the brain, but in his era the tools to study this mysterious organ properly were not adequate to the task. Now, with technological advances, psychology is gaining many of its insights from the brain itself rather than from the behavior it generates.

This new emphasis on brain science raises uncomfortable questions regarding the biological and genetic bases of behavior. Is the way we are relatively unchangeable, or are we a blank slate ready to be socialized by our environments? The old debate over "nature vs nurture" has gained new energy. Genetic science and evolutionary psychology have demonstrated that much of what we call human nature, including intelligence and personality, is wired into us in the womb or at least hormonally influenced. For cultural or political reasons, Steven Pinker notes in *The Blank Slate*, the major role that biology plays in human behavior is sometimes denied, but as knowledge increases this will become increasingly difficult to maintain. Louann Brizendine's book, for example, the result of many years' study of the effects that hormones have on the female brain, brilliantly shows the extent to which women can be shaped by their biology at different stages in life.

More fundamentally, Moir and Jessel's *Brainsex* presents a convincing case that many of our behavioral tendencies come from the sexual biology of our brains, which are largely set by the time the foetus is eight weeks old. Even our cherished ideas about the self are going under the microscope. Today's neuroscience suggests that the self is best understood as a sort of illusion that the brain creates. The remarkable writings of Oliver Sacks, for instance, show that the brain continually works to create and maintain the feeling of an "I" that is in control, even if there is in fact no part of the brain that can be identified as the locus of "self feeling." Neuroscientist V. S. Ramachandran's work with phantom limbs seems to confirm the brain's remarkable ability to create a sense of cognitive unity even if the reality (of many selves, and of many layers of consciousness) is more complex.

Jean Piaget never did any laboratory work on the brain, but grew up studying snails in the Swiss mountains. He applied an early genius for scientific observation to the study of children, noting that they progress along a definite line of stages according to age, assuming there is adequate stimulation from their environments. Equally, sex researcher Alfred Kinsey, also originally a biologist, sought to shatter the taboos surrounding male and female sexuality by pointing out how our mammalian biology drives our sexual behaviors.

The work of both Piaget and Kinsey suggests that while biology is always a dominant influence on behavior, environment is critical to its expression. Even amid the new findings on the genetic or biological basis of behavior, we should never conclude that as human beings we are determined by our DNA, hormones, or brain structure. Unlike other animals we are aware of our instincts, and as a result may attempt to shape or control them. We are neither nature nor nurture only, but an interesting combination of both.

Tapping the unconscious mind:
Wisdom of a different kind
Gavin de Becker, *The Gift of Fear*
Milton Erickson (by Sidney Rosen), *My Voice Will Go With You*
Sigmund Freud, *The Interpretation of Dreams*
Malcolm Gladwell, *Blink*
Carl Jung, *The Archetypes and the Collective Unconscious*

Psychology involves more than the rational, thinking mind, and our ability to tap into our unconscious can yield a vast store of wisdom. Freud tried to show that dreams are not simply meaningless hallucinations, but a window into the unconscious that can reveal suppressed wishes. To him the conscious mind was like the tip of an iceberg, with the submerged bulk providing the center of gravity in terms of motivation. Jung went further, identifying a whole sub-rational architecture (the "collective unconscious") that exists independent of particular individuals, constantly generating the customs, art, mythology, and literature of culture. For both Jung and Freud, greater awareness of "what lies beneath" meant someone was less likely to be tripped up by life. The unconscious was a store of intelligence and wisdom that could be accessed if we knew how, and their great task was reconnect us to our deeper selves.

As therapy, "depth" psychology has been no more than moderately successful, and tends to be only as effective as the insights or techniques of particular practitioners. Milton Erickson, for instance, a famous hypnotherapist, had the motto "It is really amazing what people can do. Only they don't know what they can do." He also understood the unconscious to be a well of wise solutions, and enabled his patients to tap into it and regain forgotten personal power.

As a bridge between the conscious and the unconscious, intuition is a form of wisdom that we can cultivate. This is chillingly demonstrated in Gavin de Becker's *The Gift of Fear*, which provides many examples of our natural ability to know what to do in critical life-or-death situations—as long as we are prepared to listen to and act on our internal voice. Malcolm Gladwell's *Blink* also highlights the power of "thinking without thinking," showing that an instant assessment of a situation or person is often as accurate as one formed over a long period. While obviously logic and rationality are important, smart people are in touch with all levels of their mind, and trustful of their feelings even when the origins of those feelings seem mysterious.

Thinking better, feeling better: Happiness and mental health

Nathaniel Branden, *The Psychology of Self-Esteem*
David D. Burns, *Feeling Good*
Albert Ellis & Robert Harper, *A Guide to Rational Living*
Daniel Gilbert, *Stumbling on Happiness*
Fritz Perls, *Gestalt Therapy*
Barry Schwartz, *The Paradox of Choice*
Martin Seligman, *Authentic Happiness*
William Styron, *Darkness Visible*
Robert E. Thayer, *The Origin of Everyday Moods*

For many years, psychology was surprisingly little interested in happiness. Martin Seligman has helped to raise the subject to serious study and observation, and his "positive psychology" is revealing through science the sometimes unexpected recipes for mental wellbeing. Barry Schwartz's distinction between maximizers and satisficers has given us the counterintuitive insight that restricting our choices in life can actually lead to greater happiness and satisfaction, and Daniel Gilbert's book points out the surprising fact that, although humans are the only animals who can look into the future, we often make mistakes in terms of what we think will lead to happiness. Turning from the macro to the micro, Robert Thayer's work into the physiological causes of daily moods has helped thousands of people gain better control over how they feel hour by hour. The fascinating insights of each of these books show that the achievement of happiness is never as simple a matter as we would like.

The cognitive psychology revolution has had a dramatic impact on mental health, and two of its major names are David D. Burns and Albert Ellis. Their mantra that thoughts create feelings, not the other way around, has helped many people to get back in control of their lives because it applies logic and reason to the murky pool of emotions. Yet their work has many implications for achieving happiness generally, in that most of us can literally "choose" to be happy, if we understand the mind's thought–emotion mechanism.

The concept of self-esteem has been criticized in recent years, but Nathaniel Branden's seminal work on the subject remains convincing in its argument that personal esteem arises from having our own set of principles and acting on them. When we fail to do this, it is easy to descend into self-hatred and depression. Yet as William Styron's classic account of his own battle with depression indicates, the causes of the condition are often mysterious and can strike anyone. He notes that it remains the cancer of the mental health world: We are close to finding a cure, but not close enough for those who do not respond quickly to drugs or therapy.

Why we are how we are:
The study of personality and the self

Isabel Briggs Myers, *Gifts Differing*
Erik Erikson, *Young Man Luther*
Hans Eysenck, *Dimensions of Personality*
Anna Freud, *The Ego and the Mechanisms of Defence*
Karen Horney, *Our Inner Conflicts*
Melanie Klein, *Envy and Gratitude*
R. D. Laing, *The Divided Self*
Gail Sheehy, *Passages*

The ancients commanded us to "know thyself," but in psychology this quest takes on many aspects. Eysenck's work on the extraverted and neurotic dimensions of personality paved the way for many other models, with contemporary psychologists commonly assessing people according to the "Big Five" personality traits of extraversion, agreeableness, conscientiousness, neuroticism, and openness to experience. Today, we can take myriad tests to determine our "personality type," and while it is wise to be skeptical of their validity, some can provide genuine insights. The best known of the modern forms is the inventory originally created by Isabel Briggs Myers.

Of course, who we are at one point in our life may be different from who we are at another. Erik Erikson coined the term "identity crisis," and in his compelling psychobiography of religious reformer Martin Luther, he conveys both the pain of uncertain identity and the power that comes when we finally know who we are. As Gail Sheehy pointed out in her 1970s hit *Passages*, we go through many crises during adult life, and not only are they somewhat predictable, we should welcome them as an opportunity for growth.

Human beings sometimes have to cope with what seem like competing selves. Anna Freud took up where her father left off in focusing on the psychology of the ego, noting that humans do just about anything to avoid pain and preserve a sense of self, and this compulsion often results in the creation of psychological defenses. Neo-Freudian Karen Horney believed that childhood experiences resulted in our creation of a self that "moved toward people" or "moved away from people." These tendencies were a sort of mask that could develop into neurosis if we were not willing to move beyond them. Underneath was what she called a "wholehearted," or real, person.

Melanie Klein focused on how a "schizoid" personality could develop as the result of an infant's relations with its mother in the first year of life, although she noted that most people grow out of this and establish healthy relations with themselves and the world. Most of us do have a strong sense of self, but as R. D. Laing showed in his landmark work on schizophrenia, some people lack this basic security and attempt to replace the vacuum with false selves. Most of the time we take it for granted, but it is only when it is lost that we can fully appreciate our brain's ability to create the feeling of self-possession, or be comfortable with who we are.

Why we do what we do:
Great thinkers on human motivation
Alfred Adler, *Understanding Human Nature*
Viktor Frankl, *The Will to Meaning*
Eric Hoffer, *The True Believer*
Abraham Maslow, *The Farther Reaches of Human Nature*
Stanley Milgram, *Obedience to Authority*
Ivan Pavlov, *Conditioned Reflexes*
B. F. Skinner, *Beyond Freedom and Dignity*

Alfred Adler was a member of Freud's original inner circle, but broke away because he disagreed that sex was the prime mover behind human behavior. He was more interested in how our early environments shape us, believing that we all seek greater power by trying to make up for what we perceive we lacked in childhood—his famous theory of "compensation."

If Adler's theory of human action relates to power, concentration camp survivor Viktor Frankl's brand of existential psychology, "logotherapy," posits that the human species is uniquely made to seek meaning. It is our responsibility to look for meaning in life, even in the darkest times, and whatever the circumstances we always have a vestige of free will.

Yet as amateur psychologist Eric Hoffer wrote in *The True Believer*, people allow themselves to be swept up in larger causes in order to be freed of responsibility for their lives, and to escape the banality or misery of the present. And Stanley Milgram's famous experiments showed that, given the right conditions, human beings exhibit a frightening willingness to put others through pain in order to be seen kindly by those in authority. Humanistic psychologist Abraham Maslow, on the other hand, identified a minority of self-actualized individuals who did not act simply out of conformity to society but chose their own path and lived to fulfill their potential. This type of person was as representative of human nature as any mindless conformist.

While poets, writers, and philosophers have long celebrated the inner motive that guides autonomous human behavior, B. F. Skinner defined the self simply as "a repertoire of behavior appropriate to a given set of contingencies." There was no such thing as human nature, and conscience or morality could be boiled down to environments that induced us to behave in moral ways. Skinner's ideas built on the work of Ivan Pavlov, whose success in conditioning dogs' behavior also brought into question the freedom of human action.

Despite these vast differences in understanding motivation, together these books provide remarkable insights into why we do what we do, or at least what we are capable of doing—both good and bad.

Why we love the way we do:
The dynamics of relationships
Eric Berne, *Games People Play*
Susan Forward, *Emotional Blackmail*
John M. Gottman, *The Seven Principles for Making Marriage Work*
Harry Harlow, *The Nature of Love*
Thomas A. Harris, *I'm OK—You're OK*
Carl Rogers, *On Becoming a Person*

Love has traditionally been the domain of poets, artists, and philosophers, but in the last 50 years the terrain of relationships has increasingly been mapped by psychologists. In the 1950s, primate researcher Harry Harlow's legendary experiments replacing the real mothers of baby monkeys with cloth ones proved the extent to which infants need loving physical attention in order to become healthy adults. Remarkably, this sort of touching went against the child-rearing views of the time.

More recently, marriage researcher John M. Gottman looked at another aspect of relationship dynamics and found that the conventional wisdom on what makes long-term romantic partnerships work is often wrong. The most valuable information on how to maintain or save relationships comes from scientific observation of couples in action, right down to the microexpressions and apparently inane comments seen in everyday conversations. Similarly, in the past we may have looked to literature to be enlightened about a subject as intensely personal as emotional blackmail, but psychologists such as Susan Forward are now providing better answers on how we can protect ourselves against this corrosive element in relationships.

Pop psychology pioneers Eric Berne and Thomas Harris understood our close personal encounters as "transactions" that could be analyzed according to the three selves of Adult, Child, and Parent. Berne's observation that we are always playing games with each other is perhaps a cynical view of humanity, but by becoming aware of those games we have the chance to move beyond them.

The contribution of humanistic psychology to better relationships is recognized by the inclusion of Carl Rogers, whose influential book reminds us that relationships cannot flower if they don't have a climate of listening and nonjudgmental acceptance, and that empathy is the mark of a genuine person.

Working at our peak:
Creative power and communication skills
Robert Bolton, *People Skills*
Edward de Bono, *Lateral Thinking*
Robert Cialdini, *Influence*
Mihaly Csikszentmihalyi, *Creativity*
Howard Gardner, *Frames of Mind*
Daniel Goleman, *Working with Emotional Intelligence*
Douglas Stone, Bruce Patton, & Sheila Heen, *Difficult Conversations*

Debates rage in the academic world over the true nature of intelligence, but in working life we are interested in its application. Two of the outstanding titles in this area, by Daniel Goleman and Howard Gardner, both suggest that intelligence involves much more than straight IQ. There are an array of "intelligences" of an emotional or social nature that can together be a decisive factor in how well a person does in life.

Unlike IQ, one's ability to communicate well can be improved relatively easily, as Robert Bolton's perennially popular book shows. And in *Difficult Conversations*, a product of extensive Harvard research, Douglas Stone and his colleagues give excellent advice on how to deal with some of the most challenging workplace encounters. As life often seems to boil down to the outcome of such interactions, it is worth understanding what is happening below the surface of what is actually said, and how to manage an encounter while keeping everyone's dignity intact.

One of the decisive factors in success in business is the ability to persuade. Robert Cialdini's landmark work on the psychology of persuasion is a must-read if you are involved in marketing, but also of interest to anyone who wishes to understand how we are made to do things we would not normally choose to do.

Another component of work success is creativity. Edward de Bono's term "lateral thinking" seemed very new in the 1960s when he coined it, but in today's entrepreneurial culture we are all expected to think outside the box. At a broader level, Mihaly Csikszentmihalyi's *Creativity*, based on a systematic study, shows why creativity is central to a rich, meaningful life, and why many people do not achieve their full flowering until their later years. Most importantly, the book provides many features of the creative person that we can emulate.

Psychology and human nature

"The science of human nature... finds itself today in the position that chemistry occupied in the days of alchemy."

Alfred Adler

"Everyone has a theory of human nature. Everyone has to anticipate the behavior of others, and that means we all need theories about what makes people tick."

Steven Pinker

William James defined psychology as the science of mental life, but it could equally be defined as the science of human nature. Some 80 years after Alfred Adler made the remark above, we still have a long way to go in terms of creating a rock-solid science that could match the certainty of, say, physics and biology.

In the meantime, we all need a personal theory of what makes people tick. To survive and thrive, we have to know who and what we are, and to be canny about the motivations of others. The common route to this knowledge is life experience, but we can advance our appreciation of the subject more quickly through reading. Some people gain insights from fiction, others from philosophy. But psychology is the only science exclusively devoted to the study of human nature, and its popular literature—surveyed in this collection—aims to convey this vital wisdom.

50 Psychology Classics

Understanding Human Nature

"It is the feeling of inferiority, inadequacy and insecurity that determines the goal of an individual's existence."

"One motive is common to all forms of vanity. The vain individual has created a goal that cannot be attained in this life. He wants to be more important and successful than anyone else in the world, and this goal is the direct result of his feeling of inadequacy."

"Every child is left to evaluate his experiences for himself, and to take care of his own personal development outside the classroom. There is no tradition for the acquisition of a true knowledge of the human psyche. The science of human nature thus finds itself today in the position that chemistry occupied in the days of alchemy."

In a nutshell

What we think we lack determines what we will become in life.

In a similar vein
Erik Erikson *Young Man Luther* (p 84)
Anna Freud *The Ego and the Mechanisms of Defence* (p 104)
Sigmund Freud *The Interpretation of Dreams* (p 110)
Karen Horney *Our Inner Conflicts* (p 156)

CHAPTER 1

Alfred Adler

I n 1902 a group of men, mostly doctors and all Jewish, began meeting every Wednesday in an apartment in Vienna. Sigmund Freud's "Wednesday Society" would eventually become the Vienna Psychoanalytical Society, and its first president was Alfred Adler.

The second most important figure in the Viennese circle, and the founder of individual psychology, Adler never considered himself a disciple of Freud. While Freud was an imposing, patrician type who had come from a highly educated background and lived in a fashionable district of Vienna, Adler was the plain-looking son of a grain merchant who had grown up on the city's outskirts. While Freud was known for his knowledge of the classical world and his collection of antiquities, Adler worked hard for better working-class health and education and for women's rights.

The pair's famous split occurred in 1911, after Adler had become increasingly annoyed with Freud's belief that all psychological issues were generated by repressed sexual feelings. A few years earlier Adler had published a book, *Study of Organ Inferiority and Its Psychical Compensation*, which argued that people's perceptions of their own body and its shortcomings were a major factor in shaping their goals in life. Freud believed human beings to be wholly driven by the stirrings of the unconscious mind, but Adler saw us as social beings who create a style of life in response to the environment and to what we feel we lack. Individuals naturally strive for personal power and a sense of our own identity, but if healthy we also seek to adjust to society and make a contribution to the greater good.

Compensating for weakness

Like Freud, Adler believed that the human psyche is shaped in early childhood, and that patterns of behavior remain remarkably constant into maturity. But while Freud focused on infantile sexuality, Adler was more interested in how children seek to increase their power in the world. Growing into an environment in which everyone else seems bigger and more powerful, every child seeks to gain what they need by the easiest route.

Adler is famous for his idea of "birth order," or where we come in a family. Youngest children, for instance, because they are obviously smaller and less powerful than everyone else, will often try to "outstrip every other member of the family and become its most capable member." A fork in the developmental path leads a child either to imitate adults in order to become more assertive and powerful themselves, or consciously to display weakness so as to get adult help and attention.

In short, every child develops in ways that best allow them to compensate for weakness; "a thousand talents and capabilities arise from our feelings of inadequacy," Adler noted. A desire for recognition emerges at the same time as a sense of inferiority. A good upbringing should be able to dissolve this sense of inferiority, and as a result the child will not develop an unbalanced need to win at the expense of others. We might assume that a certain mental, physical, or circumstantial handicap we had in childhood was a problem, but what is an asset and what is a liability depends on the context. It is whether we *perceive* a shortcoming to be such that matters most.

The psyche's attempt to banish a sense of inferiority will often shape someone's whole life; the person will try to compensate for it in sometimes extreme ways. Adler invented a term for this, the famous "inferiority complex." While a complex may make someone more timid or withdrawn, it could equally produce the need to compensate for that in overachievement. This is the "pathological power drive," expressed at the expense of other people and society generally. Adler identified Napoleon, a small man making a big impact on the world, as a classic case of an inferiority complex in action.

How character is formed

Adler's basic principle was that our psyche is not formed out of hereditary factors but social influences. "Character" is the unique interplay between two opposing forces: a need for power, or personal aggrandizement; and a need for "social feeling" and togetherness (in German, *Gemeinschaftsgefühl*).

The forces are in opposition, and each of us is unique because we all accept or reject the forces in different ways. For instance, a striving for dominance would normally be limited by a recognition of community expectations and vanity or pride is kept in check; however, when ambition or vanity takes over, a person's psychological growth comes to an abrupt end. As Adler dramatically put it, "The power-hungry individual follows a path to his own destruction."

When the first force, social feeling and community expectation, is ignored or affronted, the person concerned will reveal certain aggressive character traits: vanity, ambition, envy, jealousy, playing God, or greed; or nonaggressive traits: withdrawal, anxiety, timidity, or absence of social graces. When any of these forces gains the upper hand, it is usually because of deep-seated feelings of inadequacy. Yet the forces also create an intensity or tension that can give tremendous energy. Such people live "in the expectation of great triumphs" to compensate for those feelings, but as a result of their inflated sense of self lose some sense of reality. Life becomes about the mark they will leave on the world and what others think of them. Though in their mind they are something of a heroic figure, others can see that their self-centeredness actually restricts their proper enjoyment of the possibilities of life. They forget that they are human beings with ties to other people.

Enemies of society

Adler noted that vain or prideful people usually try to keep their outlook hidden, saying that they are simply "ambitious," or even more mildly "energetic." They may camouflage their true feelings in ingenious ways: To show that they are not vain, they may purposely pay less attention to dress or be overly modest. But Adler's piercing observation of the vain person was that everything in life comes down to one question: "What do I get out of this?"

Adler wondered: Is great achievement simply vanity put in the service of humankind? Surely self-aggrandizement is a necessary motivation in order to want to change the world, to be seen in a good light? His answer was that it isn't. Vanity plays little part in real genius, and in fact only detracts from the worth of any achievement. Really great things that serve humanity are not spurred into existence by vanity, but by its opposite, social feeling. We are all vain to some extent, but healthy people are able to leaven their vanity with contribution to others.

Vain people, by their nature, do not allow themselves to "give in" to society's needs. In their focus on achieving a certain standing, position, or object, they feel that they can shirk the normal obligations to the community or family that others take for granted. As a result, they usually become isolated and have poor relationships. So used to putting themselves first, they are expert at putting the blame on others.

Communal life involves certain laws and principles that an individual cannot get around. Each of us needs the rest of the community in order to survive both mentally and physically; as Darwin noted, weak animals never live alone. Adler contended that "adaptation to the community is the most important psychological function" that a person will master. People may outwardly achieve much, but in the absence of this vital adaptation they may feel like nothing and be perceived as such by those close to them. Such people, Adler said, are in fact enemies of society.

Goal-striving beings

A central idea in Adlerian psychology is that individuals are always striving toward a goal. Whereas Freud saw us as driven by what was in our past, Adler had a teleological view—that we are driven by our goals, whether they are conscious or not. The psyche is not static but must be galvanized behind a purpose—whether selfish or communal—and continually moves toward fulfillment of that. We live life by our "fictions" about the sort of person we are and the person we are becoming. By nature these are not always factually correct, but they enable us to live with energy, always moving toward something.

It is this very fact of goal directedness that makes the psyche almost indestructible and so resistant to change. Adler wrote: "The hardest thing for human beings to do is to know themselves and to change themselves." All the more reason, perhaps, for individual desires to be balanced by the greater collective intelligence of the community.

Final comments

In highlighting the twin shaping forces of personal power and social feeling, Adler's intention was that by understanding them we would not be unknowingly shaped by them. In the vignettes of actual people presented in his book we may see something of ourselves: Perhaps we have cocooned ourselves in our family or community, forgetting the career dreams we once had; or maybe we see ourselves as a "king of the world," able to defy social convention at will. In both cases, there is an imbalance that will lead to restriction of our possibilities.

Much of *Understanding Human Nature* reads more like philosophy than psychology, overloaded with generalizations about personal character that are anecdotal rather than empirical. This absence of scientific support is one of the main criticisms of Adler's work. However, notions such as the inferiority complex have become a part of everyday usage.

While both Freud and Adler had strong intellectual agendas to pursue, Adler had a more humble aim, influenced by his socialist leanings: a practical understanding of how childhood shapes adult life, which in turn might benefit society as a whole. Unlike the culturally élitist Freud, Adler believed that the work of understanding human nature should not be the preserve of psychologists alone but a vital task for everyone, given the bad consequences of ignorance. This approach to psychology was unusually democratic, and appropriately *Understanding Human Nature* is based on a year's worth of lectures at the People's Institute of Vienna. It is a work that anyone can read and understand.

Alfred Adler

Adler was born in Vienna in 1879, the second of seven children. After a severe bout of pneumonia at the age of 5 and the death of a younger brother, he committed himself to becoming a doctor.

He studied medicine at the University of Vienna and qualified in 1895. In 1898 he wrote a medical monograph on the health and working conditions experienced by tailors, and the following year met Sigmund Freud. Adler remained involved with the Vienna Psychoanalytical Society until 1911, but in 1912 broke away with eight others to form the Society of Individual Psychology. At this time he also published his influential The Neurotic Constitution. *Adler's career was put on hold during the First World War, when he worked in military hospital service, an experience that confirmed his anti-war stance.*

After the war, he opened the first of 22 pioneering clinics around Vienna for children's mental health. When the authorities closed the clinics in 1932 (because Adler was a Jew), he emigrated to the United States, taking up a professorship at the Long Island College of Medicine. He had been a visiting professor at Columbia University since 1927, and his public lectures in Europe and the US had made him well known.

Adler died in 1937, suddenly of a heart attack. He was in Aberdeen, Scotland, as part of a European lecture tour. He was survived by his wife Raissa, whom he had married in 1897. They had four children.

Other books include The Science of Living, The Practice and Theory of Individual Psychology, *and the popular* What Life Could Mean to You.

The Gift of Fear

"*Like every creature, you can know when you are in the presence of danger. You have the gift of a brilliant internal guardian that stands ready to warn you of hazards and guide you through risky situations.*"

"*Though we want to believe that violence is a matter of cause and effect, it is actually a process, a chain in which the violent outcome is only one link.*"

"*For men like this, rejection is a threat to the identity, the persona, to the entire self, and in this sense their crimes could be called murder in defense of the self.*"

In a nutshell

Trust your intuition, rather than technology, to protect you from violence.

In a similar vein

Malcolm Gladwell *Blink* (p 124)

CHAPTER 2

Gavin de Becker

" **H**e had probably been watching her for a while. We aren't sure—but what we do know is that she was not his first victim." With this creepy line *The Gift of Fear* begins. The book outlines real-life stories of people who became victims, or almost became victims, of violence; in each case the person either listened to their intuition and survived, or did not and paid the consequences.

We normally think of fear as something bad, but de Becker tries to show how it is a gift that may protect us from harm. *The Gift of Fear: Survival Signals that Protect Us from Violence* is about getting into other people's minds so that their actions do not come as a terrible surprise. Though this may be uncomfortable, particularly when it is the mind of a potential killer, it is better to do this than to find out the hard way.

Before he was 13 Gavin de Becker had seen more violence within his own home that most adults see in a lifetime. In order to survive, he had to become good at predicting what would happen next in frightening situations, and he made it his life's work to formularize the violent mindset so that others could also see the signs. De Becker became an expert in assessing the risk of violence, charged with protecting high-profile celebrity, government, and corporate clients, and also something of a spokesperson on domestic violence.

De Becker is not a psychologist, but his book gives more insights into the nature of intuition, fear, and the violent mind than you are ever likely to read in a straight psychology text. As gripping as a good crime novel, *The Gift of Fear* may not just change your life—it could actually save it.

Intuitive security

In the modern world, de Becker observes, we have forgotten to rely on our instincts to look after ourselves. Most of us leave the issue of violence up to the police and criminal justice system, believing that they will protect us, but often by the time we involve the authorities it is too late. Alternatively, we believe that better technology will protect us from danger; the more alarms and high fences we have, the safer we feel.

But there is a more reliable source of protection: our intuition or gut feeling. Usually we have all the information we need to warn us of certain people or situations; like other animals, we have an in-built warning system for danger. Dogs' intuition is much vaunted, but de Becker argues that in fact human beings have better intuition; the problem is that we are less prepared to trust it.

De Becker describes female victims of attacks who report: "Even though I knew what was happening leading up to the event was not quite right, I did not extract myself from it." Somehow, the attacker who helped them with their bags or got into the lift with them was able to make these women go along with what he wanted. De Becker suggests that there is a "universal code of violence" that most of us can automatically sense, yet modern life often has the effect of deadening our sensitivity. We either don't see the signals at all or we won't admit them.

Paradoxically, de Becker proposes that "trusting intuition is the exact opposite of living in fear." Real fear does not paralyze you, it energizes you, enabling you to do things you normally could not. In the first case he discusses, a woman had been trapped and raped in her own apartment. When her attacker said he was going into the kitchen, something told her to follow him on tiptoe, and when she did she saw him rifling through the drawers looking for a large knife—to kill her. She made a break for the front door and escaped. What is fascinating is her recollection of not being afraid. Real fear, because it involves our intuition, in fact is a positive feeling designed to save us.

A violent streak in everyone

De Becker debunks the idea that there is a "criminal mind" separating certain people from the rest of us. Most of us would say that we can never kill another person, but then you usually hear the caveat: "Unless I was having to protect a loved one." We are all capable of criminal thoughts and even actions. Many murders are described as "inhuman," but surely, de Becker observes, they can't be anything *but* human. If one person is capable of a particular act, under certain circumstances we may all be capable of that act. In his work, de Becker does not have the luxury of making distinctions like "human" and "monster." Instead, he looks for whether a person may have the intent or ability to harm. He concludes, "the resource of violence is in everyone; all that changes is our view of the justification."

A chain, not an isolated act

Why do people commit violence? De Becker boils it down to four elements:

❖ Justification—the person makes a judgment that they have been intentionally wronged.
❖ Alternatives—violence seems like the only way forward to seek redress or justice.
❖ Consequences—they decide they can live with the probable outcome of their violent act. For instance, a stalker may not mind going to jail as long he gets his victim.
❖ Ability—they have confidence in their ability to use their body or bullets or a bomb to achieve their ends.

De Becker's team check through these "pre-incident indicators" when they have to predict the likelihood of violence from someone threatening a client. If we pay attention, he says, violence never "comes from nowhere." It is actually not very common for people to "snap" before they commit murder. Generally, de Becker remarks, violence is as predictable "as water coming to a boil."

What also helps in predicting violence is to understand it as a *process*, "in which the violent outcome is only one link." While the police are looking for the motive, de Becker and his team are going deeper to find the history of violence or violent intent that usually precedes the act.

The Gift of Fear includes a chapter on spousal violence, noting that most spousal murder does not happen in the heat of the moment. It is usually a premeditated decision, preceded by the husband stalking his wife and sparked by the wife's rejection. For such men, being rejected is too great a threat to their sense of self and killing their partner seems the only way to restore their identity. De Becker reveals an alarming fact: Three-quarters of spousal murders happen *after* the woman leaves the marriage.

Knowing how to pick a psychopath

The features of predatory criminals usually include:

❖ recklessness and bravado;
❖ single-mindedness;
❖ not being shocked at things that would appall other people;
❖ being weirdly calm in conflict;
❖ the need to be in control.

What is the best predictor of violent criminality? De Becker's experience is that a troubled or abusive childhood is an important factor. In a study into serial killers, 100 percent were found to have suffered violence themselves, been humiliated, or simply neglected as children. Robert Bardo, who shot and killed actress Rebecca Shaeffer, was kept in his room as a child and fed like the family pet. He never learnt to be sociable. Such people form a warped view of the world—at the public's expense.

Yet violent people can be very good at hiding the signals that they are psychopaths. They may studiously model normality so that they can at first appear to be "regular guys." Warning signals include:

❖ They're *too* nice.
❖ They talk too much and give us unnecessary details to distract us.
❖ They approach us, never the other way around.
❖ They typecast us or mildly insult us, in order to have us respond and engage with them.
❖ They use the technique of "forced teaming," using the word "we" to make them and their victim seem like they are all in the same boat.

❖ They find a way to help us so we feel in their debt (called "loan sharking").
❖ They ignore or discount our "no." Never let someone talk you out of a refusal, because then they know they are in charge.

We don't have to lead paranoid lives—most of the things we worry about never happen—yet it is foolish to trust our home or office security system or the police absolutely. As it is *people* who harm, de Becker notes, it is people we must understand.

Inside the mind of the stalker

The Gift of Fear is riveting when de Becker is discussing public figures who are his clients and stalkers' attempts to get close to them. At any one time, a famous singer or actor may have three or four people after them, sending mountains of letters or trying to get through security. Only a small number of these stalkers actually want to kill their target (the rest believe they are in some kind of "relationship" with the star), but the common factor is a desperate hunger for recognition.

All of us want recognition, glory, significance to some extent, and in killing someone famous, stalkers themselves become famous. Mark Chapman and John Hinckley Jnr, for instance, are names forever linked with their targets, John Lennon and Ronald Reagan. To such people assassination makes perfect sense; it is a shortcut to fame, and psychotic people do not really care whether the attention they gain is positive or negative.

The image of a crazed person going after a movie star or president captures the public imagination, but de Becker wonders why are we so intrigued by celebrity stalkers, but are blasé about the fact that, in the US alone, a woman is killed by a husband or boyfriend every two hours. Incidentally, he has little faith in restraining orders, which he says only intensify the situation. Violent people thrive on engagement, and if they are unbalanced anyway, a restraining order will not guarantee safety.

Final comments

The Gift of Fear is a very American book, written within a cultural context of the rampant use of guns and a society that puts less emphasis than others on social cohesion. If you live in an English village or a Japanese city or even a quiet part of the United States, the book could seem a little paranoid. However, de Becker blames evening news reports for making his country seem a lot more dangerous than it actually is, noting that we have a much higher likelihood of dying from cancer or in a car accident than as a result of a violent attack by a stranger.

Since the attack on New York's World Trade Center in 2001 we have become obsessed with the possibility of random violence, but most attacks and homicides still occur in the home, and knowing the impending signs of violence may save you from harm. In terms of personal safety, de Becker says that men and women live in two different worlds. Oprah Winfrey told her television audience that *The Gift of Fear* "should be read by every woman in America."

In writing *The Gift of Fear*, de Becker was influenced by three books in particular: FBI behavioral scientist Robert Ressler's *Whoever Fights Monsters*; psychologist John Monahan's *Predicting Violent Behavior*; and Robert D. Hare's *Without Conscience*, which takes the reader into the minds of psychopaths. There is now a large literature on the psychology of violence, but de Becker's book is still a great place to start.

Gavin de Becker

De Becker is considered a pioneer in the field of threat assessment and the prediction and management of violence. His firm provides consultation and protection services to corporations, government agencies, and individuals. He headed the team that provided security for guests of President Reagan, and he has worked with the US Department of State on official visits of foreign leaders. He also developed the MOSAIC system for dealing with threats to US Supreme Court judges, senators, and congressman. De Becker has consulted on many legal cases, including the criminal and civil cases against O. J. Simpson.

He is a senior fellow at the University of California, Los Angeles (UCLA) School of Public Affairs, and has co-chaired the Domestic Violence Council Advisory Board.

Other books include Protecting the Gift, *on the safety of children, and* Fear Less: Real Truth About Risk, Safety and Security in a Time of Terrorism.

Games People Play

"*[The] marital game of 'Lunch Bag.' The husband, who can well afford to have lunch at a good restaurant, nevertheless makes himself a few sandwiches every morning, which he takes to the office in a paper bag. In this way he uses up crusts of bread, leftovers from dinner and paper bags his wife saves for him. This gives him complete control over the family finances, for what wife would dare buy herself a mink stole in the face of such self-sacrifice?*"

"*Father comes home from work and finds fault with daughter, who answers impudently, or daughter may make the first move by being impudent, whereupon father finds fault. Their voices rise, and the clash becomes more acute… There are three possibilities: (a) father retires to his bedroom and slams the door; (b) daughter retires to her bedroom and slams the door; (c) both retire to their respective bedrooms and slam the doors. In any case, the end of a game of 'Uproar' is marked by a slamming door.*"

In a nutshell

People play games as a substitute for real intimacy, and every game, however unpleasant, has a particular payoff for one or both players.

In a similar vein

Thomas A. Harris *I'm OK—You're OK* (p 148)
Karen Horney *Our Inner Conflicts* (p 156)
Fritz Perls *Gestalt Therapy* (p 216)

CHAPTER 3

Eric Berne

I n 1961, psychiatrist Eric Berne published a book with a very boring title, *Transactional Analysis in Psychotherapy*. It became the foundation work in its field, was much referenced, and was a reasonable seller.

Three years later he published a sequel based on the same concepts but with a more colloquial feel. With its brilliant title and witty, amusing categories of human motivation, *Games People Play* was bound to attract more attention. Sales for the initial print run of 3,000 copies were slow, but two years later, thanks mostly to word of mouth and some modest advertising, the book had sold 300,000 copies in hardback. It spent two years on the *New York Times* bestseller list (unusual for a nonfiction work) and, creating a template for future writers who suddenly got wealthy by writing a pop psychology bestseller, the fiftysomething Berne bought a new house and a Maserati, and remarried.

Though he did not realize it at the time, *Games People Play: The Psychology of Human Relationships* marked the beginning of the popular psychology boom, as distinct from mere self-help on the one hand and academic psychology on the other. Mainstream psychologists looked down on Berne's book as shallow and pandering to the public, but in fact the first 50 or 60 pages are written in a rather serious, scholarly style. Only in the second part does the tone lighten up, and this is the section most people bought the book for.

Today, *Games People Play* has sold over five million copies and the phrase in its title has entered the English idiom.

Strokes and transactions

Berne began by noting research that infants, if deprived of physical handling, often fall into irreversible mental and physical decline. He pointed to other studies suggesting that sensory deprivation in adults can lead to temporary psychosis. Adults need physical contact as much as children, but it is not always available so we compromise, instead seeking symbolic emotional "strokes" from others. A movie star, for instance, may get his strokes from hundreds of adoring weekly fan letters, while a scientist may get hers from a single positive commendation from a leading figure in the field.

Berne defined the stroke as the "fundamental unit of social action." An exchange of strokes is a transaction, hence his creation of the phrase "transactional analysis" (TA) to describe the dynamics of social interaction.

Why we play games

Given the need to receive strokes, Berne observed that in biological terms human beings consider any social intercourse—even if negative—as better than none at all. This need for intimacy is also why people engage in "games"— these become a substitute for genuine contact.

He defined a game as "an ongoing series of complementary ulterior transactions progressing to a well-defined, predictable outcome." We play a game to satisfy some hidden motivation, and it always involves a payoff.

Most of the time people are not aware they are playing games; it is just a normal part of social interaction. Games are a lot like playing poker, when we hide our real motivations as part of a strategy to achieve the payoff—to win money. In the work environment the payoff may be getting the deal; people speak of being in the "real estate game" or the "insurance game" or "playing the stock market," an unconscious recognition that their work involves a series of maneuvers to achieve a certain gain. And in close relationships? The payoff usually involves some emotional satisfaction or increase in control.

The three selves

Transactional analysis evolved out of Freudian psychoanalysis, which Berne had studied and practiced. He had once had an adult male patient who admitted that he was really "a little boy in an adult's clothing." In subsequent sessions, Berne asked him whether it was now the little boy talking or the adult. From these and other experiences, Berne came to the view that within each person are three selves or "ego states" that often contradict each other. They are characterized by:

❖ the attitudes and thinking of a parental figure (Parent);
❖ the adult-like rationality, objectivity, and acceptance of the truth (Adult);
❖ the stances and fixations of a child (Child).

The three selves correspond loosely to Freud's superego (Parent), ego (Adult), and id (Child).

In any given social interaction, Berne argued, we exhibit one of these basic Parent, Adult, and Child states, and can easily shift from one to the other. For instance, we can take on the child's creativity, curiosity, and charm, but also the child's tantrums or intransigence. Within each mode we can be productive or unproductive.

In playing a game with someone we take on an aspect of one of the three selves. Instead of remaining neutral, genuine, or intimate, to get what we want we may feel the need to act like a commanding parent, or a coquettish child, or to take on the sage-like, rational aura of an adult.

Let the games begin

The main part of the book is a thesaurus of the many games people play, such as the following.

"If it weren't for you"

This is the most common game played between spouses, in which one partner complains that the other is an obstacle to doing what they really want in life.

Berne suggested that most people unconsciously choose spouses because they want certain limits placed on them. He gave an example of a woman who seemed desperate to learn to dance. The problem was that her husband hated going out, so her social life was restricted. She enrolled in dancing classes, but found that she was terribly afraid of dancing in public and dropped out. Berne's point was that what we blame the other partner for is more often revealed as an issue within ourselves. Playing "If it weren't for you" allows us to divest ourselves of responsibility for facing our fears or shortcomings.

"Why don't you—yes, but"

This game begins when someone states a problem in their life, and another person responds by offering constructive suggestions on how to solve it. The subject says "Yes, but..." and proceeds to find issue with the solutions. In Adult mode we would examine and probably take on board a solution, but this is not the purpose of the exchange. It allows the subject to gain sympathy from others in their inadequacy to meet the situation (Child mode). The problem solvers, in turn, get the opportunity to play wise Parent.

Wooden leg

Someone playing this game will have the defensive attitude of "What do you expect of a person with a wooden leg/bad childhood/neurosis/alcoholism?" Some feature of themselves is used an excuse for lack of competence or motivation, so that they do not have to take full responsibility for their life.

Berne's other games include:

❖ Life games—"Now I've Got You, You Son of a Bitch"; "See What You Made Me Do."
❖ Marital games—"Frigid Woman"; "Look How Hard I've Tried."
❖ "Good" games—"Homely sage"; "They'll be glad they knew me."

Each game has a thesis—its basic premise and how that is played out—and an antithesis—the way it reaches its conclusion, with one of the players taking an action that in their mind makes them the "winner."

The games we play, Berne said, are like worn-out loops of tape we inherit from childhood and continue to let roll. Though limiting and destructive, they are also a sort of comfort, absolving us of the need to confront unresolved psychological issues. For some, playing games has become a basic part of who they are. Many people feel the need to get into fights with those closest to them or intrigues with their friends in order to stay interested. However, Berne warned, if we play too many "bad" games for too long, they become self-destructive. The more games we play, the more we expect others to play them too; a relentless game player can end up a psychotic who reads too much of their own motivations and biases into others' behavior.

Final comments

Though *Games People Play* was reviled by many practicing psychiatrists as too "pop" and inane, transactional analysis continues to be influential and has been added to the armory of many psychotherapists and counselors who need to deal with difficult or evasive patients. It seemed like a ground-breaking book because it brought a psychologist's precision to an area that was normally the preserve of novelists and playwrights. Indeed, American novelist Kurt Vonnegut wrote a celebrated review that suggested its contents could inspire creative writers for years.

Be aware that *Games People Play* is quite Freudian, with many of the games based on Freud's ideas about inhibition, sexual tension, and unconscious impulses. It is also clearly a relic of the 1960s in its language and social attitudes.

Yet it can still be a mind-opening read, and is a classic for the simple insight that people always have and probably always will play games. As Berne noted, we teach our children all the pastimes, rituals, and procedures they need to adapt to our culture and get by in life, and we spend a lot of time choosing their schools and activities, yet we don't teach them about games, an unfortunate but realistic feature of the dynamics of every family and institution.

Games People Play can seem to offer an unnecessarily dark view of human nature. However, this was not Berne's intention. He remarked that we can all leave game playing behind if we know there is an alternative. As a result of childhood experiences we leave behind the natural confidence, spontaneity, and curiosity we had as a child and instead adopt the Parent's ideas of what we can or cannot do. Through greater awareness of the three selves, we can get back to a state of being more comfortable within our own skin. No longer do we feel that we need someone's permission to succeed, and we become unwilling to substitute games for real intimacy.

Eric Berne

Eric Bernstein grew up in Montreal, Canada; his father was a doctor and his mother a writer. He graduated from McGill University in 1935 with a medical degree, and trained to be a psychoanalyst at Yale University. He became a US citizen, worked at Mt Zion Hospital in New York, and in 1943 changed his name to Eric Berne.

During the Second World War Berne worked as a US army psychiatrist, and afterwards resumed his studies under Erik Erikson (see p. 84) at the San Francisco Psychoanalytic Institute. Settling in California in the late 1940s, he became disenchanted with psychoanalysis, and his work on ego states evolved over the next decade into transactional analysis. He formed the International Transactional Analysis Association, and combined private practice with consulting and hospital posts.

Berne wrote on a range of subjects. In addition to his other bestseller, What Do You Say After You Say Hello? *(1975), which examined the idea of "life scripts," he also published the* Layman's Guide to Psychiatry and Psychoanalysis *(1957),* Structure and Dynamics of Organizations and Groups *(1963),* Sex in Human Loving *(1970), and, posthumously,* Beyond Games and Scripts *(1976). See also the biography by Elizabeth Watkins Jorgensen,* Eric Berne: Master Gamesman *(1984).*

Berne admitted that he had a well-developed Child, once describing himself as "a 56-year-old teenager." He was a keen poker player, was married three times, and died in 1970.

1979

People Skills

"Although interpersonal communication is humanity's greatest accomplishment, the average person does not communicate well. Low-level communication leads to loneliness and distance from friends, lovers, spouses, and children—as well as ineffectiveness at work."

"Communication skills, no matter how finely structured, cannot be a substitute for authenticity, caring, and understanding. But they can help us express these qualities more effectively than many of us have been able to do in the past."

In a nutshell

Good people skills not only get you what you want, they bring out the best in your relationships.

In a similar vein
Daniel Goleman *Working with Emotional Intelligence* (p 130)
Carl Rogers *On Becoming a Person* (p 238)
Douglas Stone, Bruce Patton, & Sheila Heen *Difficult Conversations* (p 272)

CHAPTER 4

Robert Bolton

O ften the best books are those that authors needed to write for their own use. In the preface to *People Skills: How to Assert Yourself, Listen to Others, and Resolve Conflicts*, Robert Bolton notes that he would never have got into the communications field were it not for the fact that his own people skills were so bad.

The book was written over a six-year period while he was running a consulting firm, and the material was tested on thousands of people doing the company's communication skills workshops. Participants involved everyone from top executives to hospital workers to small business owners to priests and nuns.

There are virtually no jobs where communicating well does not make a big difference to our success. As many people have found, particularly those in a more technical field, the actual "work" is only part of the job; the rest is managing or dealing with people. Therefore, if we can communicate well, this can account for at least half our achievements.

Removing the roadblocks

People yearn for a closer connection with one another, Bolton notes. They may be lonely not because they don't have others around them, but because they cannot communicate well. Yet if we can put a man on the moon and cure virulent diseases, why aren't we all great communicators? It is partly because we learn a good deal of our communication skills from our family; chances are our parents were not perfect communicators, and neither were their parents.

Nearly everyone wants better communication skills, yet often without knowing it our communication is full of roadblocks that prevent real communication with others. Two of the main ones are judging and sending solutions.

When talking with someone, it is difficult to listen to what they are saying without putting in our "two bits' worth." This is the nicer side of judging. The other is criticism and labeling. With people close to us we feel we should be critical, otherwise we don't see how they will ever change. With others, we feel the need to give them a label such as "intellectual," "brat," "jerk," or "nag," but by doing so we cease to see the person before us, only a type. Our "good advice" is in fact rarely constructive, because it usually represents an affront to the other person's intelligence.

We may be so used to having roadblocks that we wonder what will be left if we remove them from our style of conversation. What remains is the ability to understand and empathize with other people, and to make our concerns clearly known.

Listening skills

Are your conversations a competition in which "the first person to draw breath is declared the listener"? Not many people are good listeners. Research has found that "75 percent of oral communication is ignored, misunderstood, or quickly forgotten."

There is a huge difference between merely hearing and listening, Bolton notes. The word "listening" is derived from two Anglo Saxon words, *hlystan* ("hearing") and *hlosnian* ("waiting in suspense"). The act of listening therefore means more than just something physical, it is a *psychological* engagement with another person.

Listening is not a single skill, but if genuinely practiced involves a number of skill areas, which are described below.

Attending

The common estimate given in research papers is that 85 percent of our communication is nonverbal. Therefore attending skills, which are about the extent to which we are "there" for someone when they are speaking, are vital to good communication. You are not looking somewhere else in the room, but through your posture, eye contact, and movement show the other person that they are your focus; you are "listening with your body."

Bolton describes when painter Norman Rockwell was creating a portrait of President Eisenhower. Even though the President was amid the worries of office and about to enter an election campaign, for the hour and a half he sat for Rockwell, Eisenhower gave the painter his full attention. Think of anyone you know who is a great communicator and they will be the same: They fully attend to you with their whole mind and body.

Following

Following skills relate to how we follow up what someone says to us. Though commonly we advise or reassure, a better way is to provide a "door opener" phrase. This may involve:

* Noting the other person's body language: "Your face is beaming today."
* Inviting the other person to speak: "Tell me more." "Care to talk about this?" "What's on your mind?"
* Silence: giving the other person space to say something if they want to.
* Our body language: offering the message that we are ready to listen.

Doing any of those things shows respect; the other person can talk or not talk as they wish. There is no pressure. Bolton comments that a lot of people are initially uncomfortable with silence, but with a little practice it is not hard for us to extend our comfort zone.

In developing our skill at following, we become adept at discovering exactly how the speaker sees their situation, unlocking or bringing out whatever is waiting to be said. This is valuable to both parties.

Paraphrasing

Bolton defines paraphrasing as "a *concise response* to the speaker which states the *essence* of the other's content in the listener's own words." For example, when someone is telling us their problems, we report back to them in our own words, and in one sentence, what they are saying. This lets them know we are really listening, and indicates understanding and acceptance. We may feel strange doing this at first and think the other person will wonder what the hell we are doing, but in fact most of the time they will be glad that their feelings are being recognized.

Reflective responses

This type of listening provides a mirror to the speaker so that the state or emotion they are in is recognized. Bolton gets us to picture a young mother on a morning when everything is going wrong. The baby cries, the phone rings, the toast gets burnt. If her husband notices this and says something like "God, can't you learn to cook toast?" the woman's reaction is likely to be explosive.

But picture an alternative. The same events happen and the husband says, "Honey, it's a rough morning for you—first the baby, then the phone, now the toast." This is a reflective response, acknowledging what his wife is experiencing without any judgment or criticism. Imagine how much better she will feel!

Reflective responses work because people don't always wish to spell out what they are really feeling. They beat around the bush. Only by being reflective, not reactive, are we able to discern their real message. Psychologists talk of the "presenting problem" and the "basic problem." What presents is what a person *says* is the matter, and behind it is the real problem. This is why we have to listen for the *feeling* in a conversation. That points us in the right direction, whereas a common mistake is to try to make sense of the words only.

People complain that reflective listening takes more time and effort. It does in the short term, but it is likely to avoid major troubles that blow up later on as the result of poor communication.

Assertiveness skills

Bolton likes to think of listening as the *yin* (the receiving aspect) of communication, while assertiveness is the *yang* (the active aspect).

Because of the poor communication skills most of us have been taught, when we want something we choose between either nagging or aggression, or we avoid the issue altogether. These responses stem from the basic "fight or flight" modes we operate with as animals. But as humans we also have a third option: verbal assertion. We can stand our ground yet not be aggressive. This is easily the most effective means of communication for most situations, yet most of us either forget assertion or don't know how to use it.

The whole point of assertion statements is to produce change without invading the other person's space. There is no power or coercion involved, as the focus is on a result. We can remain very angry, and the other person knows it from what we are saying, yet at the same time it allows us not to be hostile or aggressive. They are left to decide for themselves how to respond to the message, which allows them to retain their dignity—while we have taken a big step in getting what we want.

Conflict prevention and control

What we really want in life is situations where everybody wins. Bolton presents the counterintuitive idea that if we define a problem in terms of solutions, one person wins and the other loses. To get win–win outcomes, we have to focus not on the solution but on each party's needs.

For instance, he worked with a group of nuns who only had one car between them. Several of them needed the car to make visits and go to meetings, so there were inevitable clashes. When one person had the car, the others lost out. But Bolton asked them what each of them needed. The need they identified was *transportation*, and use of the group's car was only one solution to that. Seeing the situation in terms of needs meant that many other possible solutions appeared.

As the old saying goes, "A problem well defined is a problem half solved." Bolton provides a step-by-step process for identifying needs, which then lead to a solution. Using this method surprisingly elegant answers can be found to questions we may have thought were intractable. But it first requires us to really listen to what other people require to make them happy.

Final comments

People Skills has been around for a quarter of a century and still sells well. What is the secret of its longevity? First, the book rests on a strong intellectual foundation, referencing ideas from the likes of Carl Rogers, Sigmund Freud, and Karen Horney. Secondly, it sticks to the fundamentals, not trying to cover every aspect of interpersonal relations but focusing on three vital, learnable skills: listening, asserting, and resolving conflict. Although the book seems long and there is a fair amount of repetition, it contains some highly useful tips and techniques that can be applied immediately.

Nowhere does *People Skills* ask us to change our personality to become a warm and fuzzy "people person." What it does do is show us well-researched techniques that can make a dramatic difference to our effectiveness. We suddenly understand what people are really saying, and we begin to be able to communicate what we truly want in a direct fashion.

Conversely, if we still have a tendency to think that having good people skills means the ability to manipulate others into doing or saying something that suits us, not them, Bolton's book reminds us of the three pillars of respect that *really* produce good relationships: empathy, nonpossessive love, and genuineness.

Robert Bolton

Bolton is the head of Ridge Associates, a training and consulting firm founded in 1972 that focuses on workplace communication and interpersonal skills. He previously created training programs for the New York State Department of Mental Hygiene and also founded a psychiatric clinic.

His other book, written with his wife Dorothy Grover Bolton, is People Styles at Work: Making Bad Relationships Good and Good Relationships Better *(1996).*

Lateral Thinking

"Lateral thinking is like the reverse gear in a car. One would never try to drive along in reverse gear the whole time. On the other hand one needs to have it and to know how to use it for maneuverability and to get out of a blind alley."

"The purpose of thinking is not to be right but to be effective."

In a nutshell

Learning how to think more effectively is not difficult and can dramatically improve our ingenuity in solving problems.

In a similar vein
Mihaly Csikszentmihalyi *Creativity* (p 68)

CHAPTER 5

Edward de Bono

Edward de Bono is inevitably associated with the word "thinking," and no one is better known for getting people to work on the effectiveness of their thought patterns and ideas.

De Bono's early books were among the first in the popular psychology field. The writing style is not exactly bubbly, but the quality of the ideas made them bestsellers. De Bono coined the term "lateral thinking," now listed in the *Oxford English Dictionary*, in *The Use of Lateral Thinking* (1967), but it is *Lateral Thinking* (subtitled *Creativity Step by Step* in the United States and *A Textbook of Creativity* in Britain) that is more widely read and still in print.

What is lateral thinking?

When de Bono started writing in the 1960s there were no practical, standardized ways of achieving new insights. A few people were considered "creative," but the rest had to plod along within established mental grooves. He promoted the concept of lateral thinking as the first "insight tool" that anyone could use for problem solving.

The lateral thinking concept emerged from de Bono's study of how the mind works. He found that the brain is not best understood as a computer; rather, it is "a special environment which allows information to organize itself into patterns." The mind continually looks for patterns, thinks in terms of patterns, and is self-organizing, incorporating new information in terms of what it already knows. Given these facts, de Bono noticed that a new idea normally has to do battle with old ones to get itself established. He looked for ways in which new ideas could come into being via spontaneous insight rather than conflict.

Lateral thinking is a process that enables us to restructure our patterns, to open up our mind and avoid thinking in clichéd, set ways. It is essentially creativity, but without any mystique. It is simply a way of dealing with information that results in more creative outcomes. What is humor, de Bono asks, but the sudden restructuring of existing patterns? If we can introduce the unexpected element, we need not be enslaved to these patterns.

Lateral thinking is contrasted with "vertical thinking." Our culture in general, but in particular our educational system, emphasizes the use of logic, by which one correct statement proceeds to the next one, and finally to the "right" solution. This type of vertical thinking is good most of the time, but when we have a particularly difficult situation it may not give us the leap forward we need—sometimes we have to "think outside the box." Or as de Bono puts it, "Vertical thinking is used to dig the same hole deeper. Lateral thinking is used to dig a hole in a different place."

Lateral thinking does not cancel out vertical thinking, but is complementary to it, to be used when we have exhausted the possibilities of normal thought patterns.

Techniques of creative thinkers

It is not enough to have some awareness of lateral thinking, de Bono asserts, we have to practice it. Most of his book consists of techniques to try to get us into lateral thinking mode. They include:

- Generating alternatives—to have better solutions you must have more choices to begin with.
- Challenging assumptions—though we need to assume many things to function normally, never questioning our assumptions leaves us in thinking ruts.
- Quotas—come up with a certain predetermined number of ideas on an issue. Often it is the last or final idea that is the most useful.
- Analogies—trying to see how a situation is similar to an apparently different one is a time-tested route to better thinking.
- Reversal thinking—reverse how you are seeing something, that is, see its opposite, and you may be surprised at the ideas it may liberate.
- Finding the dominant idea—not an easy skill to master, but extremely valuable in seeing what really matters in a book, presentation, conversation, and so on.
- Brainstorming—not lateral thinking itself, but provides a setting for that kind of thinking to emerge.
- Suspended judgment—deciding to entertain an idea just long enough to see if it might work, even if it is not attractive on the surface.

One of de Bono's key points is that lateral thinkers do not feel they have to be "right" all the time, only effective. They know that the need to be right prevents new ideas forming, because it is quite possible to be wrong at some stages in an idea cycle but still finish with great outcomes. What matters most is generating enough ideas so that some may be wrong, but others turn out right.

The glorious obvious

De Bono remarks, "It is characteristic of insight solutions and new ideas that they should be obvious after they have been found."

Brilliant yet obvious ideas lie hidden in our minds, just waiting to be fished out. What stops us from retrieving them is the clichéd way we think, always sticking to familiar labels, classifications, and pigeonholes—what de Bono describes as the "arrogance of established patterns."

To get different results, we need to put information together differently. What makes an idea original is not necessarily the concept itself, but the fact that most other people, thinking along conventional lines, were not led to it themselves.

We have the cult of genius, glorifying famous figures like Einstein, only because most people are not taught to think in better ways. For those who practice lateral thinking all the time, the flow of original ideas never stops.

Final comments

Though de Bono's books are the progenitors of many of the sensationally written "mind power" titles available today, *Lateral Thinking* itself has a dry style. Unlike many of the seminar gurus who followed him, de Bono has degrees in psychology and medicine, so there is more rigor in his approach.

If you have never got much out of de Bono before, the chances are you are already a lateral thinker. But everyone can become a better thinker, and his books are a good place to begin.

People take jibes at de Bono's invention of words like "po" to simplify his teachings, but he has probably done more than anyone to get us thinking about thinking itself. This is an important mission, because among the many things that make the world progress, new and better ideas are always at the heart of them.

Edward de Bono

Born in 1933 in Malta, the son of a professor of medicine and a magazine journalist, de Bono was educated at St. Edward's College and gained a medical degree at the Royal University of Malta at the age of 21. He won a Rhodes Scholarship to Christ Church, Oxford, graduating with an MA in psychology and physiology and a DPhil in medicine. He completed his doctorate at Cambridge and has had appointments at the universities of Oxford, Cambridge, London, and Harvard. He became a full-time author in 1976.

De Bono has worked with many major corporations, government organizations, teachers, and schoolchildren, and is a well-known public speaker. He has written over 60 books, including The Mechanism of Mind *(1969),* Po: Beyond Yes and No *(1973),* The Greatest Thinkers *(1976),* Six Thinking Hats *(1986),* I Am Right, You Are Wrong *(1990),* How to Be More Interesting *(1997), and* How to Have a Beautiful Mind *(2004).*

1969

The Psychology of Self-Esteem

"There is no value-judgment more important to man—no factor more decisive in his psychological development and motivation—than the estimate he passes on himself."

"Happiness or joy is the emotional state that proceeds from the achievement of one's values. Suffering is the emotional state that proceeds from a negation or destruction of one's values."

"The collapse of self-esteem is not reached in a day, a week, or a month: it is the cumulative result of a long succession of defaults, evasions, and irrationalities—a long succession of failures to use one's mind properly."

In a nutshell

Self-esteem occurs naturally when we choose to live according to reason and our own principles.

In a similar vein

Albert Ellis & Robert A. Harper *A Guide to Rational Living* (p 74)
Susan Forward *Emotional Blackmail* (p 94)

CHAPTER 6

Nathaniel Branden

This book popularized the concept of self-esteem. Previously most psychologists recognized that how we perceive ourselves is important, affecting our behavior in areas such as work and love, but few had looked into exactly why. *The Psychology of Self-Esteem* attempts to get to the roots of personal estimation—what increases it, and what diminishes it.

Nathaniel Branden was a disciple and lover of Ayn Rand, a famous Russian-American philosopher and author of the classic novels *Atlas Shrugged* and *The Fountainhead*. As a result, for a work of psychology his book is very philosophical, driven along by Rand's notions of supreme rationalism and individualism.

The Psychology of Self-Esteem takes as its premise that we are rational beings in full control of our destiny. If we accept this truth and take responsibility for it, we naturally see ourselves in a good light. If we fail to take responsibility for our life and actions, that estimation falls into danger.

Many readers find this book tough going, especially the first half, but it is one of the earliest classics of the popular psychology genre and still has the power to change minds.

Conceptual beings

Branden devotes many pages to highlighting how humans are different to other animals. His chief point is that while other animals may have consciousness, or at least awareness, only humans require a *conceptual* framework by which to view themselves. Other animals can perceive green-colored objects, but only we have the idea of "green." Dogs can perceive individual people, but only we have the concept of "humankind." Only humans can ask questions about the meaning of life. There is nothing automatic about such conceptualizing; thinking, therefore, is for us an act of *choice*.

Branden refutes the two schools of psychology that were dominant at the time he was writing. Freudian psychoanalysis had humans as an "instinct-manipulated puppet," while behaviorism saw us as a "stimulus–response machine." Neither took account of our powerful conceptual mind that gives us self-awareness and the ability to reason. Branden recalls Ayn Rand's remark: "The function of your stomach, lungs or heart is automatic; the function of your mind is not." We have the power to regulate and shape our own consciousness to achieve our goals.

We are created to think, and we must do so in order to esteem ourselves highly. If we dim our awareness, or are passive or fearful, step by step we kill our greatest gift. The result is that we hate ourselves. To love ourselves, we must cherish our ability to think.

Emotions and self-esteem

Have you ever been in a position where you know intellectually you should do something, but emotionally cannot bring yourself to do it? Psychological maturity, according to Branden, is the ability to think in terms of principles, not emotions. Psychological immaturity is being swamped by the moment and the emotion so that we lose sight of the broader picture. When we sacrifice thought and knowledge to feelings that cannot be justified rationally, Branden notes, the result is that we subvert our self-esteem.

Only if we have a rational approach to our emotions can we be free of paralyzing self-doubt, depression, and fear. This does not mean becoming a robot or a cold person, but simply having the awareness that emotions must be contained within a larger personal life philosophy. Neurosis, on the other hand, occurs when we let our feelings dictate our thoughts and actions. It is impossible to be both happy *and* irrational, Branden says; someone in command of their life, if we look carefully, lives according to reason.

We think of happiness as an emotion, but it is one that stems from *values* that have been consciously chosen and developed—we are happy when we achieve or fulfill what is most important to us. When we deny or erode those values, we suffer. Branden remarks that anxiety tends to happen only "when a person has not done the thinking about an issue he should have." By not thinking, the person has "thereby rendered himself unfit for reality."

Physical pain is a mechanism designed for our bodily survival, but Branden suggests that psychological pain also serves a biological purpose: When we feel anxiety, guilt, or depression, that is telling us that our consciousness is in an unhealthy state. To correct it, we must reassert ourselves as an individual and assess our values, perhaps forming new ones. In contrast, when we sacrifice reason to our emotions, we lose trust in our own judgment.

Not sacrificial animals

People high in self-esteem are guided by objective facts. They have a good relationship with reality, and always seek to stay true to who they are.

Their opposite is someone whose life is not really their own, who lives to satisfy the expectations, conditions, and values of other people; they want to be seen as "normal" at all costs, and feel terrible if others reject them. Branden calls such people "social metaphysicians" because their philosophy of life revolves around others, not themselves. Of course, this person will label their style of life as "practicality," as if self-sacrifice were quite rational. However, every step along this path leads them away from what is real and toward a loss of their true self.

Final comments

Branden disabuses the reader of the idea that self-esteem is a "feel-good phenomenon." Rather, it is a deep need that cannot be satisfied by shallow means. It must come from within, and like a muscle will get stronger the more we develop it. The more decisions we make that reflect our highest good, the better we will naturally feel. The more "shoulds" (I should do this, or do that, because…) we have in our life, the more justifications we have to come up with. We become covered in a cloak of excuses, while inside our confidence slowly ebbs away.

If you are a very confident person and all is going well, *The Psychology of Self-Esteem* may not mean much to you, but read it when faced with difficult choices in your life and it may come alive. For a more practical and less philosophical approach to self-esteem, you may prefer one of Branden's subsequent books, such as *The Six Pillars of Self-Esteem* or *The Art of Living Consciously*.

Nathaniel Branden

The author was born Nathan Blumenthal in Ontario, Canada in 1930. He attended the University of California, Los Angeles, where he received a BA in psychology, and completed his psychology PhD at New York University.

Branden first met Ayn Rand in 1950, later becoming leader of the "collective" or inner circle around her, which included his wife Barbara Branden and Alan Greenspan, later chairman of the US Federal Reserve Board. In the late 1950s Branden established the Nathaniel Branden Institute to promote objectivism, and was considered the movement's second voice. Despite being more than 20 years her junior, Branden had a lengthy affair with Rand, but only after they had gained the consent of their spouses. The romantic and professional relationship ended in 1968, when Rand learnt of Branden's affair with the actress Patrecia Scott. His book My Years with Ayn Rand *gives a good insight into the period, and although he has since criticized the cult of personality around Rand, her ideas continued to be reflected in his writing.*

Branden co-wrote several books with Rand, including The Virtue of Selfishness *(1964) and* Capitalism: The Unknown Ideal *(1966). Other titles include* The Psychology of Romantic Love *(1980),* Honoring the Self *(1983), and* Taking Responsibility *(1996).*

Based in Los Angeles, Branden is a practicing psychotherapist and runs self-esteem seminars.

Gifts Differing

"*[We] cannot safely assume that other people's minds work on the same principles as our own. All too often, others with whom we come in contact do not reason as we reason, or do not value the things we value, or are not interested in what interests us.*"

"*Well-developed introverts can deal ably with the world around them when necessary, but they do their best work inside their heads, in reflection. Similarly well-developed extraverts can deal effectively with ideas, but they do their best work externally, in action. For both kinds, the natural preference remains, like right- or left-handedness.*"

In a nutshell

If you know a person's personality type their behavior begins to make sense.

In a similar vein

Hans Eysenck *Dimensions of Personality* (p 90)
Carl Jung *The Archetypes and the Collective Unconscious* (p 168)

CHAPTER 7

Isabel Briggs Myers

The Myers-Briggs Type Indicator (MBTI) is a test for gauging personality type that has been around since the 1940s. It helped lay the foundations of the psychometric testing methods that employers use today.

The test's origins are somewhat interesting. The story goes that one Christmas vacation, Isabel Briggs brought home a boyfriend, Clarence Myers. Though Isabel's parents liked the young man, her mother Katherine noted that he was different to the family. Katherine became interested in the idea of categorizing people according to personality type, and through reading autobiographies developed a basic typology of "meditative types," "spontaneous types," "executive types," and "sociable types." She discovered Carl Jung's book *Psychological Types* and it became the theoretical foundation for a lifetime's work, later taken up by her daughter (who became Isabel Briggs Myers).

Though Isabel never studied psychology formally, the head of a local bank enabled her to learn about statistics and personnel tests, and the first forms of her Type Indicator were created in 1944. Briggs Myers persuaded school principals in Pennsylvania to get the test taken by thousands of students, and also by medical and nursing students. A private educational testing firm heard about the Indicator and published it in 1957, but it did not go into wide public use until the 1970s. Since then, the MBTI has been administered to millions of people, mostly for job compatibility purposes but also in relation to teaching, marriage counseling, and personal development. The test has been refined over the decades, but Katherine Briggs' original intention of discovering "why people are how they are" remains its inspiration.

Gifts Differing: Understanding Personality Type is Isabel Briggs Myers' personal explanation of her work, written with the assistance of her son Peter Briggs Myers and completed shortly before her death. If you are interested in the ideas behind personality typology, this is a key book to read.

When you do the actual MBTI test (consisting of yes or no questions) your personality preferences are expressed in a four-letter code, for example ISTJ or ESFP. Below is a summary of some of the key distinctions between the 16 types, and how this knowledge can be applied in practice.

Ways of perceiving: Sensing or intuiting

In *Psychological Types*, Jung suggested two contrasting ways in which people saw the world. Some people can appreciate reality only through their five senses ("sensing" types), while others wait for internal confirmation of what is true or real, relying on their unconscious. These are the "intuitive" types.

People who use the sensing mode are engrossed in what is around them, look only for facts, and find it less interesting to deal with ideas or abstractions. Intuitive people like to dwell in the unseen world of ideas and possibilities, distrustful of physical reality. Whatever mode people enjoy using and trust most, they tend to employ from an early age and refine over a lifetime.

Ways of judging: Thinking or feeling

In the Jung/Briggs Myers understanding, people choose between two ways of coming to conclusions or judgments: by thinking, using an impersonal process of logic; and by feeling, deciding what something means to them.

People stick to their preferred method. Trusting their own way, the thinkers consider the feelers as irrational and subjective. The feelers wonder how the thinkers can possibly be objective about the things that matter to them—how can they be so cold and impersonal?

Generally, a child who prefers the feeling mode is likely to become someone good at interpersonal relations, while a child who prefers the thinking mode will become good at collating, using, and organizing facts and ideas.

The four preferences

These orientations of Sensing (S), Intuition (N), Thinking (T), and Feeling (F) form four basic preferences that produce certain values, needs, habits, and traits. They are:

ST—Sensing plus Thinking
SF—Sensing plus Feeling
NF—Intuition plus Feeling
NT—Intuition plus Thinking

ST people like to proceed only on the basis of facts that their senses can verify. Practical minded, their best work is done in fields that require impersonal analysis such as surgery, law, accounting, and working with machinery.

SF people also rely on their senses, but the conclusions they make are more based on how they feel about the facts rather than cold analysis of them. They are "people people" and tend to be found in fields where they can express personal warmth, such as nursing, teaching, social work, selling, and "service-with-a-smile" jobs.

NF people also tend to be warm and friendly, but instead of focusing on the situation or the facts at hand, are more interested in how things might be changed or future possibilities. They like work that utilizes their gift for communication combined with their need to make things better, such as higher-level teaching, preaching, advertising, counseling or psychology, writing, and research.

NT people are also focused on possibilities, but draw on their powers of rational analysis to achieve outcomes. They are likely to be found in professions that require ingenious solving of problems, particularly of a technical nature, such as science, computing, mathematics, or finance.

Extraversion and introversion

A preference for extraversion (seeing life in terms of the external world) or introversion (greater interest in the inner world of ideas) is independent of your preferences for sensing, thinking, intuition, and feeling. You can be an extraverted NT type, for instance, or an introverted sensing and feeling type; that is, an ENT or an ISF. The first letter of the four letter code, E or I, indicates your extraversion or introversion preference.

Extraverts tend to move quickly and try to influence situations directly, while introverts give themselves time to develop their insights before exposing them to the world. Extraverts are happy making decisions in the thick of events, while introverts want to reflect before taking action. Neither preference necessarily makes better decisions than the other; it simply represents the style that each is comfortable with.

Dominant and auxiliary processes

Although we each favor certain ways of being, one will dominate above the others. Consider NT types. Although possessed of both intuitive and thinking preferences, if they find thinking more attractive this becomes their dominant process. They may intuit something as being right, but this must be confirmed by objective thinking. As thinking is a process of judgment, the final element in this person's type is "Judgment." They are ENTJs. Other people's final letter is P for "Perception," indicating their strong desire to understand better.

The need for a dominant process to bring cohesion to the self is perfectly understandable, but Jung went further to suggest that each person also needs an "auxiliary" process. Introverts have extraversion as their auxiliary so they can "put on a public face" when necessary. Extraverts use introversion as their auxiliary to take care of their inner lives. In both cases, if the auxiliary is little used, the person lives in one extreme and their life suffers accordingly. Briggs Myers noted that in our extravert-oriented society, there is a greater penalty for introverts who do not develop their auxiliary than for extraverts who fail to take account of inner things.

The aim of personality typing is to acquire greater powers of perception and judgment, which are both assisted by the use of the auxiliary. Briggs Myers observes: "Perception without judgment is spineless; judgment with no perception is blind. Introversion lacking any extraversion is impractical; extraversion with no introversion is superficial."

Better relationships through type awareness

The fact that people don't get along all the time suggests that we don't under-stand or value the ways other people see the world. A thinker, for instance, will underrate a feeling type's judgment, because the thinker cannot under-stand how the feeling type can come to good decisions without using logic. The thinker makes this assumption because their own feelings are erratic and unreliable. But the feeling type has cultivated their dominant process to such an extent that it delivers them good perceptions and judgments, even if it doesn't do so for the thinker.

In the same way, because a sensing type must perceive and judge based on what they see, hear, smell, and touch, the views and conclusions of an intuitive type, who just "knows" if something is good or bad, seem incomprehensible. For the intuitive, the sensing type seems to plod along without the "breath of life," inspiration. To take another example: Thinkers think that feeling types talk too much. When thinkers talk to someone they want information. Therefore if a feeling type wants anything from a thinker, they should try to remember to be concise.

In all these cases, what each type fails to appreciate is that the dominant process of another person works, and works well. Trying to tell that person that their perception or judgment is wrong is like telling grass that it shouldn't be green.

Dealing with the types at work

In work situations, if you have some idea of how your colleagues think, you can expect to be more effective in getting your ideas accepted and reduce any friction. You would know that:

❖ With a sensing type you have to articulate the problem very quickly before you can expect them to provide a solution.
❖ Intuitives will only be interested in helping if an enticing possibility is dangled before them.
❖ Thinkers need to know what sort of result they are looking for and to have the situation explained in a set of logical points.
❖ Feeling types will need to have the situation framed in terms of what it means to the people involved.

With all types, it is as well to remember never to focus on the people involved, but to attack the problem. If we are aware of each type's contributions, there will be less conflict, less chance of loss of face, and a greater opportunity for a perfect solution to emerge.

Final comments

Isabel Briggs Myers' lack of formal psychology qualifications ensured that she was never fully accepted by the psychological establishment. Some have questioned whether she interpreted Jung correctly, and therefore whether the whole methodology for identifying personality types is unsound. Jung himself was wary of applying his general principles to particular individuals, and skeptics also claim that the type explanations are too vague and could apply to anyone. Judge for yourself. You may find, if you take the test or a variant of it, that the description given of you is remarkably accurate.

On her own scale, Briggs Myers came out as an INFP (Introverted–Intuitive–Feeling–Perceiving). She noted that introverts often gain the most from doing the test. As three out of every four people are extraverted, and for every intuitive there are three sensing types, we therefore live in an "extravert's world." As a less common type, introverts may, not surprisingly, feel some pressure to be something they are not, and the MBTI allows them, perhaps for the first time, to feel it is OK to be who they are.

One of the fascinating insights in *Gifts Differing* is that recognition and development of our type may be more important to success in life than IQ. Isabel Briggs Myers' view was that personality type is as innate as left- or right-handedness; anyone who tries to be a right hander when they are really a leftie is asking for stress and misery, whereas going with our strengths massively increases our chances of fulfillment, happiness, and productivity.

Isabel Briggs Myers

Born in 1897, Briggs was schooled at home by her mother in Washington DC. Her father, Lynam Briggs, was a physicist and for over a decade was the director of the National Bureau of Standards. Isabel married Clarence Myers in 1918 and the following year graduated from Swarthmore College with a BA in political science.

Her tests of over 5,000 medical students were conducted at the George Washington School of Medicine. She followed up the study 12 years later, finding that the students had generally followed paths (i.e. research, general practice, surgery, administration) that might be expected of their type. The nursing study involved more than 10,000 students. The MBTI was first published in 1957 by the Educational Testing Service.

Isabel Briggs Myers died in 1980. Her work is continued today through the Myers & Briggs Foundation.

Peter Briggs Myers, born in 1926, was a Rhodes Scholar in physics. A scientific researcher and administrator, he was a staff director at the National Academy of Science. Involved in the development of the MBTI since his teens, he is now Chair of the Myers & Briggs Foundation and a Trustee of the Myers-Briggs Trust.

2006

The Female Brain

"More than ninety-nine percent of male and female genetic coding is exactly the same. Out of the 30,000 genes in the human genome, the variation between the sexes is small. But those few differences influence every single cell in our bodies—from the nerves that register pleasure and pain to the neurons that transmit perception, thoughts, feelings and emotions."

"Just as women have an eight-lane superhighway for processing emotion while men have a small country road, men have Chicago's O'Hare Airport as a hub for processing thoughts about sex whereas women have the airfield nearby that lands small and private planes. That probably explains why eighty-five percent of twenty- to thirty-year-old males think about sex every fifty two seconds and women think about it once a day—or up to every three or four hours on their most fertile days. This makes for interesting interactions between the sexes."

In a nutshell

Men and women experience the world differently thanks to each gender's vastly different exposure to sex hormones.

In a similar vein

Alfred Kinsey *Sexual Behavior in the Human Female* (p 174)
Anne Moir & David Jessel *Brainsex* (p 204)
Steven Pinker *The Blank Slate* (p 228)
Gail Sheehy *Passages* (p 260)
Robert E. Thayer *The Origin of Everyday Moods* (p 284)

CHAPTER 8

Louann Brizendine

As a medical student, Louann Brizendine was aware of conclusive studies done around the world showing that women suffer from depression at a ratio of 2:1 compared to men. Going through college at the peak of the feminist movement, along with many others she believed this was the result of the "patriarchal oppression of women." But it came to her notice that, up until puberty, depression rates between boys and girls are the same. Could the hormonal changes to girls in their early teenage years, she wondered, make them suddenly more prone to getting depressed?

Later, as a psychiatrist, Brizendine worked with women suffering from the extremes of premenstrual syndrome, and was struck by the extent to which the female brain is shaped by dramatic changes in hormonal chemistry, driving a woman's behavior and creating her reality. In 1994, Brizendine established the Women's Mood and Hormone Clinic in San Francisco, one of the first of its type in the world. *The Female Brain*, the culmination of her 20 years of practice as a neuropsychiatrist, pulls together her own research and the latest findings from a range of disciplines. Contrasting the relative stability of male hormonal brain states with those of the female, which involve an often complex cocktail of chemicals and change dramatically from girlhood to adolescence, early adulthood, motherhood, and menopause, the book brilliantly shows why women's brain states and chemistry merit independent research, and why generalities about human behavior usually relate to *male* behavior.

The Female Brain includes fascinating chapters on the female brain in love, the neurobiology of sex, the "mommy brain" (how a woman's thinking changes according to altered brain chemistry in pregnancy), and the mature female brain, post-menopause. We focus here on some of Brizendine's insights regarding the infant and pubescent female brain.

Basic differences

Even taking into account differences in body size, Brizendine notes, the male brain is about 9 percent larger than the female. This fact was once interpreted as meaning that women were not as smart as men. In fact, women and men have the same number of brain cells, but women's are more tightly packed into their skull.

In the areas of the brain dealing with language and hearing, women have a full 11 percent more neurons than men, and the part of the brain associated with memory, the hippocampus, is also larger in women. The circuitry for observing emotion on other people's faces is again larger compared to the male. In relation to speech, emotional intelligence, and the ability to store rich memory, therefore, women have a natural advantage.

Men, on the other hand, have more processors in the amygdala, a part of the brain regulating fear and aggression. This perhaps explains why males are more likely to anger quickly and take violent action in response to immediate physical danger. Women's brains also evolved to deal with possibly life-threatening situations, but in a different way. The female brain experiences greater stress over the same event as a man's, and this stress is a way of taking account of all possible risks to her children or family unit. This is why, Brizendine suggests, a modern woman can view some unpaid bills as catastrophic, as they seem a threat to the family's very survival.

Brain scanning and imaging technologies now allow us to see the workings of the brain in real time. They show the brain lighting up in different places depending on whether we are in love, looking at faces, solving a problem, speaking, or experiencing anxiety, and these hot spots differ between men's and women's brains. Women actually use different parts of the brain and different circuits than men to accomplish the same tasks, including solving problems, processing language, and generally experiencing the world.

One other basic brain difference is noteworthy. Studies have shown that men think about sex on average every 52 seconds, while for women it is once a day. As the part of the brain where sexual thought and behavior is generated is two and a half times larger in the male, this is not surprising.

The baby female brain

Until they are eight weeks old, the brains of male and female foetuses look the same—"female is nature's default setting," Brizendine observes. At about eight weeks, a male foetus's brain is flooded with testosterone, which kills off the cells relating to communication and helps to grow cells relating to sex and aggression. Biochemically, the male brain is then significantly different from a female one, and by the time the first half of the pregnancy is over, the differences between male and female brains are mostly set.

A female baby comes into the world wired to notice faces and hear vocal tones better. In the first three months of her life a baby girl's abilities at "mutual gazing" and eye contact grow by 400 percent. In the same period, these abilities do not grow at all in boys.

It is well known that girls usually begin speaking some time before boys, thanks to the better-developed language circuitry of their brains. This continues into adulthood, with women speaking on average 20,000 words a day and men averaging only around 7,000. (As Brizendine remarks, this higher ability "wasn't always appreciated," with some cultures locking up a woman or putting a clamp on her tongue to stop the chatter.)

One other important difference in infancy is that baby girls are more sensitive to the state of their mother's nervous system. It is important that infant girls do not have mothers who are stressed out, as when the girl grows up to have children of her own her ability to be nurturing will be reduced. However, armed with this knowledge, it is possible to break the cycle of mother–infant stress.

The teen girl's brain

At puberty, a girl's thinking and behavior change according to the fluctuating levels of estrogen (one of the "feel-good" hormones), progesterone ("the brain's valium"), and cortisol (the stress hormone) in her brain. Other important hormones produced are oxytocin (which makes us want to bond, love, and connect with others) and dopamine (which stimulates the brain's pleasure centers).

The effect of these chemicals is to give a teenage girl a great need for and pleasure in gossiping, shopping, exchanging secrets, and experimenting with clothing and hair styles—anything that involves connecting and communicating. Teenage girls are always on the phone because they actually *need* to communicate to reduce their stress levels. Their squeals of delight at seeing friends, and the corresponding panic at being grounded, are also part of these changes. The dopamine and oxytocin rush that girls experience is "the biggest, fattest neurological reward you can get outside of an orgasm," Brizendine remarks.

Why exactly does the loss of a friendship feel so catastrophic to a teen girl, and why is her social group so important to her? Physiologically she is reaching the optimum age for child rearing, and in evolutionary terms she knows that a close-knit group is good protection, since if she has a small child with her she is not able to attack or run away as a man can. (The concept of "fight or flight" in response to danger is an observation of men rather than women.) Close social bonds actually alter the female brain in a highly positive way, so that any loss of those relationships triggers a hormonal change that strengthens the feelings of abandonment or loss. The intensity of female pubescent friendships therefore also has a biochemical basis.

The teenage girl's confidence and ability to deal with stress also change according to the time of the month, and Brizendine has treated many "problem" girls who experience higher than average hormonal changes. The most brash and aggressive girls often have high levels of androgens, the hormones associated with aggression. At normal levels, fluctuations in androgens can cause a girl to be more focused on power, whether within the peer group or over boys.

Incidentally, why do teenage boys often become brooding and monosyllabic? The testosterone that marinates their brains not only drives them to "compelling masturbatory frenzies," but also reduces their wish to talk or socialize if it does not involve girls or sport.

Overall, in the teen years the differing hormonal effects on the brain cause males and females to go off in different directions—boys gain self-esteem through independence from others, while females gain it through the closeness of their social bonds.

Final comments

Brizendine began her career in psychiatric work and later moved to neurology. This perspective has made her less willing to speculate on psychological or sociological ideas that have little to do with how the brain actually works; though clearly a feminist, she warns that political correctness has no role in understanding behavior. Yes, we may be able to alter our cultural attitudes or policies to make a better world, but first we must understand the facts about how brain biology—so different between men and women—shapes behavior.

Brizendine weighs into the debate sparked by Harvard University president Lawrence Summers, who said that the differences in achievement between men and women in mathematics and the sciences was due to natural brain differences between the sexes. She notes that until puberty, boys and girls are exactly the same in mathematical or scientific achievement. However, the testosterone that floods the male brain makes boys extremely competitive but also more willing to spend many hours studying alone or working on their computers. With the teenage girl's flood of estrogen, in contrast, a female becomes a lot more interested in social bonding and her emotional life, and as a consequence is unlikely to sit for hours alone pondering mathematical puzzles or battling to top the class. Even as adults women are compelled by their brain chemistry to want to communicate and connect, and this favors them less for the sort of solitary work often required by mathematical, scientific, or engineering careers. Brizendine's theory in a nutshell: It is not lack of aptitude that makes women stay out of these fields, but brain-driven attitudes to the work involved.

Yet Brizendine says, "Biology powerfully affects, but does not lock in our reality." That is, if we know about the physiological or genetic forces that shape us, we are able to take account of them. The availability of estrogen in pill form and the fact that we can replace hormones (*The Female Brain* includes a long appendix on hormone replacement therapy) means that women can now have more control over their daily experience of reality; perhaps such treatments will end up having as great an impact on women's lives and destinies as the contraceptive pill did.

Subtracting the copious appendices and notes, *The Female Brain* is only 200 pages long. As an enjoyable and often witty popular synthesis of the latest research on the subject, it is likely to be read for many years to come. With many additional insights into the male brain, this is a book for everyone.

Louann Brizendine

Brizendine's first degree was in neurobiology from the University of California, Berkeley (1972–6), followed by medicine at Yale University, and psychiatry at Harvard Medical School (1982–5).

After a stint teaching at Harvard, in 1988 she accepted a post at the Langley Porter Psychiatric Institute at the University of California, San Francisco, where in 1994 her Women's Mood and Hormone Clinic was established. She continues to combine research work with clinical practice and teaching, focusing on the effects on mood, energy, sexual function, and hormonal influences on the brain.

Feeling Good

"If you're willing to invest a little time in yourself, you can learn to master your moods more effectively, just as an athlete who participates in a daily conditioning program can develop greater endurance and strength."

"What is the key to releasing yourself from your emotional prison? Simply this: Your thoughts create your emotions; therefore, your emotions cannot prove that your thoughts are accurate. Unpleasant feelings merely indicate that you are thinking something negative and believing it. Your emotions follow your thoughts just as surely as baby ducks follow their mother."

In a nutshell

Feelings are not facts; you can change your feelings by changing your thinking.

In a similar vein

CHAPTER 9

David D. Burns

Consider this statistic: In the United States, 5.3 percent of the population will at any given time have depression, and the lifetime risk is 7–8 percent in adults, higher for women. Forty years ago, the mean age for onset of depression was 29.5; today, it has halved to 14.5 years. And though rates differ around the developed world, the incidence of depressive illness has risen dramatically since 1900.

Prior to the 1980s, David Burns writes, depression had been the cancer of the psychological world—widespread but difficult to treat—and the taboos associated with it made the problem worse for most people. As with cancer, finding a "cure" had been its holy grail; everything from Freudian psychoanalysis to shock treatment was applied to the problem, with not very good results.

Burns helped to establish a new method of treatment, cognitive therapy, and *Feeling Good: The New Mood Therapy* is his attempt to explain how it works and why it is different. The book has been a bestseller because it was the first to tell the general public about cognitive therapy, and also because it is a surprisingly enjoyable and useful read for the nondepressed, providing possibly life-changing insights into how our thoughts and emotions interact.

The cognitive way

In his work at the University of Pennsylvania as a psychiatric resident, Burns collaborated with pioneering cognitive psychologist Aaron T. Beck, who believed that most depression or anxiety was simply a result of illogical and negative thinking. He noted the remarkable contrast between how the depressed person feels—that they are a loser or that their life has gone horribly wrong—and the actual conditions of their life, which are often high in achievement. Beck's conclusion was that depression therefore had to be based on problems in *thinking*. By straightening out one's twisted thoughts, one could get back to normal.

Beck's three principles of cognitive therapy were:

❖ All our emotions are generated by our "cognitions," or thoughts. How we feel at any given moment is due to what we are thinking about.
❖ Depression is the constant thinking of negative thoughts.
❖ The majority of negative thoughts that cause us emotional turmoil are plain wrong or at least distortions of the truth, but we accept them without question.

For Burns this sounded a little too obvious and simple, but when he actually tried Beck's new talking treatment for depression called cognitive therapy, he was amazed at how many of his chronic patients were relieved of their destructive feelings. People who had been suicidal a couple of weeks earlier now looked forward to rebuilding their lives.

Seeing through black magic

Cognitive therapy's revolutionary idea is that depression is *not* an emotional disorder. The bad feelings we have in depression all stem from negative thoughts, therefore treatment must be about challenging and changing those thoughts.

Burns lists ten "cognitive distortions," such as all-or-nothing thinking, overgeneralization, disqualifying the positive, jumping to conclusions, and giving ourselves labels. By understanding these distortions, we are led to the awareness that "feelings aren't facts," they are only mirrors of our thoughts.

If that is true, should we trust our feelings? They seem valid, the "truth," but as Burns points out, it is like trusting the funny mirrors we see in amusement parks to be an accurate reflection of ourselves. He notes, "Unpleasant feelings merely indicate that you are thinking something negative and believing it." This is why, he suggests, "depression is such a powerful form of black magic."

Because thoughts come before emotions, our emotions don't prove anything about the accuracy of our thoughts. Feelings are not special at all, particularly when based on distortions. Burns asks the question: When we are in a great mood, do our good feelings determine what we are worth? If not, how can we say that the feelings we have when feeling blue *do* determine our worth?

Burns is not saying that all emotions are distortions. When we experience real sadness or joy, for instance, these are healthy and normal reactions. Genuine sadness, say at the loss of a relative, is of the "soul," whereas depression is always of the mind. It is not an appropriate response to life but a disease of wrong, circular thinking.

Creating a new self-image

Burns notes the catch-22 nature of depression: The worse we feel, the more distorted our thoughts become, and this thinking plunges us even lower into black feelings about ourselves. Nearly all his patients considered that their situation was hopeless. They really believed that they were bad people, and the conversations they had with themselves were like a broken record of self-blame and self-deprecation. Depressed people feel wretched even when they are loved, have a family, have good jobs, and so on. We can have "everything," but if self-love and self-worth have fled, we feel that we are nothing.

Cognitive therapists will often be engaged in a spirited back-and-forth with their patients, trying to point out the silliness or fallacy of their assertions. Eventually patients learn to challenge their wrong thoughts on their own, which is the beginning of feeling good about themselves.

Final comments

Do the ideas in *Feeling Good* really work? Researchers followed two groups of similar patients, one that was given Burns's book to read within a month, and another that was not. Not only did the *Feeling Good* group experience a significant amelioration of depressive symptoms compared to the "blind" group, but their symptoms stayed away. Perhaps the key to the book's efficacy is that we feel we are not being "worked on" but given the tools to change ourselves.

Prescribing books like *Feeling Good* to mental illness patients is called "bibliotherapy," and Burns's is usually ranked highly by professionals in this respect. Could reading a book really be as effective, or even better, than drugs or psychotherapy in helping people with depression? It is certainly worth trying. As Burns himself points out in an introduction to the revised 1999 edition, his book costs about the price of two Prozac pills, and there are no side effects.

Indeed, the great benefit of cognitive therapy is that there is no need to take any drugs. But in the last chapter of *Feeling Good*, Burns explains that, for really serious depression, the most effective treatment is a combination of cognitive therapy and antidepressants, the former to improve patients' thinking, the latter to lift their overall mood.

Burns points out that the basic idea of cognitive therapy—that our thoughts affect our emotions and mood, not the other way around—goes back a long way: The ancient philosopher Epictetus rested his career on the idea that it is not events that determine your state of mind, but how you decide to *feel* about the events. This secret is shared by all happy people, yet it is a skill that can be learnt by anyone.

David D. Burns

Burns attended Amherst College and received his MD from Stanford University. He completed his psychiatric training at the University of Pennsylvania, where he was Acting Chief of Psychiatry of its Medical Center. In 1975 he won the A. E. Bennett Award for research on brain chemistry from the Society for Biological Psychiatry.

Burns has been a Visiting Scholar at Harvard Medical School, and is currently Adjunct Clinical Professor of Psychiatry and Behavioral Sciences at the Stanford University School of Medicine.

Feeling Good has sold over four million copies. As well as the successful spinoff* The Feeling Good Handbook, *Burns has published* Love Is Never Enough, *on relationships,* Ten Days to Self-Esteem, *and* When Panic Attacks.

Influence

"*Just what are the factors that cause one person to say yes to another person? And which techniques most effectively use these factors to bring about such compliance? I wondered why it is that a request stated in a certain way will be rejected, while a request that asks for the same favor in a slightly different fashion will be successful.*"

"*When viewed in this light, the terrible orderliness, the lack of panic, the sense of calm with which these people moved to the vat of poison and to their deaths, seems more comprehensible. They hadn't been hypnotized by Jones; they had been convinced—partly by him but, more importantly, also by the principle of social proof—that suicide was correct conduct.*"

In a nutshell

Know the techniques of psychological influence to avoid becoming their victim.

In a similar vein
Gavin de Becker *The Gift of Fear* (p 20)
Malcolm Gladwell *Blink* (p 124)
Eric Hoffer *The True Believer* (p 152)
Stanley Milgram *Obedience to Authority* (p 198)
Barry Schwartz *The Paradox of Choice* (p 248)

CHAPTER 10

Robert Cialdini

nfluence: The Psychology of Persuasion has sold more than a million copies and been translated into 20 languages. In his introduction, Robert Cialdini admits he had always been an easy mark for salespeople, peddlers, and fundraisers. It had never been easy for him to just say "no" when asked to donate money. An experimental social psychologist, he began wondering about the actual techniques that are used to make a person agree to do something when normally they would not be interested. As part of his research, Cialdini answered newspaper ads for various sales training programs so that he could learn at first hand about persuasion and selling techniques. He penetrated advertising, public relations, and fundraising agencies in order to glean the secrets of the "psychology of compliance" from its professional practitioners.

The result is a classic work of both marketing and psychology that shows us why we are so vulnerable to persuasion, in the process telling us much about human nature.

Getting our tapes to play

Cialdini starts by discussing the mothering instinct of turkeys. Mother turkeys are very protective, good mothers, but their mothering instinct has been found to be triggered by one thing and one thing only: the "cheep-cheep" sound of their chicks. The polecat is the turkey's natural enemy, and when a mother turkey sees one she instantly goes into attack mode; she will do so even at the sight of a stuffed version of a polecat. But when the same stuffed polecat is made to make the same "cheep-cheep" sound that her chicks make, something strange happens: The mother turkey becomes a devoted protector of the polecat!

How dumb are animals, you may be thinking. Press a button, and they act in a certain way, even if those actions are ridiculous. But Cialdini tells us about turkey behavior only to prepare us for the uncomfortable truth about *human* automatic reactions. We also have our "preprogrammed tapes" that usually work for us in positive ways—for instance, to ensure our survival without having to think too much—but they can also play to our detriment when we are unaware of the triggers.

Cialdini identifies half a dozen "weapons of influence," ways of getting us to act automatically that sidestep our normal rational decision-making processes. Psychologists call these easily triggered behaviors "fixed-action patterns"—know the trigger, and you can predict with reasonable likelihood how someone will react.

A more accurate title for *Influence* could be "How to get automatic reactions from people before they can think rationally about your proposition." Cialdini's six basic weapons that compliance professionals use to get people to say "yes" without thinking include reciprocation, commitment and consistency, social proof, liking, authority, and scarcity.

Always return a favor

The rule of reciprocation, found in every culture, is that we should repay anything given to us, whether it's a gift, an invitation, a compliment, and so on.

Do you prefer doing favors for someone you like? Most of us would say yes, but psychological studies have found that the liking factor makes no difference to our sense of obligation to repay a favor. We will feel obligated to individuals or organizations who give us something, even if it is small and even if we don't want it. Cialdini mentions the Hare Krishna movement's tactic of giving flowers or small books to people in the street or in airports. Though most people don't want the flower and often try to give it back, once it is in their hand they feel an obligation to offer a donation. Straightforward mailings by charity groups usually get a response rate of less than 20 percent. But this jumps dramatically when the mailing includes a gift, such as stick-on labels printed with the receiver's own name and address.

It is not just the obligation to repay that is powerful, but the obligation to receive. Not feeling able to say "no," plus our unwillingness to be seen as a person who doesn't repay things, makes us prey to canny marketers. Next time you receive an unsolicited "gift," Cialdini warns, be aware of the lack of goodwill involved; that may allow you to receive it and not give anything back while retaining a good conscience.

He refers to the famous Watergate break-in that brought down the Nixon presidency. In hindsight, the break-in was stupid, risky, unnecessary (Nixon was set to win the next election anyway), and expensive. But the Republican re-election committee that agreed the job only did so to placate one of its more extreme members. G. Gordon Liddy had previously presented two much more outlandish, expensive proposals involving everything from mugging to kidnapping, so when he submitted the idea of a small break-in at Democratic headquarters, the committee felt obligated to say "yes." As committee member Jeb Magruder put it later, "We were reluctant to send him away with nothing." Beware the influence of the reciprocation impulse.

Being consistent

Human beings like to be consistent. We feel better about something if we are committed to it, and once we are, we do what we can to justify the decision in our minds. Why are we like this? Part of the reason is social pressure. No one likes someone who see-saws from one idea or state of mind to another—we like to be seen as knowing what we want. This, unfortunately, creates a goldmine for marketers. They are very aware of the internal pressures against changing our mind, and take full advantage. When charity phone callers ask "How are you feeling tonight, Mrs...?" nine times out of ten we give a positive response. Then when the caller asks us to give a donation to the unfortunate victims of some disaster or disease, we can't very well suddenly turn mean and grumpy and refuse others who are in a bad way. To be consistent, we feel compelled to offer a donation.

Marketers know that if you get someone to offer a small commitment, you have their self-image in your hands. This is why some unscrupulous car dealers offer an initially very low price for a car, which gets us into the showroom, but later, with all the extras, it doesn't turn out to be such a low price at all. Yet by this stage we feel committed to the purchase. Another trick is for salespeople to get customers to fill out an order form or sales agreement themselves, dramatically reducing the chances of them changing their mind. Public commitments are a strong force.

Cialdini notes Emerson's famous quote, "A foolish consistency is the hobgoblin of little minds." Especially when you are marketed to, remember your natural tendency to be consistent and you will find it easier to back out of deals that really aren't that good. Go with your gut feeling about the worth of something before you feel the pressure of consistency—and before you make an initial commitment.

Social proof

Why is canned laughter still added to the recordings of television comedy shows, even when the creative people who make the shows feel insulted by it and most viewers say they don't like it? Because research shows that viewers find the gags funnier when they hear other people laughing, even if the laughter isn't real.

Human beings need the "social proof" of other people doing something first before they feel comfortable doing it themselves. Cialdini provides a very dark example, the famous case of Catherine Genovese, a woman who was murdered in the street in Queens, New York City in 1964. Despite the fact that her assailant attacked her three times over the course of half an hour before finally killing her, despite the sound of screams and scuffles, and incredibly even though 38 people saw what was happening, no one stopped to intervene. Was this just a case of the heartlessness of New Yorkers? Possibly, although the witnesses seemed shocked themselves that they had done nothing. Finally an answer emerged. It seemed that everyone thought *someone else* would do something, and so no one did anything. A person in dire straits, Cialdini notes, has a greater chance of getting help if only one person is around, rather than a number of people. In a crowd or in a city street, if people see that no one has gone to someone's aid, they feel disinclined to help. We need "social proof" before we act.

Before it became a common notion, Cialdini discussed the idea of "copycat" suicides. The most famous case of social proof in relation to suicide was the ghastly Jonestown, Guyana incident in 1978, when 910 members of Jim Jones's People's Temple cult took their lives by drinking from vats of poisoned soft drink. How was it possible that so many died so willingly? Most of the cult members had been recruited in San Francisco, and Cialdini suggests that the isolation of being in a foreign country contributed to the natural human tendency to "do what others like us are doing."

On a lighter note, advertising and marketing are often built around our need for social proof. Often our unwillingness to use a product until plenty of other people are is a useful way of knowing if something is good or not (a shortcut), but marketers get around this easily. Consider the use of "testimonials," which, even when done by actors, still have the ability to influence our buying decisions.

Not missing out

G. K. Chesterton said, "The way to love anything is to realize that it might be lost." It is human nature to value something more when it is scarce. In fact, we are more motivated by the thought of losing something than we are by gaining something of equal value in its place. Retailers know this, which is why they perpetually scream "stocks won't last" to make us fear not getting something we were not sure we wanted anyway.

When a film or book has been censored or banned, Cialdini notes, demand for it usually jumps. Whatever we have been told we shouldn't have gains cachet. According to his "Romeo and Juliet" effect, teenage lovers are much more likely to intensify their relationship if both parents oppose the union and it is difficult for them to meet.

We should be aware of our reaction to scarcity because it affects our ability to think straight. We do silly things like get into bidding wars and then have to pay for something we never budgeted for. We fall victim to salespeople who "only have one left in stock" or real-estate agents who tell us about "a physician and his wife from out of town who are also interested in the house." Be careful to make a cool evaluation of the worth of something, instead of being hijacked by the fear of missing out.

Final comments

You will have to get the book to learn about the two other categories of influence, "liking" and "authority." As a clue to the second, Cialdini refers to Stanley Milgram's famous experiments (see p 198) on the tendency of human beings to respect authority, even when the authority figure is highly questionable.

Though Cialdini offers many salutary and often scary lessons about our vulnerability to psychological techniques, awareness of them should not necessarily lower our view of human nature. In fact, an appreciation of our automatic behavior patterns may increase the chance that we retain a mind of our own. The best way of reducing the effectiveness of compliance tactics on the unaware is to have more people knowing about them—and in this *Influence* has done a great public service.

One interesting feature of the revised edition of the book is the letters sent in from readers who have witnessed, or been the victim of, the techniques discussed in the book and wish to share them. *Influence* is a great primer on how marketers succeed in getting us to buy, but on a deeper level it is about the way we make decisions. Are your decisions the result of someone trying to pull your mental or emotional strings, or are you thinking rationally?

Robert Cialdini

Cialdini received his PhD in psychology from the University of North Carolina and did postdoctoral training at Columbia University. He has also held posts as a visiting scholar at Ohio State University and Stanford University.

He is considered the world's leading authority on the subject of influence and persuasion and is currently Regents' Professor of Psychology at Arizona State University, and president of a consultancy, Influence At Work, which works with corporate clients.

Cialdini has also written Influence: Science and Practice, *designed for teaching persuasion and compliance principles to groups.*

Creativity

"The real story of creativity is more difficult and strange than many overly optimistic accounts have claimed. For one thing, as I will try to show, an idea or product that deserves the label 'creative' arises from the synergy of many sources and not only from the mind of a single person... And a genuinely creative accomplishment is almost never the result of a sudden insight, a light-bulb flashing on in the dark, but comes after years of hard work."

"Creativity is a central source of meaning in our lives for several reasons... First, most of the things that are interesting, important, and human are the results of creativity. We share 98 percent of our genetic makeup with chimpanzees... Without creativity, it would be difficult indeed to distinguish humans from apes."

In a nutshell

Real creativity can only emerge once we have mastered the medium or domain in which we work.

In a similar vein
Edward de Bono *Lateral Thinking* (p 38)
Martin Seligman *Authentic Happiness* (p 254)

CHAPTER 11

Mihaly Csikszentmihalyi

Before turning his mind to creativity, psychologist Mihaly Csikszentmihalyi (pronounced Chick-sent-me-hi) wrote a celebrated book called *Flow*. Its insight was that it is a mistake to pursue happiness itself. Rather, we should recognize when we are genuinely happy—what we are doing when we feel powerful and "true"—and do more of those things. Flow activities we do for the sheer enjoyment or intellectual satisfaction, rather than to gain some extrinsic reward. You might want to win a game of chess, for instance, but you play it because it engages your mind totally. You might want to become a good dancer, but it is the learning and dancing that are the main reward.

Csikszentmihalyi took these ideas and applied them to the question of how some people become genuinely creative. He was not interested in what he calls the "small c" creativity involved in making a cake or choosing curtains or the imaginative talk of a child, but the kind that changes a whole "domain" or area of human endeavor. Truly creative people have a capacity to change the fundamental way we see, understand, appreciate, or do things, whether it is by inventing a new machine or writing a set of songs, and Csikszentmihalyi wanted to know what made them different.

Creativity: Flow and the Psychology of Discovery and Invention is the culmination of 30 years of work into creativity. There is a small industry of how-to-be-more-creative books and seminars, and many are glib, but this is one of the few serious treatments that understands the complexity of the creative person and process.

Studying the creative

At the beginning of *Creativity*, Csikszentmihalyi provides information on what he claims was the first systematic study of living creative people, involving interviews with 91 people considered to have had an outstanding impact on their domain, whether that was the arts, business, law, government, medicine, or science (the scientists encompassed 14 Nobel Prize winners). The names included Mortimer J. Adler, philosopher; John Bardeen, physicist; Kenneth Boulding, economist; Margaret Butler, mathematician; Subrahmanyan Chandrasekhar, astrophysicist; Barry Commoner, biologist; Natalie Davis, historian; Gyorgy Faludy, poet; Nadine Gordimer, writer; Stephen Jay Gould, paleontologist; Hazel Henderson, economist; Ellen Lanyon, artist; Ernst Mayr, zoologist; Brenda Milner, psychologist; Ilya Prigogine, chemist; John Reed, banker; Jonas Salk, biologist; Ravi Shankar, musician; Benjamin Spock, pediatrician; and Eva Zeisel, ceramic designer.

It is worth getting *Creativity* just to read about these people, some of whom are outright famous and others who are known mainly within their own field. Nearly all the subjects were over 60, allowing Csikszentmihalyi a better chance to survey fully developed careers and elicit insights into the secrets of mature creative success.

Creativity in context

Csikszentmihalyi suggests that the common idea of a creative individual coming up with great insights, discoveries, works, or inventions in isolation is wrong. Creativity results from a complex interaction between a person and their environment or culture, and also depends on timing.

For instance, if the great Renaissance artists like Ghiberti or Michelangelo had been born only 50 years before they were, the culture of artistic patronage would not have been in place to fund or shape their great achievements. Consider also individual astronomers: Their discoveries could not have happened unless centuries of technological development of the telescope and evolving knowledge of the universe had come before them.

Csikszentmihalyi's point is that we should devote as much attention to the development of a domain as we do to the people working within it, as only this can properly explain how advances are made. Individuals are only "a link in a chain, a phase in a process," he notes. Did Einstein really "invent" the theory of relativity? Did Edison "invent" electricity? This is like saying that the spark is responsible for the fire, when of course fire involves many elements.

The products of creativity also need to have a receptive audience to evaluate them. A creation vanishes if it is not recognized. "Memes" are the cultural equivalent of genes, things such as language, customs, laws, songs, theories, and values. If they're strong they survive, otherwise they are lost. Creative people seek to create memes that can have an impact on their cultures. The greater the creator, the longer lasting and deeper the impact of the memes.

First, love your work

Creative breakthroughs never just come out of the blue. They are almost always the result of years of hard work and close attention to something. Many creative discoveries are lucky, particularly those of the scientific type, but usually the "luck" comes after years of detailed work in the area in which the discovery is made. Csikszentmihalyi tells of the astronomer Vera Rubin, who discovered that stars in some galaxies do not all rotate in the same direction—some go clockwise, and others anticlockwise. She would not have made the discovery if she had not had access to a new type of clearer spectral analysis, and this access came from her already being known for her substantial contributions to the field. Rubin was not out to make a big discovery; rather, it was the result of close observation of stars and a love of her work. Her goal was to record data, but it was her dedication that yielded the surprise findings. Truly creative people work for work's own sake, and if they make a public discovery or become famous that is a bonus. What drives them, more than rewards, is the desire to find or create order where there was none before.

Be a master before a creator

A popular image of the creative person is their defiance of all norms, dogma, and customs. This gives the wrong impression, however, as everyone who creates genuine change has first needed to master their domain, which means soaking up and mastering its skills and knowledge. It is only later, having mastered their domain, that people can truly make a creative mark, as incorporation of the "rules" of the domain allows those rules to be bent or broken to create something new. In short, to do new things, you first have to have done the old things well.

Common creative features

Csikszentmihalyi's other insights include:

* The idea of the tortured creative person is largely a myth. Most of his respondents were very happy with their lives and their creative output.
* Successful creative people tend to have two things in abundance: curiosity and drive. They are absolutely fascinated by their subject, and while others may be more brilliant, their sheer desire for accomplishment is the decisive factor.
* Creative people take their intuition seriously, looking for patterns where others see confusion, and are able to make connections between discrete areas of knowledge.
* Creative people are often seen as arrogant, but this is usually because they want to devote most of their attention to their exciting work.
* Though creative people can be creative anywhere, they gravitate to centers where their interests can be satisfied more easily, where they can meet like-minded people, and where their work can be appreciated.
* Beautiful or inspiring environments are better at helping people to be more creative thinkers than giving them a seminar on "creativity."
* School does not seem to have had a great effect on many famous creative people, and even in college they were often not stars. Many people later considered geniuses were not particularly remarkable as children; what they always had more than others was curiosity.
* Many creative achievers were either orphaned or had little contact with their father. On the other hand, they frequently had a very involved, loving mother who expected a lot from them.

❖ Most fell into one of two family categories: They were poor or disadvantaged, but their parents nevertheless pushed them to educational or career attainment; or they grew up in families of intellectuals, researchers, professionals, writers, musicians, and so on. Only 10 percent were middle class. The lesson: To be a powerfully creative adult, it is best to be brought up in a family that values intellectual endeavor, not one that celebrates middle-class comfort.

❖ The creative are both humble and proud, with a selfless devotion to their domain and what might be achieved, yet also confidence that they have much to contribute and will make their mark.

❖ It is a myth that there is one "creative personality." Something all creative people seem to share is complexity—they "tend to bring the entire range of human possibilities within themselves."

Final comments

Csikszentmihalyi says that it would be too easy to see creative people as a privileged elite. Rather, their lives are a message that we should all be able to find work that is fulfilling and that we love. As he notes, most of the people in the study did not come from privileged backgrounds, but had to struggle to do what they wanted in the face of economic or family pressures. Some of the respondents felt that their greatest achievement, in fact, was having created their own lives or careers without recourse to social expectation.

Why should we really care about creativity? Csikszentmihalyi's work on the flow experience found that it occurs most readily when people are engaged in "designing or discovering something new." We are happiest when we are being creative because we lose our sense of self and get the feeling that we are part of something greater. We are actually programmed to get satisfaction and pleasure from discovery and creativity, he says, because its results lead to our survival as a species. New ideas are needed more than ever if the planet is going to survive, and the best ones are likely to come from genuinely creative people.

Mihaly Csikszentmihalyi

Mihaly Csikszentmihalyi was born in 1934 in Fiume on the Adriatic, and his father was the Hungarian consul of what was then an Italian city. The family name means "Saint Michael from the province of Csik," Csik being originally a Hungarian province.

Csikszentmihalyi spent his adolescence in Rome, helping to run the family restaurant while receiving a classical education. After graduating he worked as a photographer and travel agent. He enrolled at the University of Chicago in 1958, where he received a BA and PhD. Though he was more interested in the ideas of Carl Jung, he was required to study behaviorist psychology, and only later during his years as a professor at Chicago was he able to develop his theories on flow, creativity, and the self.

Since 1999 Csikszentmihalyi has been a professor at Claremont Graduate University in California, where his Quality of Life Research Center explores aspects of positive psychology.

Other books include Beyond Boredom and Anxiety *(1975),* The Evolving Self: A Psychology for the Third Millennium *(1993), and* Finding Flow: The Psychology of Engagement with Everyday Life *(1997).*

A Guide to Rational Living

"*You can never expect to be deliriously happy at all times in life. Freedom from all physical pain is never likely to be your lot. But an extraordinary lack of mental and emotional woe may be yours—if you think that it may be and work for what you believe in.*"

"*Man is a uniquely language-creating animal and he begins to learn from very early childhood to formulate his thoughts, perceptions, and feelings in words, phrases, and sentences... If this is so (and we know of no evidence to the contrary), then for all practical purposes the phrases and sentences that we keep telling ourselves usually are or become our thoughts and emotions.*"

In a nutshell

If we know how we generate negative emotions through particular thoughts, especially irrational ones, we have the secret to never being desperately unhappy again.

In a similar vein

Nathaniel Branden *The Psychology of Self-Esteem* (p 42)
David D. Burns *Feeling Good* (p 58)
Martin Seligman *Authentic Happiness* (p 254)

CHAPTER 12

Albert Ellis & Robert A. Harper

A *Guide to Rational Living* is one of the most enduring books in the popular psychology literature, selling over a million copies. Since it was published over 40 years ago, thousands of "inspirational" titles have come and gone, but it continues to change people's lives.

The book brought to public attention a new form of psychology, "rational emotive therapy" (RET), that went against decades of orthodox Freudian psychoanalysis and sparked a revolution in psychology. RET says that emotions do not arise as a result of repressed desires and needs, as Freud insisted, but directly from our thoughts, ideas, attitudes, and beliefs. It is not the mysterious unconscious that matters most to our psychological health, but the humdrum statements we say to ourselves on a daily basis. Added up, these represent our philosophy of life, one that can quite easily be altered if we are willing to change what we habitually say to ourselves.

Reasoning your way out of emotional tangles seems doubtful, but Ellis's pioneering ideas, and four decades of cognitive psychology, have shown that the theory does indeed work.

Watching our internal sentences

Human beings, Ellis and Harper note, are language-creating animals. We tend to formulate our emotions and our ideas in terms of words and sentences. These effectively become our thoughts and emotions. Therefore, if we are basically the things we tell ourselves, any type of personal change requires us to look first at our internal conversations. Do they serve us or undermine us?

Talk therapy aims to reveal the "errors in logic" that people believe to be true. If, for instance, we are having terrible feelings of anxiety or fear, we are asked to track back to the original thought in the sequence of thoughts that led to our current anxiety. We invariably find that we are saying things to ourselves such as "Wouldn't it be terrible if…" or "Isn't it horrible that I am…" It is at this point that we have to intervene and ask ourselves *why* exactly it would be so terrible if such and such happened, or whether our current situation is *really* as bad as we say. And even if it is, will it last forever?

This sort of self-questioning at first seems naïve, but by doing it we begin to see just how much our internal sentences shape our life. After all, if we label some event a "catastrophe," it surely will become one. We can only live up to our internal statements, whether they make something good, bad, or neutral.

Never being desperately unhappy again

How is it that human beings have conquered space and the atom, but most of us can't get ourselves out of bad moods? As we have advanced materially, it seems that the level of neurosis and psychosis in society has only risen; the main challenge for people today is gaining control over their emotional lives.

In a chapter titled "The art of never being desperately unhappy," Ellis and Harper argue that misery and depression are always states of mind, since they are self-perpetuated. When we are dejected after the loss of a relationship or a job, for instance, this is quite understandable. However, if we allow the feeling to linger, it builds strength. Things snowball so that we become "miserable with our own misery," instead of trying to see the situation rationally. *A Guide to Rational Living* notes that it is "virtually impossible to sustain an emotional outburst without bolstering it by repeated ideas." Something will remain "bad" in our mind only as long as we tell ourselves it is. If we do not keep creating the bad feeling, how can it possibly endure? Granted, if we are experiencing physical pain we cannot simply ignore it, but once it is over there is no automatic link between stimulus and feeling.

Even in the 1960s, Ellis was saying that drugs were problematic in treating depression, because once a person stopped taking them, they tended to become depressed again. Permanent change required them to actually change their thinking so that they could "talk themselves out of" persistent negative feelings whenever they surfaced. He shrewdly observed that some people secretly enjoy being depressed, because they don't have to take any action to change. In some cases, we have to decide that we will not be depressed and our feelings alter accordingly.

Final comments

Are human beings rational or irrational? We are both, Ellis and Harper say. We are brainy, but we still go in for puerile, idiotic, prejudiced, and selfish behavior anyway. The key to a good life is applying rationality to the most irrational sphere of life, the emotions.

In the emphasis on disciplining our own thinking and finding a middle way between extreme emotions, there are some definite echoes of Buddhism in the rational emotive approach. It acknowledges that whatever happened in our past, it is the present that matters and what we can do now to alleviate it. Ellis discovered this himself as a boy. With a troubled bipolar-affected mother, and a father often away on business trips, he took responsibility for his younger siblings, making sure they got dressed and off to school each day. When he was hospitalized with kidney problems, his parents rarely visited him. Ellis learnt that we don't have to get upset by situations unless we allow ourselves to be, that there is always room for control of our reactions. While his brand of therapy may seem hard-nosed, in fact it represents a very optimistic view of people.

A *Guide to Rational Living* helps anyone to understand how their emotions are generated and, crucially, how a reasonably happy and productive life can be yours through more care and discipline in your thinking. Its topics include lessening the need for approval, conquering anxiety, "how to be happy though frustrated," and eradicating fear of failure. Consistent with its content, the book has a wonderfully clear and straightforward style. Get the updated and revised third edition, which contains a new chapter on research supporting the principles behind, and the techniques of, RET.

Albert Ellis

Born in 1913 in Pittsburgh, Pennsylvania, Ellis was raised in New York City. He gained a business degree at the City University of New York, and unsuccessfully attempted a career in business. He also tried and failed to become a novelist.

Having written some articles on human sexuality, in 1942 Ellis entered the clinical psychology program at Columbia University. On obtaining his master's degree in 1943 he launched a part-time private practice in family and sex counseling, and in 1947 earned his doctorate. He held positions at Rutgers and New York University, and as a senior clinical psychologist at the Northern New Jersey Mental Hygiene Clinic.

Ellis's ideas were slow to be accepted by the American psychological establishment, but today he is considered, along with Aaron Beck, to be the father of cognitive behavior therapy. The Institute for Rational-Emotive Therapy, founded in 1959, continues to disseminate his ideas. See also the biography The Lives of Albert Ellis *by Emmet Velten.*

Ellis was the author of more than 600 academic papers, and his 50-plus books include How to Live with a Neurotic, The Art and Science of Love, Sex Without Guilt, The Art and Science of Rational Eating, *and* How to Make Yourself Stubbornly Refuse to be Miserable About Anything—Yes, Anything.

Robert A. Harper is a former president of the American Association of Marriage Counselors and the American Academy of Psychotherapists. He has a PhD from Ohio State University, and since 1953 has been in private practice in Washington DC. Other books include Creative Marriage *(with Albert Ellis) and* 45 Levels to Sexual Understanding and Enjoyment *(with Walter Stokes).*

1982

My Voice Will Go With You: The Teaching Tales of Milton Erickson

"If one reads these stories in the so-called waking state, one might dismiss them as being 'clichéd,' 'corny,' or 'of interest, but not enlightening.' Yet, in the hypnotic state, where everything that is said by the therapist is heightened in meaning, a story, or a single word in a story, may trigger a mini satori—the Zen term for enlightenment." Sidney Rosen

"It is really amazing what people can do. Only they don't know what they can do." Milton Erickson

In a nutshell

The unconscious mind is a well of wise solutions and forgotten personal power.

In a similar vein

Robert Cialdini *Influence* (p 62)
Sigmund Freud *The Interpretation of Dreams* (p 110)
Carl Jung *The Archetypes and the Collective Unconscious* (p 168)
Fritz Perls *Gestalt Therapy* (p 216)
Carl Rogers *On Becoming a Person* (p 238)

CHAPTER 13

Sidney Rosen

Sigmund Freud experimented with hypnosis, but could never induce trances easily or get patients to accept his suggestions. Milton Erickson, born 45 years after Freud, in many ways fulfilled the potential of hypnosis and made it into a bona fide psychological tool, which can often bring about instant changes in people who have labored with complexes and phobias for years.

Perhaps the answer to why Freud failed and Erickson so brilliantly succeeded can be found in the dynamics of the psychotherapeutic relationship. Conventionally, because doctors have the knowledge, they are the healers. The patients, in their ignorance, are the ones to be healed. As a young doctor in mental institutions, Erickson inherited this understanding, but later began to comprehend the relationship as simply two people working together to tap their unconscious minds for solutions. By going into a trance himself, Erickson's voice would "become" the patient's voice ("My voice will go with you," he would tell them), so creating a great power of suggestion.

The Erickson way

Erickson's secret was his "teaching tales," not old fairytales but anecdotes about his own family life or the cases of previous patients that carried with them special meaning for a person's problem. They usually involved an element of shock or surprise, and were designed to provoke an "aha" moment that allowed the person to get outside the normal circularity of their thoughts. Instead of saying "I see what's wrong, this is what you should do," Erickson would let patients glean the message from the anecdote, as if they had figured it out on their own.

An alcoholic who came to Erickson seemed a hopeless case. His parents were alcoholics, his grandparents on both sides were drinkers, even his wife and brother were alcoholics. Erickson could have sent him to Alcoholics Anonymous, but given the man's environment—he worked on a newspaper, which he said encouraged a hard-drinking lifestyle—Erickson thought he would try something different. He asked the man to go the local botanical gardens and just sit and contemplate the cactus plants, which "could go for three years without water and not die." Many years later the man's daughter contacted Erickson, and told him that after the "cactus treatment" both her father and her mother had stayed sober. The image of a flourishing cactus needing little "drink" had obviously been a powerful one.

Erickson admitted that this treatment would never have been found in a textbook, but that was the point of his style of therapy: We are all different and we respond to the cure that means most to us. Sometimes his tales seem more like Zen *koans* or riddles, not making perfect sense. When you hear them in a normal state you may consider they are corny or think "So what?" but in a trance the loaded language, meaningful pauses, and element of surprise can jolt a sudden connection with the unconscious mind that triggers change.

Erickson gave psychiatrist Sidney Rosen permission to collate many of his tales and put them into a book with commentary. Though over 20 years old now, *My Voice Will Go With You* is a perfect introduction to Erickson, capturing his magic and unique contribution to psychology. Below is a brief look at a handful of tales and an interpretation of their meaning, but it is worth getting the actual book for the rest.

Establishing rapport

When working with patients, rather than trying to find out a lot of background history Erickson's priority was to establish "rapport." He became very aware of how a person responded to a tale in terms of body language, breathing, and small facial cues.

One summer Erickson was selling books door to door to help pay for his college tuition. He visited a farmer, but the farmer wasn't interested in books. He was only concerned with raising his hogs. Giving up trying to sell anything, Erickson began scratching the hogs' backs; having grown up on a farm himself, he knew they liked this. The farmer noticed and was pleased, saying, "Anyone who likes hogs, and knows how to scratch their backs, is someone I want to know." He asked the young Erickson to stay for supper, and then agreed to buy his books.

Erickson told the story to show that everything about us communicates something—we cannot *not* communicate. When we need to make judgments, just as the farmer did we have to let our subconscious minds have a role; feelings or hunches are usually correct and we must take in the "whole" situation.

Mirroring

A related technique is mirroring. By "going along with" what a patient was saying, Erickson could make them see more objectively how they were acting.

In a hospital where he worked there were two men claiming to be Jesus Christ. He made them sit on a bench and talk to each other. Eventually, by seeing the idiocy of the other person's claims each was able to see the silliness of their own. When a hospital was building a new wing, Erickson got another "Jesus" to help out with the carpentry, knowing that the man could not deny that Jesus was famously a carpenter before emerging as the Messiah. This unusual remedy got the man engaged with reality and other people again.

Ruth was a beautiful 12-year-old girl with a great personality. People did things for her because they liked her so much. However, she was apt to suddenly kick people in the shins, tear their clothes, or stamp on their foot and break their toes. One day Erickson heard that she was on a rampage in a ward. When he got there she was tearing plaster off walls, but he didn't tell her to stop—he began trashing the surroundings himself, tearing sheets off beds and breaking windows. "Let's go somewhere else," he said, "this is fun," and he went into the corridor. When he saw a nurse he ripped her clothes off, revealing only her bra and panties. At this Ruth said, "Dr. Erickson, you shouldn't do a thing like that," and brought a sheet to the nurse to cover her up. With her own behavior revealed to her, she became a good girl. (The nurse who "happened" to be in the corridor had agreed to be part of the scene.)

Indirect logic

Often, when someone came to Erickson with a control or addiction problem, he would not tell them to stop doing whatever they were doing, but to go on doing it more intensely. When a man came to him who wanted to lose weight and stop smoking and drinking, he did not tell him to cease any of these things. Instead, he ordered him to buy his food, cigarettes, and alcohol not from the local shops but from shops at least a mile away, so that frequent exercise would lead him to reconsider his habits.

A woman came to Erickson who weighed 180lb and wanted to weigh 130lb. She was stuck in a pattern of gaining then losing weight. Erickson said he would help her if she first made a promise. She agreed, and he told her to first *gain* weight until she reached 200lb. She fought against this, but once she had reached 200lb she was so desperate to be "allowed" to lose weight that she went down to 130lb without difficulty.

These examples of Erickson's "indirect" logic reveal his larger philosophy: You can only really get a person to change when they feel they "own" the change. Compared to coercion or instruction, change will always be more powerful and lasting this way.

Reframing

A woman came to see Erickson who hated living in Phoenix, Arizona. Her husband wanted to go on holiday to Flagstaff (another city in Arizona), but she said she felt better staying in Phoenix and *hating* it than she did going elsewhere for relief. Erickson made her curious about why she hated Phoenix so much and why she punished herself with her thoughts. During a hypnosis session he told her to go to Flagstaff and watch for a "flash of color." He secretly had nothing in mind he wanted her to see, but it made the woman curious, and when she found her flash of color (a red bird against a green background) she was elated.

Erickson wanted to change her mindset so that she would begin to see things she didn't normally see—in a deeper sense in addition to the physical faculty of vision. The woman ended up spending a month in Flagstaff, and thereafter went on vacations in different parts of America, looking for the "flash of color" that provided meaning. In one or two sessions, Erickson had facilitated a change from strong negative feeling to life-affirming curiosity.

The wisdom within

If there is one thing that can be drawn from Erickson's work it is that inside each of us there is "something which knows." He believed that every person had a healthy, powerful core, and that hypnosis was a useful tool in allowing this self to guide us again.

He illustrated this in an anecdote from his boyhood. One day a horse wandered onto the family property and they didn't know whose it was; it had no marks. Milton decided to mount the horse and take it back to the road, but instead of riding it different places to find the owner, he let the horse guide *him*. When the horse walked back to its owners' property, they asked how he knew it was theirs. He replied: "*I* didn't know—but the *horse* knew. All I did was keep him on the road."

The "horse" is of course the unconscious mind, which if accessed in a trance state can solve any problem and return us to our true, powerful self. Erickson believed that most of our limitations are self-imposed, but that the barriers are mainly put up by our conscious mind. By accessing and reshaping the contents of our unconscious, we can reshape our lives. It is up to us to reprogram ourselves with information that is a better approximation of reality, not to be stuck with negative or twisted thought patterns.

Final comments

Erickson's ability to pick up on tiny cues in a person's facial movements and body language often caused people to believe he was psychic. When he contracted polio at 17 he could hardly move, and with nothing else to do, he began watching and analyzing the behavior of his numerous siblings. He noticed that sometimes when they said one thing they meant another, and that communication involved a lot more than merely speech. His famous ability to read people had begun.

If you have ever gone to a hypnotist to stop smoking, lose weight, or be cured of a phobia you are evidence that hypnosis is now respectable, and this is part of Erickson's legacy. His idea of "brief therapy"—that change can happen in an instant, instead of a patient spending years in psychoanalysis—is also now part of the psychotherapeutic landscape. In addition, his followers Richard Bandler and John Grinder went on to create neurolinguistic programming (NLP), a more codified version of Ericksonian techniques that has been taken up by business and personal coaches to provide an edge at work.

Yet as Rosen shows, Erickson was hardly technological in his approach. He recognized human beings as a story-telling species. A tale, myth, or anecdote is always the most effective way to express insights about life and personal transformation.

Milton Erickson

Born in Aurum, Nevada in 1901, Erickson was color blind, tone deaf, and dyslexic. When he was young his family traveled in a covered wagon to Wisconsin, where they established a farm.

Erickson studied psychology at the University of Wisconsin, where he learnt how to hypnotize people. He gained his medical degree through the Colorado General Hospital, and worked as a junior psychiatrist at Rhode Island State Hospital. From 1930–34 he was at Worcester State Hospital, becoming chief psychiatrist, followed by clinical and teaching appointments in Eloise, Michigan. There he married Elizabeth Erickson; they had five children, in addition to three he had in a previous marriage.

In 1948 Erickson moved to Phoenix for health reasons, where his "miracle" cures brought people to him from across America. He hypnotized writer Aldous Huxley, and counted among his friends anthropologist Margaret Mead and philosopher Gregory Bateson. He was founder of the American Society of Clinical Hypnosis and a fellow of the American Psychological and Psychiatric Associations.

Erickson died in 1980. His ashes were scattered on Squaw Peak in Phoenix, which he had often ordered patients to climb as part of their treatment.

Sidney Rosen is assistant clinical professor in the psychiatric department of the New York University Medical Center. He has presented workshops on Ericksonian techniques, and wrote the foreword to Erickson's Hypnotherapy: An Exploratory Casebook *(1979), written with Ernest L. Rossi.*

Young Man Luther

"I have called the major crisis of adolescence the identity crisis; it occurs in that period of the life cycle when each youth must forge for himself some central perspective and direction, some working unity, out of the effective remnants of his childhood and the hopes of his anticipated adulthood."

"No doubt when Martin learned to speak up, much that he had to say to the devil was fueled by a highly compressed store of defiance consisting of what he had been unable to say to his father and to his teachers; in due time he said it all, with a vengeance, to the Pope."

In a nutshell

Crises of identity, while painful at the time, are necessary to forge a stronger, more commanding self.

In a similar vein

Nathaniel Branden *The Psychology of Self-Esteem* (p 42)
William James *The Principles of Psychology* (p 162)
Gail Sheehy *Passages* (p 260)

CHAPTER 14

Erik Erikson

f you have ever talked about having an "identity crisis" you have psychologist Erik Erikson to thank for inventing the term. Erikson's focus on identity was shaped by his own background. The product of a brief affair between his married Jewish mother, Karla Abrahamsen, and an unidentified Danish man, he grew up in Germany as Erik Homberger, taking the surname of his physician stepfather. At school he was teased for being Jewish, while at the synagogue he was pilloried for his "Nordic god" appearance; he was tall, blond, and blue-eyed. When three half-sisters came along, this only intensified his feeling of being an outsider. In his late 30s, on taking up US citizenship, Erik Homberger changed his surname to Erikson; that is, son of himself.

While Erikson paid particular attention to the formation of identity in adolescence, his great contribution was to note that the question "Who am I?" will raise itself many times over the course of an average person's lifetime. Freud identified five stages of psychological development from infancy to the teenage years, but Erikson went further to cover the whole life cycle, with eight "psychosocial" stages from birth to old age. As one stage ends, we experience a crisis when our identity comes into question, and at these points we can choose either growth or stagnation. Each choice, he said, lays another cornerstone in the structure of the adult personality. In fully appreciating the intensity of these turning points, he shattered the myth that life after we turn 20 is one long flat line of stability.

Erikson is famous for another reason. Although Freud had written a celebrated study of Leonardo da Vinci, it was Erikson's books on Gandhi and Martin Luther that established a new genre, "psychobiography" or the application of psychological analysis to famous people's lives. In Luther he found an example of identity crisis *par excellence*, described in *Young Man Luther: A Study in Psychoanalysis and History*.

The Luther story in brief

The Christian Europe of Luther's childhood and adolescence was preoccupied with the "Last Judgment," a final accounting of one's life in which all sins would be balanced against the good. People lived in fear of going to hell, and prayed relentlessly for the souls of those who had died. Public torture of criminals was common, as were caning and whipping children in school. The theme of life was total obedience: to one's elders, to the Church, to God.

Into this "world-mood of guilt and sadness," as Erikson described it, Martin Luther was born in 1483. His father came from peasant stock, but through hard work became a small-scale capitalist with an ownership stake in a mine. Hans Luther created a nest egg for his son's education, intending him to become a high-ranking lawyer who would vault the family out of its humble origins. Martin Luther duly went to Latin school and did well, and at 17 entered university. In 1505 he graduated and enrolled in law school. However, while at home for the summer break he was almost struck by lightning during a thunderstorm. Already having misgivings about the life path laid out for him, he took the event as a sign and vowed to become a monk. His parents were devastated, but in 1501 he entered the Augustinian monastery at Erfurt.

At first all went well, as he enjoyed the holy atmosphere of the monastery. Nevertheless, like any young man he was tempted by sexual thoughts and consumed by guilt over them. As the many Luther biographers tell the story, he had some kind of panic attack in the choir of his monastery church, crying out "I am *not*!" Erickson saw the event as indicating a classic identity crisis. Luther had left behind the secular career (not to mention marriage) his father had so wanted him to follow, yet now, after a promising "godly" beginning, the monastery path seemed wrong as well, despite his desperate efforts to cling to his vows. He was caught in a terrible no-man's-land of identity. Whatever he thought he was, it was painfully clear he was not.

Yet Martin stayed with the Church, ascending quickly. He became a doctor of theology and by 1515 was a vicar in charge of 11 monasteries. All the time, though, a gap was growing between his understanding of genuine spiritual faith and his perception of the Church. According to medieval Catholic doctrine, sins required some kind of worldly punishment, which could be alleviated by doing "good works." But even this responsibility could be sidestepped by the purchase of "indulgences," pieces of paper sold by the Church that poured money into its coffers. Even this issue was just the tip of the iceberg for Luther. Quite radically, he had come to the belief that the authority of the Bible (the "Word") was far more important than the authority of an institution.

Things came to a head when, in October 1517, he nailed a document—the famous "95 Theses"—to the door of the Castle Church in Wittenberg (a usual place for posting public notices), outlining the areas where the Church had to reform. The document was a bombshell, but might never have had the impact it did were it not for the recent invention of the printing press, which enabled this and Luther's later writings to be spread far and wide. Anyone, from peasant to prince, who had a gripe with the status quo now had a focus. Luther became a celebrity, and his rebellion sparked off the Protestant Reformation.

Erikson's interpretation

Rebellion is usually manifested in one's younger years, but Luther was 34 by the time he properly spoke out against the Church. Erikson's explanation was that young people must first believe in something intensely before they turn against it, and Luther was desperate to believe in the Church's divine authority. He may never have become its most vocal critic if he had not first gone through the experience of complete devotion and attachment. Erikson commented that great figures in history often spend years in a passive state. From a young age they feel that they will create a big stamp on the world, but unconsciously they wait for their particular truth to form itself in their minds, until they can make the most impact at the right time. This was the case with Luther.

Erikson gave a great deal of space to a psychoanalytical discussion of Luther's relationship with his father. He surmised that Luther's courage in standing up to the Holy Roman Church can only be understood in the context of his initial disobedience to his father. Perhaps surprisingly, Erikson suggested that Luther was not rebellious by nature, but having once defied the major figure in his life, this put him on a trajectory of disobedience.

Erikson's most intriguing point was that Luther did change the world via his theological position, but that position was the result of working out his own personal demons and identity crises. Was he Luther the good monk, Luther the good son, or Luther the great reformer?

Erikson likened major identity crises to a "second birth," an idea that he got from William James. While once-born people "rather painlessly fit themselves and are fitted into the ideology of their age," twice-born people are often tortured souls who seek healing in some total conversion experience that will give them direction. The positive aspect of the twice born is that if they do successfully transform themselves, they have the potential to sweep the world along with them. It took a while for Luther to work out who he was, but once he had done so not even the Pope could stop him.

The importance of time out

Erikson considered a society's ability to accommodate youthful identity crises as extremely important. He wrote about the concept of "moratorium," a period of time or an experience that a culture deliberately creates so that young people can "find themselves" before embarking on proper adulthood. Today, we may take a "gap year" between finishing school and starting college. In Luther's time a period in the monastery gave many young men an opportunity to decide "what one is and is going to be."

What would have happened if Luther had done what his father wanted and entered the legal profession? He may have done well in a conventional sense, but he may never have fulfilled his potential.

Erikson remarked that the real crisis in a person's life often comes in their late 20s, when they realize they are overcommitted to some path they feel is "not them," even if they entered it enthusiastically in the first place. Their very success has put them into a hole that may require all their psychological strength to climb out of.

Erikson's broader point was that if at certain vital junctures people feel pressured to choose stagnation over growth, society at large suffers. All wise cultures acknowledge the youthful identity crisis and seek to accommodate it. Though troublesome in the short term, the new ideas and energies that are unleashed by these personal turning points can bring rejuvenation, not just to the person experiencing it but to the wider community.

Luther's final crisis

Even at the height of his fame and power, Luther was still writing to his father trying to defend and justify his actions—and like his dad, in middle age and later he became something of a reactionary. The firebrand ended up living in comfort, defending Germany's system of princely government, and urging the peasants to accept their station in life. In outlook and habits, he remained a "provincial" rather than a worldly figure. He became just as his father wanted him to be: influential, well off, and married.

You would have thought this would have been the happiest time in Luther's life. In fact, it ushered in what Erikson called the mature adult crisis of "generativity," in which people ask,"Has what I have created been worth it? Would I do it all over again, or have I wasted all those years?" Luther's first crisis was of pure identity; this one, Erikson noted, was of integrity. Despite being a "great man" Luther still had to go through this phase, as every older adult inevitably does.

Erikson's point was that the issue of identity is never completely solved. When one aspect of us achieves wholeness, there is still some larger self that is trying to make sense of our experience. Luther's life might be characterized as a succession of statements to himself of "what he is *not*." That, in a way, is the easy half of identity formation. We are still left with the task of deciding what we *are*.

Final comments

How we change our conception of ourselves over a lifetime is one of the most intriguing questions in psychology, because identity—who or what we know ourselves to be, or at least hope we are—is so fundamental.

There is a tendency to belittle someone going through an identity crisis, to emphasize the normality of it. Yet Erikson's observation of Luther could be said of all of us in the same position: "He acts as if mankind were starting all over with his own beginning as an individual... To him, history ends as well as starts with him." This may sound like the self-absorption of the adolescent, yet at all ages we must come to some kind of resolution about where we stand in relation to the world. Unless society does what it can to help with a successful passage through major life turning points, the cost will be not only mental illness, but also the loss of potential.

The obvious danger of psychobiography is that we can read too much into a person's childhood and its effect on their later life. However, Erikson made a convincing connection between a severe childhood and domineering father on the one hand, and the tenor of the times in which Luther lived. He showed that Luther's personal crises could not be separated from the social changes happening around him, and that the whole Reformation could be seen as Luther's personal issues being worked out on a global scale. It was Luther's own conscience, for instance, that drove him to reposition the Church as secondary to a person's direct relationship with God. And as a true believer, his insistence on faith above "good works" also reshaped Christendom.

Psychology matters, Erikson was saying, because history is essentially the acting out of individual psychologies.

Erik Erikson

Born in Frankfurt in 1902, Erik was cared for by his mother alone until her marriage to Theodor Homberger, his pediatrician. The family moved to Karlsruhe in southern Germany, where Erik's three sisters were born. After school he traveled around Europe for a year before enrolling in art school. He taught art for a while in Vienna, where he met his wife Joan Serson, his lifelong collaborator. In 1927 he began studying psychoanalysis at the Vienna Psychoanalytic Institute, working under Anna Freud (see p. 104) and specializing in child psychology.

In 1933, Erik moved to the United States, and changed his name to Erikson. He taught for three years at Harvard Medical School and also became Boston's first child analyst. At Harvard he was strongly influenced by his friendships with anthropologists Ruth Benedict, Gregory Bateson, and Margaret Mead. He later had positions at Yale University, the Menninger Foundation, the Center for Advanced Study in the Behavioral Sciences at Palo Alto, California, and the Mount Zion Hospital in San Francisco. Erikson's well-known studies of the Lakota and Yurok Native American peoples were made while he was at the University of California at Berkeley. After leaving Berkeley he worked in private practice for many years before returning to Harvard.

Erikson's breakthrough work was Childhood and Society *(1950), a wide-ranging study of individuals and cultures that won the Pulitzer prize and America's National Book Award. Other books include* Identity: Youth and Crisis *(1968),* Gandhi's Truth *(1970), and* The Life Cycle Completed *(1985). Erikson died in 1994.*

Dimensions of
Personality

"*Personality is determined to a large extent by a person's genes; he is what the accidental arrangement of his parents' genes produced, and while environment can do something to redress the balance, its influence is severely limited. Personality is in the same boat as intelligence; for both, the genetic influence is overwhelmingly strong, and the role of environment in most cases is reduced to effecting slight changes and perhaps a kind of cover-up.*"

In a nutshell

All personalities can be measured according to two or three basic biologically determined dimensions.

In a similar vein
Isabel Briggs Myers *Gifts Differing* (p 46)
Ivan Pavlov *Conditioned Reflexes* (p 210)
Steven Pinker *The Blank Slate* (p 228)

CHAPTER 15

Hans Eysenck

E ysenck was one of the twentieth century's most controversial and prolific psychologists. In a career spanning five decades, 50 books, and more than 900 journal articles, he shed new light on a number of areas. Born in Germany, his opposition to the Nazi party during the 1930s led to his fleeing to Britain. At the time of his death in 1997, he was the most-cited researcher in psychology.

Dimensions of Personality was Eysenck's first book, and has a dry, academic style. However, in grounding for the first time in science the concept of introversion/extraversion, it laid the foundation for 50 years' work in the field of personality difference.

The two dimensions

Though Eysenck acknowledged the ancient Greek division of people into the four temperaments of sanguine, choleric, phlegmatic, and melancholy, and was obviously in debt to Carl Jung's distinction between introverts and extraverts, he was also adamant that any study of personality differences had to be objective and statistically based. *Dimensions of Personality* was grounded in a method of research, factor analysis, which enabled Eysenck to draw conclusions about personality differences from large amounts of survey data. He had worked at the Mill Hill Emergency Hospital in wartime London, and used several hundred war-weary soldiers as his sample. The men were asked a battery of questions about their habitual reactions to certain situations and they gave themselves ratings. The collated answers led Eysenck to confidently place a person according to two broad dimensions or "supertraits" of extraversion/ introversion and neuroticism.

Eysenck believed that these supertraits were genetically determined and were manifested in our physiology, specifically the brain and nervous system. In this he was inspired by Ivan Pavlov. The source of extraversion or introversion was in the varying levels of excitability of the brain; the driver of the neurotic dimension was an aspect of the nervous system that handled emotional responses to events.

Later, Eysenck added another dimension, psychoticism. Though it could indicate mental instability, more commonly a person's placement within this dimension was an indicator of how much they were likely to be rebellious against the system or wild and reckless. Unlike the extraversion/introversion dimension, which measures sociability, psychoticism measures the extent to which someone is a socialized being living according to conventions, or in the extreme an antisocial psychotic or sociopath.

Together, the three dimensions of psychoticism–extraversion–neuroticism became known as the PEN model. Characteristics included:

Extraversion

❖ The extravert's brain is the opposite of what we would expect; it is *less* excitable than the introvert's.
❖ Because there is less going on inside, extraverts naturally seek outside stimulation and contact with others to really feel alive.
❖ Extraverts have a more even-handed approach to events, with less anguish about how they are personally perceived.
❖ Extraverts are also generally lively and optimistic, but can be restless risk takers and unreliable.

Introversion

❖ The introvert's brain is more excitable, making them more vulnerable to moods and having intense inner lives.
❖ As a result of this inner sensory overload, as a form of self-protection they naturally avoid too much social interaction, which they find mentally taxing. Or, because they have such a rich inner life, they simply do not need a lot of social interaction.
❖ Because they seem to experience things more intensely, introverts have a deeper and more anguished response to life.
❖ They are generally more reserved and serious, pessimistic, and can have issues with self-esteem and guilt.

Neuroticism

❖ Neuroticism is an indicator of how upset, nervous, worried, anxious, or stressed we have a tendency to be.
❖ Scoring high on this dimension does not mean that people are neurotic, only that they have the sort of brain that predisposes them to neuroses. A low score indicates that they are more emotionally stable.
❖ The neurotically minded over-respond to stimuli, while those who are not are calmer and can put things into perspective.
❖ Neurotically minded introverts, in an effort to control the stimulation that comes into their minds, are susceptible to phobias and panic attacks. Neurotically minded extraverts tend to undervalue the impact of life events, and may develop neuroses of denial or repression.

Final comments

Though Eysenck's work on the biological basis of personality has been frequently criticized, it has also been increasingly validated by research. As Steven Pinker notes in *The Blank Slate*, studies of identical twins raised apart have demonstrated that only a small portion of personality is due to socialization. The rest is shaped by genetics.

There are now many other models of personality type—including the commonly used five-factor model of extraversion, agreeableness, conscientiousness, neuroticism, and openness—but Eysenck was the first to make the effort toward a statistical way of understanding the issue. It is unlikely that personality will ever be an exact science, but his work laid a foundation for better understanding of people that did not rely on mere social observation or folk wisdom.

As both a serious scientist and a writer of popular psychology books, Eysenck contributed greatly to increased public understanding of psychological issues. In the 1950s he made a celebrated attack on the scientific validity of psychoanalysis, stating that there was no evidence at all that it helped cure patients' neuroses—and in the process he helped make psychotherapy more scientifically accountable and focused.

Eysenck was also known as an intelligence researcher who, going against the ethos of social conditioning, maintained that intelligence levels were largely heritable and genetic. His 1971 book *Race, Intelligence and Education*, which laid out evidence of IQ differences according to racial type, led to demonstrations and Eysenck's famously being punched in the face at a university lecture. He also delved into astrology, gave some support to paranormal phenomena, suggested that smoking-related cancer was linked to personality, and presented evidence that some people had a biological disposition to be criminals.

Despite such controversies, toward the end of his life the American Psychological Society made Eysenck a William James Fellow for a lifetime of distinguished contribution to psychological science.

Hans Eysenck

Born in Germany in 1916, after his parents' divorce Hans Jürgen Eysenck was brought up by his grandmother.

As a young man he opposed the Nazi regime and left Germany for good. He settled in England, completing his PhD in psychology at the University of London in 1940. During the Second World War he worked at Mill Hill emergency hospital as a psychiatrist, and from 1945–50 was a psychologist at the Maudsley Hospital. He also established and became director of the psychology department at the University of London's Institute of Psychiatry, a post he held until 1983.

Eysenck died in 1997.

Emotional Blackmail

"Though we may be skilled and successful in other parts of our lives, with these people we feel bewildered, powerless. They've got us wrapped around their little fingers."

"They swathe us in a comforting intimacy when they get what they want, but they frequently wind up threatening us in order to get their way, or burying us under a load of guilt and self-reproach when they don't."

"Perhaps worst of all, every time we capitulate to emotional blackmail, we lose contact with our integrity, the inner compass that helps us determine what our values and behavior should be."

In a nutshell

We maintain our integrity only by withstanding other people's controlling behavior.

In a similar vein

Nathaniel Branden *The Psychology of Self-Esteem* (p 42)
Anna Freud *The Ego and the Mechanisms of Defence* (p 104)
John M. Gottman *The Seven Principles for Making Marriage Work* (p 136)
Karen Horney *Our Inner Conflicts* (p 156)

CHAPTER 16

Susan Forward

If you have ever done something you did not want to, but felt you had to in order to preserve a relationship, this book is for you. It is not until you read Susan Forward's bestselling *Emotional Blackmail: When the People in Your Life Use Fear, Obligation, and Guilt to Manipulate You* that you realize how pervasive emotional blackmail may be.

The actual playing out of blackmail, while worrying on its own, is only indicative of deeper issues in both the blackmailer and the blackmailed. Why does one person feel that threat or intimidation is the only way to get what they want? Why do their victims allow themselves to be victimized?

What is emotional blackmail?

Most of us have had someone in our lives—be it a spouse, child, or work-mate—whom we placate because we don't want to cause trouble in the relationship. Or we may be in constant open conflict with them because we resent the pressure to do something we know is not right for us.

An emotional blackmailer can be summed up by the one basic threat of "If you do not do what I want you to, you will suffer." Because they know us well, they use their knowledge of our vulnerabilities to gain our compliance. In a normal relationship there is a give-and-take balance in which we get what we want some of the time, the other person getting what they want at other times. However, the emotional blackmailer does not really care if we are happy as long as they get what *they* want.

Blackmailers create a "FOG" of "Fear, Obligation, and Guilt," which makes it sometimes difficult to see how we are actually being treated. When fear and guilt are present, it often seems as if *we* are the problem, not the one who is trying to blackmail us. If a spouse or workmate or friend or relative does some of the following, Forward warns, we are a potential target of blackmail:

❖ Threaten to make things difficult if we don't go along with them, including ending the relationship.
❖ Imply that their misery is the result of our noncompliance.
❖ Make big promises if we agree to do something, which don't ever materialize.
❖ Ignore or discount our thoughts and feelings on something.
❖ Tell us we are bad in some way if we don't give in to them.
❖ Use money or affection as rewards to be given or withdrawn depending on whether we give them what they want.

Often, the more we resist the blackmailer's demands, the more FOG they pump into the relationship. We become confused and resentful about what is happening, but we don't seem to have the ability to act decisively. After all, is it us being unreasonable?

Forward identifies six steps of emotional blackmail:

- ❖ The blackmailer makes a demand.
- ❖ The target resists.
- ❖ The blackmailer exerts pressure, e.g., "I only want what's best for us," "Don't you love me?"
- ❖ As the target continues to resist, the blackmailer makes threats, e.g., "If you can't commit to this, maybe we should start seeing other people."
- ❖ Compliance—not wanting to jeopardize the relationship, the target agrees to the demand.
- ❖ Repetition—the blackmailer has seen that the pattern works, so the groundwork is laid for future manipulation.

The most important step is the last, for now the blackmailer knows that whatever they have done to get our compliance, it worked. They have discovered a pattern for manipulation, and we are the victim.

Inside the mind of the blackmailer

Why is it so important to blackmailers that they get their way, even to the extent of punishing us if we don't acquiesce? In a chapter on the inner world of the blackmailer, Forward observes that they are usually frustrated individuals who feel they have to take drastic action in order to get things they consider vital to them. Partners are amazed how hard their other half can suddenly become; the normal compromises of an intimate relationship are replaced by dogmatic decisions. People who cling, or are angry, or who continually test us are like this because this is the method they have adopted to protect themselves from possible loss. Though we are made to feel as if we are doing something wrong, it is more likely to be their past problems coming back to haunt the present relationship.

By punishing us blackmailers feel they are maintaining order or teaching us a lesson, and an inflexible stance makes them feel better about themselves. Yet invariably, the punishment they mete out has unintended consequences, and does not achieve their objective. Instead of being pulled into line, the target resents the whole situation and draws away.

Much blackmail comes in the form of neediness or possessiveness. If we have to go away on business or decide to take a weekend course, the partner left at home makes us feel horribly guilty. They let us know how lonely and depressed they are when we are not there. Naturally we empathize with them, but as Forward suggests, in time our compassion only increases the manipulative behavior. To stay sane and healthy ourselves, we have to draw limits and recognize that what we want to do is quite normal, and that their demands are unreasonable, even if they apparently come from a loving place.

There are many different styles of emotional blackmail. Some people issue aggressive threats; others quietly let us know what will result if they don't get their way; others give us the "silent treatment" until we find out what they want and, in desperation to reestablish normal relations, give it to them.

The closer the relationship, Forward writes, the more vulnerable we are to blackmailers. Not many of us would find it easy to stand our ground when being threatened with being cut off financially, with being divorced, or in the face of extreme anger or even physical abuse. On a more subtle level, who would find it easy to refuse a request when it is framed by the pleading question, "Don't you love me?" A daughter in the fragile stage of trying to wean herself off drugs knows she can get a loan from her mother to buy a house, because the threat is there: "If you don't, I will go back to how I was."

If nothing else, Forward asks us to remember that emotional blackmail "*sounds* like it's all about you, and *feels* like it's all about you, but for the most part, *it's not about you at all*. Instead, it flows from and tries to stabilize some fairly insecure places inside the blackmailer."

The effect of emotional blackmail
There is a difference between the familiar conflicts and arguments found in most relationships, and a *pattern* of manipulation. While the former allows us to get into skirmishes and then go back to the basically firm emotional ground of the relationship, the latter involves the attempted or real diminishment of the other person's self—one person grows their power at the expense of another. Forward notes that even very strong disagreements don't have to involve insults or aspersions being cast on a person's character; healthy conflict never involves trying to "beat the other person up emotionally."

Blackmailers always try to make out that their motives are superior to ours, and that there is something wrong with us, for example that we're selfish or uncaring. They are skilled spin doctors, turning around their unreasonable demands so that they are "obviously" good for everyone. Whoever has a different opinion is mad or bad.

Such twisting of reality corrodes relationships, sucking out all the fun, good will, and intimacy. What may be left is a shell, the trust and caring gone. The number of topics we can talk about lessens as the rift grows, and we develop a life of avoidance and walking on eggshells. "What used to be a graceful dance of caring and closeness," Forward poetically puts it, "becomes a masked ball in which the people involved are hiding more and more of their true selves."

Every time we capitulate, we stop trusting our "inner compass" that normally tells us what to do to maintain our integrity. The more we become what the blackmailer wants us to be, the more we lose sight of who we are.

Why we are vulnerable

Many people who came to Forward for help from blackmailers mentioned a feeling she calls the "black hole." The thought of their partner leaving them was so horrible that they reverted to a very reactive mindset—they would do anything to keep them. "We may function at a high level in the rest of our lives," Forward notes, "only to turn to jelly at any rejection or perceived rejection from a partner."

This fear of abandonment is the mother of most other fears, and all blackmailers need to do to achieve their aims is to start this rolling in us. But our integrity and peace of mind depend on confronting fears, and this is what Forward addresses in the second part of *Emotional Blackmail*. She provides tools and techniques for identifying our own emotional vulnerabilities, so that we will never be held hostage by another person again. We learn how to stand our ground, confront the real issues, set limits, and be able to tell the blackmailer that what they are doing is not acceptable.

Final comments

This is only a bare-bones treatment of *Emotional Blackmail*. The first part, "Understanding the blackmail transaction," is worth the price of the book alone, but it is in the second that even greater value is to be found. Here Forward goes beyond telling us what blackmail consists of and outlines how to combat and defeat it.

One drawback of the book is that there is no list of sources or bibliography. It would have been interesting to know Forward's influences, or whether her insights are all based on her therapy practice. Her ideas on the emotional makeup and history of the blackmailer echo the work of Karen Horney (see p 156), who wrote about the neurotic tendencies we develop in childhood in order to feel more secure, but erroneously take into adulthood as well.

Forward's books—she also wrote the marvelously titled *Men Who Hate Women and the Women Who Love Them*—have helped millions, and *Emotional Blackmail* is a perfect example of how a good self-help book can make a significant contribution to psychology. You finish reading it with a greater appreciation of the complexity of behavior and emotions that can be found within one person. Many of the people quoted in the book say that their partner can be both "the most wonderful, caring person in the world" and a cold-hearted blackmailer thinking only of themselves. The fact is, human nature can accommodate both. But we should never accept blackmail in our relationships because, even if they survive its stranglehold, the life is slowly squeezed out of them. Don't let this happen to yours.

Susan Forward

Susan Forward's career in psychology began when she was a volunteer at the University of California, Los Angeles (UCLA) Neuropsychiatric Institute. Enrolling as a graduate student, she gained her master's degree in psychiatric social work at UCLA and later her PhD. She has run a private therapy practice for many years, in addition to working with many Southern Californian psychiatric and medical institutions.

Her first book, Betrayal of Innocence *(1978), made her an authority on child abuse, followed by* Men Who Hate Women and the Women Who Love Them *(1986), and* Toxic Parents *(1989), also a bestseller. Other books include* Obsessive Love, Money Demons, *and* When Your Lover Is a Liar; *the latter and* Emotional Blackmail *were written with Donna Frazier.*

Forward is a well-known media and public speaker, and has been a consulting witness at high-profile court trials. In her role as Nicole Simpson's therapist, she testified at the O. J. Simpson trial.

The Will to Meaning

"What I term the existential vacuum constitutes a challenge to psychiatry today. Ever more patients complain of a feeling of emptiness and meaninglessness, which seems to derive from two facts. Unlike an animal, man is not told by instincts what he must do. And unlike man in former times, he is no longer told by traditions what he should do. Often he does not even know what he basically wishes to do. Instead, he either wishes to do what other people do (conformism), or he does what other people wish him to do (totalitarianism)."

In a nutshell

The conscious acceptance of suffering or fate can be transformed into one of our greatest achievements.

In a similar vein

Nathaniel Branden *The Psychology of Self-Esteem* (p 42)

CHAPTER 17

Viktor Frankl

F rankl's most famous work is *Man's Search for Meaning* (see the commentary in *50 Self-Help Classics*), a gripping account of his time in a Nazi concentration camp and of fellow prisoners who either developed a survival mindset or gave up on life. Many readers treasure it as an antidote to the boredom and meaninglessness of modern life.

While that book includes some explanation of Frankl's psychology of meaning—logotherapy (from the Greek *logos*, or meaning)—*The Will to Meaning: Foundations and Applications of Logotherapy* is fully devoted to explaining its tenets and philosophical basis. This makes it a more challenging read, but a highly rewarding one.

Frankl's brand of therapy is sometimes considered, after Freud's psychoanalysis and Adler's individual psychology, to be the third school of Viennese psychotherapy, and *The Will to Meaning* clearly points out the differences between his ideas and those of his compatriots. It also refutes the behaviorist school of psychology and its attempts to reduce human beings to complex products of their environment.

Psychology's blind spot

What psychology failed to appreciate, Frankl believed, is the multidimensional nature of human beings. He did not deny that biology or conditioning shapes us, but he also insisted that there is room for free will—to choose to develop certain values or a particular course in life, or to retain our dignity in difficult situations.

Frankl denied that things like love and conscience can be reduced to "conditioned responses" or the result of biological programming. As a neurologist, he actually agreed that substantial aspects of the human can be compared to a computer. However, his point was that we cannot be boiled down to the workings of such a machine. We may have problems relating to the balance of chemicals in our body or mental issues such as agoraphobia, but we have another group of complaints (which he called noogenic) that relate to moral or spiritual conflicts. These cannot by treated by conventional psychiatrists, who may completely miss the point of why a person has come to see them—the patient may get more out of visiting a priest or a rabbi. Could the same profession that would have dismissed Joan of Arc as a schizophrenic, Frankl wondered, be trusted to make judgments on issues such as guilt, conscience, death, and dignity?

Logotherapy's answer

Frankl considered his psychology to be existential, but unlike the existentialism of Albert Camus or Jean-Paul Sartre, which is associated with the meaninglessness of life, logotherapy is basically optimistic. Its aim is to convince people that life always has meaning, even if it is not yet clear what that is. We may not discern a meaning in difficult or painful situations until later, when we have grown as a result of what happened.

The greatest human achievement is not success, Frankl said, but facing an unchangeable fate with great courage. A dying woman whom Frankl attended to in hospital, petrified at what was to come, came to realize that her courage in death might be her finest hour. Instead of a "meaningless" early death, she found great meaning in the way she chose to die.

Frankl argued that the "existential vacuum" that people feel is not a neurosis. It is rather something very human, signaling that our will to meaning is alive and well. He quoted the novelist Franz Werfel, "Thirst is the surest proof for the existence of water."

Responsibility and guilt

Frankl once gave a talk in the notorious San Quentin prison. The prisoners loved him because he did not pretend they were all wonderful people or say they were victims of society or their genes. Instead, he recognized them as free and responsible people who had taken decisions that had led them to where they were. He acknowledged the reality of guilt.

Frankl was fond of saying that a Statue of Responsibility should be erected on the West Coast of America, to complement the Statue of Liberty on the East. We live in an age of relativism, which waters down real values and meaning that exists independent of our judgments. But by choosing to be free of such universals, over time we paradoxically hem in our own freedoms.

Conscience

If you have read *Man's Search for Meaning* you may be surprised to discover that Frankl had an opportunity to avoid the concentration camps. While living in Vienna, because he was a neurologist he was offered a visa to live in America—but it was only for him, not his parents. Knowing the fate that lay in store for them, he could not bring himself to leave.

Each person, he wrote, comes into life with a unique set of potential meanings to fulfill. It is up to us whether we decide to grasp these meanings and accept them, or try to avoid them. There is no ultimate "meaning of life," only individual meanings of the lives of individual people. To ask "What is the meaning of life?" makes no sense unless we ask it of our own life and our own set of issues and challenges. This uniqueness of meaning is called conscience.

Final comments

At the end of *The Will to Meaning*, Frankl asked the obvious question: If logotherapy is all about meaning, what distinguishes it from religion? His answer was that religion is by nature about salvation, whereas logotherapy is about mental health.

Notwithstanding this distinction, a spiritual faith in ultimate meaning underlay his form of psychology, which instantly marked it as suspect in many people's eyes. Yet Frankl was a doctor of neurology and of psychiatry, and had survived two concentration camps. He was not a mystic or a dreamer. That human beings have a will to meaning cannot be denied, even if we doubt that life itself has some ultimate meaning.

While Freud wrote of the drive toward pleasure or sex, and Adler of a drive toward power, Frankl believed that the human will to meaning was at least as strong a force in making us into who we are. While we are pushed by drives, we are *pulled* by meaning, and though he did not deny that biology or conditioning shaped us, he also insisted that there was room for free will—to choose to develop certain values or a particular course in life, or to retain our dignity in difficult situations. For Frankl, if psychology was to achieve anything, it had to take account of this will to meaning as much as it did the pleasure or power instinct.

Viktor Frankl

Born in Vienna in 1905, Frankl studied medicine at the University of Vienna, where he received his MD and PhD. During the 1930s he worked in the suicide department of the General Hospital in Vienna, and built up a private psychiatry practice. From 1940–42 he was head of neurology at the Rothschild Hospital.

In 1942, Frankl, his parents, and his wife Tilly were sent to a concentration camp, initially Theresienstadt. The rest of the family did not survive, but Frankl was freed from Dachau in 1945 by the advancing US Army.

Returning to Vienna after the war, Frankl wrote Man's Search for Meaning *and was appointed to head the Vienna Neurological Policlinic, a post he held until 1971. He received 29 honorary doctorates, and was a visiting professor at Harvard and other US universities and at the University of Vienna Medical School.*

His other books include The Doctor and Soul *(1965),* The Unheard Cry for Meaning *(1985), and* The Unconscious God *(1985). Frankl died in 1997, in the same week as Mother Teresa and Princess Diana.*

1936

The Ego and the Mechanisms of Defence

"*In all these situations of conflict the ego is seeking to repudiate a part of its own id. Thus the institution which sets up the defence and the invading force which is warded off are always the same; the variable factors are the motives which impel the ego to resort to defensive measures. Ultimately all such measures are designed to secure the ego and to save it from experiencing 'pain.'*"

"*My patient was an exceptionally pretty and charming girl and already played a part in her social circle, but in spite of this she was tormented with a frantic jealousy of a sister who was still only a child. At puberty the patient gave up all her former interests and was thenceforth actuated by a single desire—to win the admiration and love of the boys and men who were her friends.*"

In a nutshell

We do just about anything to avoid pain and preserve a sense of self, and this compulsion often results in us creating psychological defenses.

In a similar vein

CHAPTER 18

Anna Freud

Anna Freud was the youngest of her father Sigmund's six children, and the only one to become a well-known psychologist in her own right. By the age of 14 she had read his books and was intent on following in his footsteps, and though inevitably tagged "Daddy's girl," in fact she was a pioneer in two important areas: ego psychology and child psychoanalysis.

While Sigmund famously focused on the unconscious (the id), Anna made the ego seem more important, particularly in respect of therapy and psychoanalysis. Her work looked at how exactly the ego, id, and superego interacted, and it was through this understanding that she was able to explore the concept of psychological defense mechanisms. In her work with children and adolescents, she demonstrated to her father why they were quite different to adults in terms of psychoanalytical practice.

The Ego and the Mechanisms of Defence is her best-known work. Although it presumes that the reader has some familiarity with psychoanalytical terms, laypeople can still read the book and it contains interesting case studies to spice up the theory. She used many classic Freudian terms such as "hatred of the mother," "penis envy," and "castration anxiety," which contemporary readers will take with a grain of salt. Yet behind these notions is a compelling explanation of why some people act as they do, and despite much debunking of Freudian psychology in recent years, Anna Freud's explanation of how defense mechanisms come about and their function is convincing.

What is a defense mechanism?

The term "defense" in relation to psychology was first used by Sigmund Freud in 1894. He meant it to describe, as Anna Freud said, "the ego's struggle against painful or unendurable ideas or effects," which may lead to neurosis. The ego develops a defense in order to protect itself against being overcome by unconscious demands such as sex and aggression. The work of the psychoanalyst is to get the person to become conscious of their instinctual urges, which may involve isolating the pain experienced when they were originally confronted by an unsatisfied impulse.

The ego is always alert to the dangers that the unconscious may overthrow it. It may try to intellectualize away unconscious urges, inhibit them, project them onto others, or deny them. Freud noted that when someone succeeds in creating defense mechanisms against anxiety and pain, their ego has won the battle between the "three institutions" of ego, id, and superego. When they have lost an internal battle to unconscious instinct, or societal "musts" and "shoulds," it is their ego that has lost. The ego continually endeavors to create harmony between itself, the unconscious, and the outside world, but this does not always lead to perfect mental health. In fact, sometimes when the ego "wins" the person as a whole may have lost, since the win may involve the creation of a defense in order to have the ego maintain its sense of itself at all costs.

Slave to the superego

While the ego is the normal thinking mind, and the id represents the unconscious, the superego in Freudian terminology is that part of us that responds to social or societal rules.

When a natural instinct surfaces, the ego wants to have it satisfied, but the superego does not allow that. The ego submits to the "higher" superego, but is left with the problem. It begins a struggle with the impulse and, to reduce the pain of not satisfying it, engineers a defense that allows itself to make sense of its decision to submit.

The superego, Freud wrote, is the "mischief maker which prevents the ego's coming to a friendly understanding with the instincts." It creates a high standard in which sex is seen as bad and aggression is antisocial. But renouncing the instincts may simply mean that the impulses are pushed out of the ego's view, and what the ego cannot incorporate into its sense of self is expressed elsewhere as unhealthy personality traits or neuroses. When the ego becomes merely an instrument for the execution of the superego's wishes, we get the bottled-up, prim-and-proper type of person, who lives in fear of being attacked and overcome by their instincts.

Freud described one woman whose life was shaped by her very strong superego, to the extent that her natural impulses, which she did not allow herself to fulfill, were "projected" into other areas of her life. As a child she was a passionate "wanter," demanding certain objects and clothing in order to be as good as or better than other children. Her desires were everything to her. As an adult she became an unmarried and childless governess, dull in her outlook, not ambitious, and the wearer of rather plain clothing. What had happened? At some point, she felt she should attune herself to society's values and standards, and so repressed her natural wishes and went to the other extreme. In place of her own concerns, she spent her time empathizing with others and looking out for them. She was highly interested in the love lives of her friends, and enjoyed talking about clothes, yet she did not allow herself these pleasures. Her defense mechanism against the perception that her desires were too strong was to gratify her desires through other people. Her ego and id had fully lost the battle with her superego, and this was the only way they could be expressed.

Repression

While this example involved projecting instincts onto the world, Freud argued that this is a comparatively healthy form of defense. A more powerful and often more damaging defense is repression, because it requires the most energy to keep it in place.

She told of a girl who, having grown up around brothers and resenting her mother's continual pregnancies, developed a hatred of her mother. Repressing these feelings because she felt they were not nice, her ego tried to protect itself against their returning by evolving the opposite reaction: over-tenderness for her mother and concern for her safety. The girl's envy and jealousy were transformed into unselfishness and thoughtfulness for others. Though this helped her fit in to the family environment, her repression of natural feelings led to a loss of normal reactions and spirit in a girl her age.

In another example, a young girl developed a fantasy of biting off her father's penis, but to avoid this feeling her ego created a disinclination to bite altogether, which led to problems with eating.

In both cases, although the ego was "at peace" in the sense that it no longer had to resolve an inner conflict, the girls suffered at another level when the conflict was repressed. Repression is the most dangerous form of defense, Freud observed, because it takes away consciousness of a whole area of our instinctual life, so deadening the personality.

Children's defenses

Not all defenses are necessarily bad; they may simply be a person's way of coping with real external danger. When looking at defenses created by children, Freud noted that kids experience themselves as comparatively weak in a world of powerful adults and dangers, and as a result make up for this in fantasy and role playing. Often, when a child feels threatened by an image, perhaps a ghost or a violent man, they incorporate the characteristics of this external object by pretending they are a ghost themselves, or by dressing up like a cowboy or a robber. They pass from a passive to an active role. In this way they get back power from their environment.

Freud analyzed children's stories in which a boy or a girl manages to tame a bad old man who is rich or powerful or fearsome, such as *Little Lord*

Fauntleroy. The child touches the man's heart like no one else has been able to, and as a result he is transformed into a real human being. In other stories, wild animals are tamed or beasts made human. What these fantasies commonly show is a reversal of reality. They may enable children to come to grips with the lack of power in a real relationship, such as between a son and his father, and they help children reconcile themselves to reality, paradoxically because they allow them to deny it.

The adolescent ego

Freud observed that teenagers often become antisocial and try to isolate themselves from other members of the family. Another feature of the adolescent is their changeable nature. At no other time in life do they so quickly and earnestly adopt new styles of clothing or hair, but also form intense attachment to particular political and religious ideals. At the same time, adolescents see themselves as the center of the world and are therefore narcissistic. They "identify" with things and people as opposed to clearly seeing them and loving them for what they are.

Freud noted that in every time of life in which there is a heightened sex drive there is a danger of neurotic or psychotic disease if the ego is not able to process the urges properly. To the ego, increased instinctual drives mean danger and in response it does anything it can to reassert itself. This was her explanation for why adolescents are so self-centered—it is how they maintain their identity against a barrage of new and powerful feelings that seem to come from nowhere.

Final comments

Freud admitted that describing the various defenses that emerge in response to anxieties and fears is not an exact science. How can it be, when we are dealing with subterranean caverns of the mind, wishes and desires, and people's response to social pressure? Freudian psychology has been accused of being unscientific, and in many respects it is. Psychoanalysts have been replaced by psychotherapists and cognitive psychologists who are not really interested in a person's past or their longings. Their task is to fix erroneous ways of thinking that have led to unsatisfactory emotions or behavior.

This is all well and good, but perhaps we will come to miss some aspects of Freudian psychology: its "sex and aggression" take on humanity, its deep knowledge of dreams and mythological symbols, and its emphasis on the competing selves of ego, id, and superego. These concepts remain useful, and as for defense mechanisms, they are real enough that most of us can probably describe at least one of our own without trying too hard. The neurological reality of defense mechanisms has recently been noted (see V. S. Ramachandran, p 232), so maybe psychoanalysis has some scientific validity after all. Anna Freud's main contribution was in putting her father's theories into practice, and if Freudian psychology makes a comeback her work is set to become more influential.

Anna Freud

Born in 1895 in Vienna, Anna Freud had a close relationship with her father from the start. She was restless at school, a voracious reader, and from guests in the family home she picked up several languages. Her older sister Sophie was considered the "beauty" and Anna the "brains" of the family.

Anna graduated from school in 1912, and after travels to Italy passed exams to be an elementary school teacher. Working on translations of her father's writings, she became a sort of apprentice to Sigmund, but also continued her teaching career. In 1918 she underwent psychoanalysis with her father, and in 1922 was accepted as a member of the International Psychoanalytic Congress. The following year she began practicing as a psychoanalyst in Berlin, but Sigmund's jaw cancer brought her back to Vienna, and until his death in 1939 she was his primary carer.

From 1927 to 1934 she headed the International Psychoanalytical Association and continued to develop her child analysis practice. In 1935 she became the director of the Vienna Psychoanalytical Training Institute, and from 1937 helped establish a nursery for poor children. When Austria was taken over by the Nazis, Anna organized for the Freuds to move to England. She established the Hampstead War Nursery for the children of single mothers, and in 1947 the Hampstead Child Therapy Clinic, a world center in child psychology.

Anna never married, and considered it her task to maintain and develop her father's legacy. She received several honorary doctorates from American universities, where she gave many lectures and seminars. After she died in 1982, her home in London became the Freud Museum.

The Interpretation of Dreams

"The dream never wastes its time on trifles; we do not allow a mere nothing to disturb our sleep. The apparently innocuous dreams turn out to be pretty bad when we take the trouble to interpret them: if I may be permitted the expression, the dream 'wasn't born yesterday.'"

"What animals dream of I do not know. There is a proverb, mentioned to me by one of my students, which claims to know, for it asks the question: What does a goose dream of? And answers: Corn. The entire theory that the dream is a wish-fulfillment is contained in these two sentences."

"It concerns a set of dreams which have their basis in my longing to go to Rome... So I dream on one occasion that I am seeing the Tiber and the Ponte Sant' Angelo through a train window; then the train starts moving, and it occurs to me that I have not even set foot in the city. The view I saw in the dream was copied from a familiar engraving which I had noticed briefly the previous day in the drawing-room of one of my patients. Another time someone is leading me to a hill and showing me Rome, half-veiled in mist and still so far away that I wonder at the clarity of the view... The motif to 'see the Promised Land from afar' is easy to recognize."

In a nutshell

Dreams reveal the desires of the unconscious mind, and its great intelligence.

In a similar vein

Alfred Adler *Understanding Human Nature* (p 14)
Anna Freud *The Ego and the Mechanisms of Defence* (p 104)
Carl Jung *The Archetypes and the Collective Unconscious* (p 168)

CHAPTER 19

Sigmund Freud

N ot many people realize that Freud was a relatively slow starter. Although he was at the top of his class for most of his school life, he spent eight years studying medicine and other subjects at university before graduating. He slowly entered the field of neurology, writing scientific papers on speech disorders, the effects of cocaine as an anesthetic, and child cerebral paralyses, before shifting his interests to psychopathology. But his ambition to be a renowned medical researcher came up against his desire to marry his fiancée Martha Bernays, and to provide for a home he had to get work practicing medicine.

The result was that the book that made his name, *The Interpretation of Dreams (Die Traumdeutung* in German), was not published until he was in his mid-40s, and even then it took over a decade for it to become famous. Only 600 copies were printed of the first edition of one of the most influential works in history, and these took eight years to sell. Reviews, and there were not many, were mostly unfavorable, and the first English translation, by A. A. Brill, was not released until 1913.

The book provides a semi-autobiographical look into the bourgeois world of late nineteenth-century Vienna, taking us behind the "great man" myth to reveal Freud enjoying time with his children, taking holidays in the Alps, dealing with his friends and colleagues, and seeking professional success. The main pleasure for the reader lies in the description and analysis of the dreams themselves (mostly those of patients, but including quite a few of his own), which can easily run to a dozen pages each and draw on Freud's considerable learning in mythology, art, and literature.

The Interpretation of Dreams brought a medical and scientific approach to a subject that had always defied real analysis, and in doing so created a science of the unconscious mind. After finishing the book Freud wrote, "Insight such as this falls to one's lot but once in a lifetime." It had taken him 40 years to fulfill his early promise, yet it was really just the beginning of his career.

The causes of dreams

It is surprising how much had been written about dreams before Freud. He began his book with a lengthy survey of the literature, going as far back as Aristotle and giving due credit to more contemporary figures such as Louis Alfred Maury, Karl Friedrich Burdach, Yves Delage, and Ludwig Strumpell. Summing up his reading, he noted, "In spite of being concerned with the subject over many thousands of years, scientific understanding of the dream has not got very far."

From a conception of dreams as "an inspiration from the divine," humans had arrived at a scientific view that they were simply the result of "sensory excitation." While sleeping, for instance, we hear a noise outside, and that noise becomes woven into the dream in order to make sense of it. According to this explanation, common dreams such as finding ourselves naked are the result of our bedclothes falling off, flying dreams are caused by the rising and falling of the lungs, and so on.

But Freud felt that sensory stimuli did not explain all dreams. Physical stimuli while we were asleep could certainly shape what we dreamed about, but they could equally be ignored and not incorporated into our dreams. There was also the ethical or moral dimension to many dreams that did not suggest merely physical causes.

Freud's interest in dreams originally came via his work with people with psychoses. He realized that the content of patients' dreams were a good indicator of their state of mental health, and that dreams were like other symptoms in being capable of interpretation. By the time he came to write *The Interpretation of Dreams*, Freud had clinically interpreted over 1,000 dreams.

Among his conclusions were:

❖ Dreams have a preference for using impressions from days just past, yet they also have access to early childhood memories.
❖ The method of memory selection in dreams is different to that of the waking mind—the unconscious mind generally does not focus on major events, but remembers the trivial or unnoticed.
❖ Despite their reputation as being random or absurd, in fact dreams have a unifying motive that easily pulls disparate people, events, and sensations into one "story."
❖ Dreams are always about the self.
❖ Dreams can have multiple layers of meaning, and a number of ideas can be condensed into a single image. Equally, ideas can be displaced (a familiar person can become someone else, a house takes on a different purpose, and so on).
❖ Nearly all dreams are "wish fulfillments," that is, they reveal a deep motivation or desire that wants to be fulfilled, often a wish going back to earliest childhood.

While some writers believed that the memory of daily events was the prime cause of dreams, Freud came to the view that both physical sensations while asleep and memories of what happened during the day were "like a cheap material always available and put to use whenever needed." They were, in short, not the *cause* of dreams but simply elements used by the psyche in its creation of meaning.

The disguised message

Having concluded that dreams were the arena in which the unconscious mind could express itself, and that they were primarily concocted to represent the fulfillment of a wish, Freud wondered why the wish was so poorly articulated, so wrapped up in strange symbols and images. Why the need to avoid the obvious?

The answer could be found in the fact that many of our wishes are repressed, and may only have a chance of reaching our consciousness if they are somewhat disguised. A dream can seem like the opposite of what we wish for, because we may be defensive about or want to cover up many of our wishes, so the only way a dream can make an issue known is by raising it in its opposite sense. Freud explained this phenomenon of "dream distortion" by analogy: A political writer may criticize a ruler, but in doing so may endanger himself. The writer therefore has to fear the ruler's censorship, and so "moderates and distorts the expression of his opinion." With dreams, if our psyche wants to give us a message, it may only be able to get it across by censoring it to make it more palatable, or by dressing it up as something else. The reason we so easily forget dreams, he believed, is that the conscious self wants to reduce the impact of the unconscious on its domain, the waking life.

One of Freud's key points was that dreams are always self-centered. When other people appear in a dream, often they are merely symbols of ourselves or symbolize what another person means to *us*. Freud believed that whenever a strange figure entered his dreamscape, the person undoubtedly represented some aspect of himself that could not be expressed in waking consciousness. He wondered about all the stories in history of someone being told to do something in a dream, perhaps given a wise urging that proved to be correct. Dreams can forcefully express an empowering message that someone is wont to suppress during waking consciousness—and that message is always about *them,* not family or society or any other social influence.

All about sex

Freud's psychoanalysis of patients led him to the belief that neuroses evolved from repressed sexual desires, and that dreams were also expressions of these repressed feelings. It was in *The Interpretation of Dreams* that Freud first discussed Sophocles' play *Oedipus the King* to support his idea of a universal tendency that a child is sexually attracted to one parent and wants to vanquish the other—what was later termed the "Oedipus complex."

Freud told of a significant event from his childhood. Before going to bed one night he broke one of his parents' cardinal rules and wet himself in their bedroom. As part of a general rebuke, his father muttered, "Nothing will come of the boy." This remark must have hit him hard, Freud admitted, as references to the scene had been a recurring motif in his dreams into adulthood, usually in connection with his achievements. In one of these dreams, for instance, it was now Freud's father who urinated in front of him. It was as if, Freud said, he wanted to tell his father, "You see, something did become of me." This competitor for his mother's affections had now been put in his place, complete with the shameful image of illicit urination.

In Freud's cosmology, civilization barely kept a lid on our instincts, and sex was the most powerful of these. Dreams were therefore much more than idle nighttime entertainments—in revealing our unconscious motivations they were a key to understanding human nature.

Final comments

Freud famously wrote that there were three great humiliations in human history: Galileo discovering that the Earth was not the center of the universe; Darwin discovering that humans were not the center of creation; and Freud's own discovery that we were not as in charge of our own minds as we believed.

This attack on the idea of human free will inevitably brought damnation, particularly in America, and as a result the whole of psychoanalysis was painted as unscientific. Though Freud was an atheist, it was pointed out that psychoanalysis had taken on the aura of a religion, creating a whole "culture of the couch" that Woody Allen satirized so well. Not only did Freudian therapy have too great a dependence on the psychoanalyst, there was a lack of standard procedures and verifiable outcomes, and little evidence of effectiveness in healing people. Neurology even discounted the idea that dreams could be linked to desire or motivation. In this climate, Freud was quietly bypassed on the reading lists of university psychology classes, and the number of professional psychoanalysts dwindled. By the early 1990s, *Time* magazine felt it appropriate to ask on its cover: "Is Freud dead?"

Today, if you visit a psychologist or psychiatrist, you may not be asked about your dreams or your past at all; these are deemed irrelevant next to cognitive psychology's more precise methods of changing your mental state. Yet today's practitioners too easily forget their debt to Freud's original "talking cure" of listening to and analyzing the content of a patient's mind, and his insight that a person can simply be sabotaged by the irrational within. In addition, recent research at the Royal London School of Medicine has lent cautious support to Freud's ideas on dreams. Brain scan imaging shows that they are not simply the by-product of random neuron firings; in fact, the limbic and paralimbic areas of the brain, which control the emotions, desires, and motivations, are very active during deep sleep. Dreams are therefore a higher mental function related to motivation, although the jury is out on whether this proves Freud's theory that they exist for wish fulfillment.

Just after the 150th anniversary of his birth, can we be sure of saying anything definite about Freud's legacy? Though his "discovery" of the unconscious changed the intellectual and imaginative landscape, perhaps his greatest contribution was to make psychology fascinating to the average person. It was the possibility he gave of seeing into our *own* minds that made his ideas so compelling.

Sigmund Freud

Born as Sigismund Freud in 1856 in Freiburg, Moravia (now known as Pribor, Czech Republic), Freud was the first of five children of parents Jacob and Amalia, who had come from Western Ukraine. The family moved to Leipzig in 1859 and then Vienna a year later.

Sigismund's parents recognized his intelligence from early on, giving him an education in the Latin and Greek classics and a separate room to study in. He was set to study law at the University of Vienna, but changed his mind at the last minute and enrolled in 1873 as a medical student. After graduating in 1881 he became engaged to Martha Bernays and worked at the Vienna General Hospital, specializing in cerebral anatomy. Later he worked under J. M. Charcot at the Saltpetriere Hospital in Paris, and with Austrian psychologist Josef Breuer, with whom he wrote Studies on Hysteria *(1893).*

After the death of his father in 1896, Freud entered a period of deep reflection, study, and self-analysis, and began work on The Interpretation of Dreams. *Within a few months of its publication* The Psychopathology of Everyday Life *came out, which introduced the idea of verbal mistakes ("Freudian slips") that reveal the unconscious mind. In 1902 the first meetings of the "Wednesday Group" of like-minded Jewish professional men were held, and Freud was made a professor of psychopathology at the University of Vienna. In 1905 he published* Three Essays on the History of Sexuality *and* Jokes and Their Relation to the Unconscious. *Psychoanalysis grew into an international movement, with its first major meeting in 1908.*

In 1920, the Freuds' second daughter Sophie, pregnant with her third child, died in a flu epidemic. Writings from this decade include Beyond the Pleasure Principle *(1920),* The Ego and the Id *(1923), an* Autobiography *(1925), and* The Future of an Illusion *(1927), which aimed to debunk religion. Freud's long essay* Civilization and its Discontents *(1930) crystallized his ideas about human aggression and the "death instinct." With Albert Einstein he wrote* Why War? *in 1933.*

After the Nazi regime's annexation of Austria in 1938 and its banning of psychoanalysis, Freud and family relocated to London. A lifelong heavy smoker of cigars, he died of cancer in 1939.

Frames of Mind

"*Only if we expand and reformulate our view of what counts as human intellect will we be able to devise more appropriate ways of assessing it and more effective ways of educating it.*"

"*In my view, it is fine to call music or spatial ability a talent, so long as one calls language or logic a talent as well. But I balk at the unwarranted assumption that certain abilities can be arbitrarily singled out as qualifying as intelligence while others cannot.*"

In a nutshell

Many different forms of intelligence are not measured by IQ testing.

In a similar vein
Mihaly Csikszentmihalyi *Creativity* (p 68)
Daniel Goleman *Working with Emotional Intelligence* (p 130)
Jean Piaget *The Language and Thought of the Child* (p 222)

CHAPTER 20

Howard Gardner

When Harvard psychology professor Howard Gardner wrote *Frames of Mind: The Theory of Multiple Intelligences* over 20 years ago, the general public largely accepted the idea that intelligence could simply be measured through an IQ, or Intelligence Quotient, test. A high IQ meant you were smart and were given certain opportunities in life, and a low IQ meant you were a bit slow, with your opportunities restricted accordingly.

Gardner's book popularized the idea that the logical-mathematical or "general" intelligence normally measured by IQ tests might not actually be a good measure of a person's potential. IQ testing may have been reasonably effective at predicting how well you did on school subjects, but not great at gauging your ability to compose a symphony, win a political campaign, program a computer, or master a foreign tongue. Gardner replaced the question "How smart are you?" with a wiser, more inclusive *"How* are you smart?"

We intuitively know that how well we do in school does not determine our success in life, and everyone knows very brainy people who have not amounted to much. Similarly, we would find it hard to believe that the achievements of figures such as Mozart, Henry Ford, Gandhi, or Churchill were merely the result of "high IQ." *Frames of Mind*, while going against conventional wisdom, actually gives us an appreciation of intelligence close to what we already know: that we each have different ways of being intelligent, and that success comes from refining and utilizing these intelligences across a lifetime.

Types of intelligence

Gardner claims that all human beings possess a unique blend of seven intelligences through which we engage with the world and seek our fulfillment. These "frames of mind" include two that are typically valued in traditional education, three that are usually associated with the arts, and two that he calls "personal intelligences."

Linguistic intelligence

This involves appreciation of language, the ability to learn new languages, and the capability to use language to accomplish certain goals. Those high in this intelligence may be good persuaders or storytellers, and can use humor to their advantage. Writers, poets, journalists, lawyers, and politicians are among those likely to have high linguistic intelligence.

Logical-mathematical intelligence

This is the capacity to analyze problems, carry out mathematical operations, and approach subjects scientifically. In Gardner's words, it entails the ability to detect patterns, reason deductively, and think logically. Along with linguistic intelligence, it is what IQ tests mainly measure. Logical-mathematical intelligence is often associated with scientists, researchers, mathematicians, computer programmers, accountants, and engineers.

Musical intelligence

People with musical intelligence actually think in terms of sounds, rhythms, and musical patterns. It encompasses skill in the performance, composition, and appreciation of musical patterns. Typical occupations employing this intelligence include musicians, disc jockeys, singers, composers, and music critics.

Bodily-kinesthetic intelligence

This involves the ability to control and coordinate complex physical movements, to express ourselves in movement. This can include body language, mime, and acting, as well as the full range of sporting pursuits. Bodily-kinesthetic intelligence is expected to be particularly high in sports people, dancers, actors, jugglers, and gymnasts, but also professions where balance and coordination are vital, such as firefighting.

Visual-spatial intelligence

This is the ability to perceive objects in space accurately, to have an idea of "where things should go." Sculptors and architects need a high degree of spatial intelligence, as do navigators, visual artists, interior designers, and engineers.

Interpersonal intelligence

Interpersonal intelligence is the capacity to understand other people's objectives, motivations, and desires. It is instrumental in building relationships. Educators, marketing executives, salespeople, counselors, and political figures are examples of individuals with high interpersonal intelligence.

Intrapersonal intelligence

This is the ability to understand the self with a heightened awareness of our feelings and motivations. This intelligence helps us to develop an effective working model of ourselves and use our self-understanding to regulate our lives. Writers and philosophers tend to have this intelligence in abundance.

Implications for how we learn

Gardner's theory presents a huge challenge to established educational models, because if we accept the idea that each person combines a unique array of intelligences, we require a carefully tuned educational system to enable their potential to be realized. Gardner admits that psychology cannot directly dictate education policy, and that further study is required to prove the existence of multiple intelligences in the first place. Yet his general inference is that an education system that takes account of the specialness of each child cannot be a bad thing.

Final comments

Will we always be measured in terms of "IQ," or will Gardner's ideas overthrow current systems of intelligence testing, such as America's famous SAT test for college entry? Most people don't realize that intelligence testing has been with us for over 100 years, with the first attempts at measurement devised by French psychologists Alfred Binet and Theodore Simon in 1905. It is a relatively easy and cheap way to sort large numbers of people according to "merit," and has become well established as a result. Yet the idea of multiple intelligences will not go away as long as people feel their true worth has not been recognized.

What ultimately matters is not a supposedly objective test of intelligence, but our own beliefs about whether we are capable of something and our discipline to follow through. Gardner calls this the "ability to solve problems within our environment." The people we most admire are smart in certain ways, they have refined their way of thinking and doing to an unusual extent. More than raw intelligence, they have *judgment*.

Perhaps the lesson of Gardner's book, therefore, is that we should stop worrying about how we measure up to some arbitrary standard of brain power, because the really smart people are those who know exactly what they are good at and live their life around that knowledge. There is a big distinction between simply possessing mental, physical, or social abilities, and actually deploying them to achieve success.

Howard Gardner

Born in 1943, the son of refugees from Nazi Germany, Howard Gardner initially went to Harvard University to study history. After a year at the London School of Economics, he entered Harvard's developmental psychology doctoral program in 1966, and subsequently became part of the research team for Project Zero (a long-term study of human intellectual and creative development). His interest in human cognition was influenced by his tutor Erik Erikson (see p 84).

Gardner is currently Hobbs Professor of Cognition and Education at Harvard Graduate School of Education; adjunct Professor of Neurology at Boston University School of Medicine; and Co-Director of Harvard's Project Zero. He has received many honorary degrees and awards.

Other books include The Unschooled Mind: How Children Think and How Schools Should Teach *(1991),* Multiple Intelligences: The Theory in Practice *(1993),* The Disciplined Mind: Beyond Facts and Standardized Tests *(1999), and* Changing Minds: The Art and Science of Changing Our Own and Other People's Minds *(2004).*

Stumbling on Happiness

"Before we can decide whether to accept people's claims about their happiness, we must first decide whether people can, in principle, be mistaken about what they feel. We can be wrong about all sorts of things—the price of soybeans, the life span of dust mites, the history of flannel—but can we be wrong about our own emotional experience?"

In a nutshell

Due to way the brain works, our predictions of how we will feel in the future are not always accurate, and that includes what will make us happy.

In a similar vein
Barry Schwartz *The Paradox of Choice* (p 248)
Martin Seligman *Authentic Happiness* (p 254)

CHAPTER 21

Daniel Gilbert

As a boy, Daniel Gilbert loved poring over a book of optical illusions, such as the Necker cube and the famous vase/faces picture (as on the cover of this book). What amazed him was how easy it was for the eyes and the brain to be fooled.

When, many years later, he became a psychologist, he was interested in the regular mistakes and exercises of "filling in" that our brain makes in order to provide us with a quick picture of reality. Just as we could make predictable mistakes with our eyesight, he found, we could also with our *foresight*. That is, we spend most of our time doing things that we hope will make us happy in the future, but our understanding of that future and how we will feel when we get there is far from reliable.

Though people have been puzzling over the question of foresight for thousands of years, Gilbert claims that *Stumbling on Happiness* is the first book to bring together ideas from psychology, neuroscience, philosophy, and behavioral economics to provide an answer. This is quite a complex area of psychology in which the author is pre-eminent, yet he spins the material into a fascinating and often fun read. With a style reminiscent of Bill Bryson, there are at least one or two chuckles per page.

Anticipation machines

Gilbert notes that most psychology books have somewhere in them the phrase, "Human beings are the only animals that..." In his case, he fills in the sentence by saying that we are the only animals that are able to think about the future. Squirrels may *seem* like they can do this in the way that they put away acorns for the winter, but in fact it is just their brain's recording of a reduction in hours of daylight that prompts them to do this. There is no awareness, only a biological instinct. Humans, however, are not only aware of the future, we are veritable "anticipation machines" focused on what is to come almost as much as we are on what is now. How did this happen?

Millions of years ago the first type of humans experienced a massive increase in the size of their brains in a relatively short space of time. But not every part of the new brain had grown. Most of the growth was in the frontal lobe region, above the eyes, which partly accounts for why our ancestors had foreheads that dramatically sloped back while ours are almost vertical—we needed the room for all those millions of new brain cells.

For a long time it was thought that the frontal lobe had no particular function, but observation of patients with frontal lobe damage revealed problems with planning, and also, strangely, a reduction in feelings of anxiety. What was the link between the two? Both planning and anxiety are related to thinking about the future. Frontal lobe damage leaves people living in a permanent present, and as a result they don't bother to make plans, so they can't be anxious about them.

The huge growth in the human frontal lobe thus gave humans a distinct survival advantage: the ability to imagine different futures, choose between them, and thereby control our environment. We can make predictions about what will make us happy in the future.

Flawed forecasting

It is possible for the brain to cram in all of a person's experiences, memories, and knowledge, Gilbert says, because we do not remember everything in its entirety, but instead preserve a few threads of each experience. We recall only these and the brain "fills in the rest" to make the memory seem complete.

The brain also creates ingenious shortcuts when it comes to perception. German philosopher Immanuel Kant suggested that perceptions are like portraits, which tell us as much about the hand of the artist (the perceiver) as they do about the subject. The brain creates an *interpretation* of reality, but it is so good that we do not grasp that it is only an interpretation.

In the same way that our memories and our perceptions can be faulty, when it comes to imagining the future the details that we imagine happening frequently do not give us the whole picture. It is not so much the things we *do* imagine happening that are incorrect, but more that we *leave out* things that do happen. As many psychological experiments have shown, the human mind is not well structured to note *absences* of things. But our brain does such a brilliant conjuring trick in making us believe that our interpretations are fact that we accept what it gives us without question.

Do we really know what makes us happy?

Gilbert's chief point about happiness is that it is subjective. He tells of conjoined twins Lori and Reba, who have been joined at the head since birth and share a blood supply and part of their brain tissue. Despite this, they go about their lives and have said to anyone who asks that they are very happy. Most people hearing this will say that these twins don't know what happiness is, a response that presumes happiness can only come from being a "single" person. In the same way, people overestimate how bad they would feel if they became blind. But the blind still go on living and doing most of the things the sighted do, and they can be as happy and satisfied as anyone.

What makes us happy colors all our perceptions of what happiness is, but even our own perceptions of what happiness is will change at different times in our lives. Lovers can never see that how they feel about each other may be different in ten years' time, and mothers can never imagine going back to work when they are in love with their newborn. There is a neurological reason for these mistakes in perception. When we imagine things in the future, we use the same sensory parts of the brain that we use to experience real things in the present. We are generally not rational about future events, carefully weighing up the pros and cons, but run them through in our mind to see what *emotional* reaction we get. What we imagine happening is defined by what we are feeling *now*. How do we know what will make us happy in 20 years' time?

In short, the human brain is set up to imagine the future quite well, but not perfectly, and this accounts for the gulfs we often experience between what we thought would make us happy and what actually does. This means that we can spend all our lives making money then decide it wasn't worth it, but also that we can be pleasantly surprised when people, situations, or events that we were certain would make us miserable turn out not to be so.

Final comments

Gilbert spends virtually the whole book identifying the problems we have in accurately predicting our future emotional states, but does he provide a solution that could make happiness more reliable? His slightly anti-climactic answer is that the best way to find out how we will feel about a particular future course of action (a certain career, a move to a particular city, having children) is to ask people who have already done it how they felt. As we are creatures of control with a strong belief in our uniqueness, we are naturally averse to relying on the experience of others. However, such a strategy, while not particularly exciting, is the best available to deliver us life satisfaction and wellbeing, whereas the happiness from relying purely on ourselves is only ever to be stumbled on.

Daniel Gilbert

Daniel Gilbert is Harvard College Professor of Psychology at Harvard University, and is also the director of the Hedonic Psychology Laboratory at Harvard. He has written numerous influential articles in the social psychology field, and is the editor of The Handbook of Social Psychology.

Blink

"*They didn't weigh every conceivable strand of evidence. They considered only what could be gathered in a glance. Their thinking was what the cognitive psychologist Gerd Gigerenzer likes to call 'fast and frugal.' They simply took a look at the statues and some part of their brain did a series of instant calculations, and before any kind of conscious thought took place, they felt something, just like the sudden prickling of sweat on the palms of the gamblers... Did they know why they knew? Not at all. But they knew.*"

"*[There] can be as much value in the blink of an eye as in months of rational analysis.*"

In a nutshell

Assessments we make in the blink of an eye can be as good as those we make after much deliberation.

In a similar vein

Gavin de Becker *The Gift of Fear* (p 20)
Robert Cialdini *Influence* (p 62)

CHAPTER 22

Malcolm Gladwell

M alcolm Gladwell has become a celebrity in the book world. A writer for *The New Yorker* magazine since 1996, he came to the public's attention with *The Tipping Point*, which considered how small ideas or trends reach a critical mass, pushing them into the mainstream.

Blink: The Power of Thinking Without Thinking, Gladwell's follow-up bestseller, is a more purely psychological work, leaning on the research of Timothy Wilson, a professor at the University of Virginia who has written about the "adaptive unconscious," that part of our mind that can lead us to good decisions even though we don't know how we make them; and Gary Klein, a cognitive psychologist who is an expert on how people arrive at decisions under pressure.

Gladwell's talent is for weaving together scientific research findings from fields as diverse as sociology, psychology, criminology, and marketing with an anecdotal style to create new ways of looking at things for the popular reader, and *Blink* is an attempt to bring to the public eye an emerging area of psychology, rapid cognition, that has so far received little popular attention.

First impressions and snap judgments

The ability to come to lightning-quick conclusions, Gladwell notes, evolved for the sake of survival. In life-threatening situations, humans needed to be able to make accurate snap judgments based on the available information.

Much of our functioning occurs without us having to think consciously, and we move back and forth between conscious and unconscious modes of thought. We work with, in effect, two brains: the one that has to deliberate over things, analyze, and categorize; and the one that sizes matters up first and asks questions later.

Often, the snap judgments we make about someone are as accurate as if we had observed them for much longer periods. The psychologist Nalini Ambady, for instance, did a study that found that the assessment college students gave of a professor's effectiveness after watching a two-second film clip of them was the same as the assessment given by students who had sat in their class for a whole semester.

As children we are taught not to trust these first impressions, but to "stop and think," "look before you leap," and not to judge a book by its cover. While there is merit in these approaches, Gladwell points out that it is not always the best strategy to gather as much information as possible before acting. Often, the extra information does not make our judgment any better, yet we continue to put all our trust in rational, conscious deliberation.

"Thin-slicing"

Gladwell introduces the concept of "thin-slicing," which is "the ability of our unconscious to find patterns in situations and behavior based on very narrow slices of experience." Even the most complex situations, he says, can be "read" quickly if we can identify the underlying pattern. Most of one chapter of *Blink* is devoted to the work of psychologist John Gottman (see p 136), who on the basis of many years observing couples in action is able to predict whether they will stay together or divorce with 90 percent accuracy—after watching them for only a few minutes.

Art experts can often assay the authenticity of a work of art very quickly, getting an actual physical feeling as they stand before a sculpture or a painting. Something tells them whether it is genuine or a fake. Basketballers are said to have "court sense," to be able to read the play of the game in an instant, and great generals have *coup d'oeil*, meaning "power of the glance." Gladwell tells of the fireman who ordered his team out of a burning house just in time. His men were trying to put out a fire in the kitchen, but there was something not quite right about the fire—it was too hot. Only later did it emerge that the main fire was in the basement, hence the greater heat coming up through the floors. A moment after the team left the house it erupted, and probably would have killed them if they had stayed inside. The fireman could not say why exactly he suddenly decided to withdraw his men—he "just knew."

By the laws of probability, most decisions made under pressure should be flawed ones, yet psychologists have found that people routinely make correct judgments most of the time, even with limited information. One of Gladwell's surprising points is that we can actually *learn* how to make better snap judgments, in the same way that we can learn logical, deliberative thinking. But first we have to accept the idea that thinking long and hard about something does not always deliver us better results, and that the brain actually evolved to make us think on our feet.

Looking like a leader

The positive aspect of thin-slicing is the ability to make quick and correct judgments. But it also carries the negative aspect of decisions that are hasty and wrong.

The people of the United States elected Warren Harding to be president, Gladwell suggests, essentially because he was tall, dark, good-looking, and had a deep voice. The "Warren Harding effect" is when we believe a person has courage, intelligence, and integrity according to their appearance—even if, as in Harding's case, there is not much going on below the surface (he was considered to have been one of America's worst presidents in the short time he was in office).

Gladwell organized a study on the height of chief executive officers of large American corporations. He found that as well as the CEOs being predominantly white and male, their average height was just under 6 feet; 58 percent of CEOs of Fortune 500 companies are over 6 feet tall, compared to only 14.5 percent of the American population. This suggests that beyond the need for leadership, we require a leader to have a particular appearance. The taller people are, the more confidence we tend to have in them—whether that is justified or not.

Tragic first impressions

Wrong first impressions can have more tragic consequences. Gladwell provides a lengthy analysis of the shooting of an innocent man, Amadou Diallo, in the Bronx area of New York. Diallo, an immigrant from Guinea, was standing outside his house getting a breath of fresh air when a car of four young, white, male undercover police happened to be driving down his street. They wondered what he was doing, leaping to the conclusion he was dealing drugs or acting as the lookout for a robbery. When they called out to him, because he was afraid he went back inside the house. For the policemen this only seemed to confirm his guilt. They ran in after him, shooting, and Diallo died on the spot from bullet wounds.

Gladwell does not believe that the police were particularly racist, but he quotes the psychologist Keith Payne: "When we make a split-second decision, we are really vulnerable to being guided by our stereotypes and prejudices, even ones we may not necessarily endorse or believe." When we are under pressure to make an instant judgment, we cannot consciously cancel out our implicit associations, or prejudices, because our first impression is coming from below the level of our consciousness.

Older, more experienced police may be wiser in similar situations, because their decisions are based more on past experience of what is likely to happen next rather than appearances. Or they may have an excellent ability to read the micro expressions on people's faces, which may last for a fraction of a second yet reveal much about their motivation.

Too much information

Cook County Hospital in Chicago—the hospital that television show *ER* is based on—found that a lot of its resources were being spent on hospital beds for people who *might just* have a heart attack. There was no standard way of making a judgment about how at risk a person was, so the hospital had to err on the side of caution. To save money, it decided to try out a quick way of assessing people at risk from cardiac arrest called the Goldman algorithm. No other hospital had been willing to try this because they did not believe that a condition so serious could be so quickly diagnosed one way or the other. Doctors were used to getting as much information as possible about a patient's history before making a judgment. But the algorithm worked superbly, freeing up doctors' time and the hospital's money.

In the medical field, it is commonly assumed that the more information practitioners have, the better their decisions. However, this is frequently not so. More information can confuse the issue, leading to a wide variety of methods of treating the same condition. It has been demonstrated that the more information a doctor takes in about a patient, the more convinced they become of the validity of their diagnosis. But the rate of correctness of the diagnosis does not increase with the amount of information they obtain.

The lesson: We feel we need a lot of information to be confident in our judgments, but often that extra information, while giving us the illusion of certainty, makes us more prone to mistakes.

Final comments

This is only a glimpse of the contents of *Blink*. There are many fascinating cases, anecdotes, and intellectual detours—from Tom Hanks's star appeal, to speed dating, to military strategy, to fake Greek statues, to how orchestras handle auditioning—that illustrate Gladwell's thesis of the power of first impressions.

It has been suggested that Gladwell's books are essentially an unsatisfying cobbling together of columns he has written for *The New Yorker*, but his writing style, leaping from one idea and example to another, is more accurately the result of a fascination with ideas about human motivation and action, whatever their source.

While the shortish *Blink* makes a perfect companion for a plane trip, the fact that it is so easy to read should not lessen its achievement: bringing a complex area of psychology to the attention of the public, and possibly improving our lives in the process.

Malcolm Gladwell

Born in 1963 in the UK, Malcolm Gladwell is the progeny of an English mathematics professor father and a Jamaican psychotherapist mother. Growing up in Ontario, he attended the University of Toronto, where he graduated in 1984 with a degree in history.

For almost a decade Gladwell worked at The Washington Post, *first as a science writer and then as its New York City bureau chief. Since 1996 he has been with* The New Yorker, *writing regular feature articles.* Time *magazine named him one of its 100 Most Influential People. His previous book,* The Tipping Point: How Little Things Can Make a Big Difference, *was published in 2000.*

To date, Blink *has sold around 1.5 million copies and been translated into 25 languages; it has also spawned a couple of parody titles, including* Blank: The Power of Not Actually Thinking at All. *It is also likely to be made into a movie; actor Leonardo di Caprio has purchased the film rights for $1 million.*

1998

Working with Emotional Intelligence

"*Emotional intelligence matters twice as much as technical and analytic skill combined for star performances... And the higher people move up in the company, the more crucial emotional intelligence becomes.*"

"*People are beginning to realize that success takes more than intellectual excellence or technical prowess, and that we need another sort of skill to survive—and certainly to thrive—in the increasingly turbulent job market of the future. Internal qualities such as resilience, initiative, optimism, and adaptability are taking on a new valuation.*"

In a nutshell

In the vast majority of fields, what makes a star performer is the ability to deploy exceptional emotional intelligence.

In a similar vein
Robert Bolton *People Skills* (p 32)
Howard Gardner *Frames of Mind* (p 116)

CHAPTER 23

Daniel Goleman

Daniel Goleman's 1995 book *Emotional Intelligence* (see the commentary in *50 Self-Help Classics*) was a surprise hit, selling over five million copies worldwide. Inspired by a couple of obscure academic papers by John Mayer and Peter Salovey linking the emotions with intelligence, Goleman combined journalistic flair (he was a writer for *The New York Times*) with his academic psychology background (as a Harvard PhD) to produce a popular psychology work of unusual impact.

Though *Emotional Intelligence* attracted the general reader, Goleman was also surprised by the strong response from the business world. Many people contacted him with their stories, usually along the lines of, "I wasn't at the top of my class in college, far from it, but here I am running a large organization." Emotional intelligence (EQ) seemed to explain why they had been successful while other, more intellectually gifted, colleagues had not done as well.

Most follow-ups to bestselling titles fail to meet expectations, but *Working with Emotional Intelligence* is as fascinating a read as its predecessor. Dividing the book into five parts, Goleman attempts to define 25 "emotional competencies" that can determine whether we move ahead or lag behind in our career, and provides a rationale for why we should be attempting to create emotionally intelligent organizations.

What employers want

Goleman begins by describing how much the rules have changed in the world of work. Job security no longer exists. Once, what sort of job we ended up in depended on how well we did in college or our technical skills. But now, academic or technical ability is simply the threshold requirement to gain entry to a career. Beyond this, what makes us a "star" is our possession of abilities such as resilience, initiative, optimism, adaptability to change, and empathy toward others. Very few employers give as a reason for hiring someone that they are "emotionally intelligent," but it will often be the decisive factor. Other terms such as character, personality, maturity, soft skills, and a drive for excellence might be used in its place.

Goleman lays out the reason emotional intelligence matters to companies now and why they want to increase it among their staff: because in competitive industries, growth from new products is limited. Companies do not compete just on products, but on how well they utilize their people. In a challenging business environment, it is emotional intelligence skills that will take a company further.

Goleman reveals research done at 120 companies, in which employers were asked to describe the abilities that made for excellence in their workforce; 67 percent of these were emotional competencies. That is, two out of three were generic behavioral skills beyond IQ or expertise requirements. Specifically, employers wanted in their staff:

❖ Listening and communication skills.
❖ Adaptability to change and ability to get over setbacks.
❖ Confidence, motivation, wish to develop one's career.
❖ Ability to work with others and handle disagreements.
❖ Wanting to make a contribution or be a leader.

Are you emotionally competent?

In 1973, Goleman's mentor David McLelland published a celebrated paper in *American Psychologist* arguing that traditional academic and intelligence testing was not a good predictor of how well a person would actually do in a job. Instead, people should be tested for "competencies" that were important to the job. This marked the beginning of competency testing, now widely used to select from applicants or create teams, in addition to the conventional consideration of academic skills and experience. Today, McLelland's concept is almost conventional wisdom, but at the time it was groundbreaking. Goleman took McLelland's ideas further, presenting 25 emotional competencies based around the following core five:

Self-awareness
Awareness of our own feelings and the ability to use them as a guide to better decision making. Knowledge of our own abilities and shortcomings. The sense that we can tackle most things.

Self-regulation
Being conscientious and delaying gratification in order to achieve our goals. Ability to recover from emotional distress and manage our emotions.

Motivation
Developing an achievement or goal orientation, so frustrations and setbacks are put into perspective and qualities such as initiative and perseverance are refined.

Empathy

Awareness of what others are feeling and thinking, and in turn the ability to influence a wide range of people.

Social skills

Handling close personal relationships well, but also having a sense of social networks and politics. Interacting well with people and the ability to cooperate to produce results.

Emotional intelligence can make the most of whatever technical skills we have, Goleman notes. Scientists want the rest of the world to know what they are doing. Programmers want people to feel that they are service oriented and not just "techies." Most tech companies have well-paid troubleshooters who can liaise with clients to get things done. They are just as smart and often as skilled as the regular technical staff, but they also have the ability to listen, influence, motivate people, and get them collaborating.

Emotional intelligence, Goleman points out, is not about "being nice" or even expressing our feelings—it is learning how to express those feelings in an appropriate way and at appropriate times, and being able to empathize with others and work well with them.

IQ explains 25 percent of job performance, Goleman argues, which leaves a full 75 percent for other factors. In most fields, a reasonable degree of cognitive ability or IQ is assumed. So are basic levels of competence, knowledge, or expertise. Beyond these, it is emotional and social competencies that separate the leaders from the rest.

What distinguishes the best

Goleman observes that the more senior we are in an organization, the more "soft skills" matter for doing the job well. At the top leadership level, technical skills are of no great import. What matters, in addition to the obvious factors such as the desire to achieve and the ability to lead teams, are:

❖ Capacity for "big-picture" thinking; that is, the ability to chart future directions accurately from the mass of current information.
❖ Political awareness, or having a picture of how certain people or groups interact and influence one another.
❖ Confidence. Psychologist Albert Bandura coined the term "self-efficacy" to describe a person's belief in their potential and ability to perform, aside from actual ability. This belief alone is an excellent predictor of how well you actually do in your career.
❖ Intuition. Studies of both entrepreneurs and top executives discovered that intuition is at the heart of their decision-making processes. They need to

provide "left-brained" analyses to convince others of their view, but it is the subconscious analysis that brings them to correct decisions.

It is instructive also to look at executive *failure*, and *Working with Emotional Intelligence* mentions several studies of executives who were working at a high level but who were then fired or demoted. According to the well-known "Peter Principle," such people "rise to the level of their incompetence" and go no further. Goleman believes that they are held back by shortcomings in the key emotional intelligence competencies. They are either too rigid, unable or unwilling to make changes or adapt to change, or have poor relationships within the organization, alienating those who work for them.

The executive search firm Egon Zehnder found that executives who failed were usually high in both IQ and expertise, but often had a fatal flaw such as arrogance, unwillingness to collaborate, inability to take account of change, or overreliance on brainpower alone. In contrast, the most successful managers stayed calm in crises, took criticism well, could be spontaneous, and were perceived to be strongly concerned for the needs of those they work with.

Final comments

Goleman mentions possibly the most important difference between IQ and emotional intelligence: Whereas we are born with a certain level of native intelligence that does not change much after the teenage years, emotional intelligence is largely *learnt*. Over time we have the chance to improve our ability to manage our impulses and emotions, to motivate ourselves, and to be more socially aware. The old-fashioned terms for this process are "character" and "maturity"; unlike native intelligence, their development is our responsibility.

A fair amount of controversy has swirled around the concept of emotional intelligence. John Mayer and Peter Salovey, the psychologists who originated it, have stated that Goleman's delineation of what constitutes emotional intelligence (including words such as zeal, persistence, maturity, and character) goes far beyond, and distorts, their original definition. They have also noted their unease with Goleman's thesis that EQ can be a predictor of success in life. Yet Goleman notes the considerable research on emotional competencies, going back 30 years, plus studies done in over 500 organizations. The weight of this research suggests that IQ is secondary to emotional intelligence as a predictor of how well someone will do in a job.

There is still plenty of debate about whether emotional intelligence exists at all. Many of its attributes, some argue, are simply facets of personality, while other psychologists maintain that IQ is still the most reliable indicator of likely work success. Yet Goleman's argument has been distorted. Nowhere does he say that IQ does not matter. He says that, all things being equal (intelligence level, expertise, education), people who work well with others, are far sighted, are empathic, and are aware of their emotions will go a lot further in their career. This thesis will make sense to anyone who has begun work and discovered that their ability to "get ahead" depends little on what they learnt in training school or university.

The second two-thirds of *Working with Emotional Intelligence* simply fill out what was said in the first, but it is fascinating to read Goleman's examples from corporate life. Though the specific references to late 1990s companies will inevitably date, the book is a blueprint for how an emotionally intelligent organization should operate, and it may change your views on how things should be done where you work.

Daniel Goleman

Daniel Goleman grew up in Stockton, California and went to Amherst College. His doctorate in psychology from Harvard University was supervised by David McClelland.

For 12 years Goleman wrote a column for The New York Times *in the behavioral and brain sciences, and he has also been a senior editor at* Psychology Today. *He has a Career Achievement award for journalism from the American Psychological Association. In 1994 he co-founded the Collaborative for Academic, Social, and Emotional Learning (CASEL), which seeks to promote social, emotional, and academic learning to enhance children's success at school and in life. Goleman is currently co-chairman of the Consortium for Research on Emotional Intelligence in Organizations at Rutgers University.*

Other books include The Meditative Mind *(1996),* Primal Leadership *(2002, with Richard Boyatsis & Annie McKee), and* Destructive Emotions: A Scientific Dialogue with the Dalai Lama *(2003).*

1999

The Seven Principles for Making Marriage Work

"*What can make a marriage work is surprisingly simple. Happily married couples aren't smarter, richer, or more psychologically astute than others. But in their day-to-day lives, they have hit upon a dynamic that keeps their negative thoughts and feelings about each other (which all couples have) from overwhelming their positive ones. They have what I call an emotionally intelligent marriage.*"

"*At the heart of my program is the simple truth that happy marriages are based on a deep friendship. By this I mean a mutual respect for and enjoyment of each other's company.*"

In a nutshell

What makes a marriage or partnership strong is not such a mystery— psychological research provides answers if we care to look.

In a similar vein
Louann Brizendine *The Female Brain* (p 52)
Susan Forward *Emotional Blackmail* (p 94)
Douglas Stone, Bruce Patton, & Sheila Heen, *Difficult Conversations* (p 272)

CHAPTER 24

John M. Gottman

When Dr. John Gottman began researching the subject in the early 1970s, there was very little solid scientific data on marriage and the factors that make it work. Marriage counselors depended on conventional wisdom, opinion, intuition, religious beliefs, or the ideas of psychotherapists to give advice to couples, with the result that their assistance was not particularly effective.

In 1986, Gottman, a psychology professor at the University of Washington in Seattle who had previously studied mathematics at MIT, set up his Family Research Lab, colloquially known as the "Love Lab." A furnished apartment overlooking a lake, the laboratory was set up to film and record the conversations, arguments, and body language of couples living together.

Surprisingly, the project was the first to scientifically observe real married couples in action. By the time Gottman published *The Seven Principles for Making Marriage Work* (written with Nan Silver), his team had observed more than 650 couples over a 14-year period. Most of those who came to his marriage classes were on the brink of divorce, but after learning his principles their relapse rate back to marital misery was less than half the average for marriage counseling.

There are hundreds of titles on improving relationships, but Gottman's book has the edge because its advice is founded on actual data rather than well-meaning generalities. As a consequence, many of its answers are counter-intuitive, and Gottman delights in busting a few myths about what makes for a happy and stable romantic partnership.

The biggest myth

Attendees at Gottman's workshops are always relieved to hear that even the happiest and most stable couples have their fights. What makes a good marriage is not simply "chemistry" but how the partners handle conflict.

Under the heading "Why most marriage therapy fails," Gottman reveals the biggest myth of professional counseling: that communication between partners is the key to a happy, lasting marriage. Counselors tell you that your problems relate to poor communication, and that "calmly and lovingly" listening to your partner's point of view will transform your marriage. In place of screaming matches, repeating back and validating what your partner is saying, and then calmly stating what you want, will create breakthroughs in understanding.

This idea originated with psychologist Carl Rogers (see p 238), who taught that nonjudgmental listening and acceptance of another person's feelings create rapport. Applied to the marriage relationship, however, Gottman says that this approach definitely does not work. Most couples who use it become distressed, and of those who do seem to benefit, most relapse into their old conflicts within a year. However well each partner is made to air their grievances, it was still a case of one person trashing the other, and very few people—maybe the Dalai Lama, Gottman suggests—can remain magnanimous in the face of criticism.

More myths

Major differences of opinion will destroy a marriage
Gottman reveals a shocking truth about marital conflict: "Most marital arguments cannot be resolved." His research found that 69 percent of conflicts involve perpetual or unresolvable problems. For example, Meg wants to have children, but Donald does not. Walter always wants more sex than Dana does. Chris always flirts at parties, and Susan hates it. John wants to bring the kids up Catholic, Linda wants to raise them Jewish.

Couples spend years and huge amounts of energy trying to change each other, but significant disagreements are about values and different ways of seeing the world—things that don't change. Successful couples know this and therefore decide to accept each other "warts and all."

Happy marriages are unusually open and honest
The truth is, plenty of good marriages shove a lot of issues "under the rug." When many couples have a fight, the man storms off to watch television, and the woman rushes off for some retail therapy. A couple of hours later, the argument has blown over and they are pleased to see each other again. Many partnerships remain stable and satisfied without airing deep feelings.

Gender differences are a big problem
The fact that men are from Mars and women are from Venus may have an impact on marriage problems, Gottman notes, but it does not actually cause them. Some 70 percent of couples said that the quality of the friendship with their partner was the determining factor in happiness, not gender or anything else.

Predicting divorce

After many years of research, Gottman's astonishing claim is to be able to make 91 percent accurate predictions of whether a couple will divorce or stay married—after observing them for only five minutes.

Couples do not end up in the divorce courts because they have arguments, he writes, it is the *way* they argue that massively increases the chance of them splitting up. In watching endless hours of taped interaction between couples, Gottman identified several signs that they may be on the road to divorce—if not in the next year, then some years hence. These include the following.

Harsh startups

Discussions that begin with criticism, sarcasm, or contempt have what Gottman calls a "harsh startup." What begins badly, ends badly.

Criticism

There is a difference between complaints, which refer to a particular action by your spouse, and personal criticism.

Contempt

This includes any form of sneering, eye rolling, mockery, or name calling that aims to make the other person feel bad. A worse version of contempt is belligerence, often expressed in the phrase, "What are you going to do about it?"

Defensiveness

Trying to make the other person seem like they are the problem, as if you have not made any contribution.

Stonewalling

Stonewalling is when one partner "tunes out," unable to take regular criticism, contempt, and defensiveness. By disengaging they are less exposed to being hurt. Gottman notes that in 85 percent of marriages, it is the man who is the stonewaller. This is because the male cardiovascular system recovers from stress more slowly. A man's response to conflict is likely to be more indignant, with thoughts of getting even or "I don't have to take this." Women, on the other hand, are better able to soothe themselves down following a stressful situation, which also explains why women nearly always have to raise the issues of conflict in the relationship and men try to avoid them.

Flooding

Regular emotional "flooding" is when either partner is overwhelmed by verbal attacks from the other. When we are attacked, heart rate and blood pressure increase and hormones are released, including adrenaline. On a physiological level we experience verbal attacks as a threat to our survival. As Gottman puts it, the response is the same "whether you're facing a saber-toothed tiger or a contemptuous spouse demanding to know why you can never remember to put the toilet seat back down." When frequent flooding occurs, each partner's wish to avoid the experience results in them emotionally disengaging from each other.

Failure of repair attempts
Unhappy couples fail to stop a heated argument in its tracks by saying, for instance, "Wait, I need to calm down," or employing an amusing expression to prevent the conflict escalating. Happy couples all have this vital ability.

On their own, these signs do not necessarily predict divorce, but if they occur on top of one another over a sustained period, they are very likely to end a relationship. Gottman describes defensiveness, stonewalling, criticism, and contempt as the "four horsemen of the apocalypse." The level of negative sentiment slowly starts to overtake the positive, so that the "set point" of happiness in the relationship declines to a degree that it becomes too painful. The partners emotionally disengage, stop bothering to try to sort things out, and begin leading parallel lives within the same house. This is the time at which affairs are most likely, because one or both of the partners becomes lonely and seeks attention, support, or care elsewhere. An affair, Gottman points out, is usually a symptom of a dying marriage rather than the cause.

What makes a marriage good
Most of Gottman's principles for creating sustainable and happy marriages revolve around one crucial factor: friendship. The partners are able to maintain a mutual respect for each other and enjoyment of each other's company. Friendship kindles romance, but also protects against a relationship getting adversarial. As long as you can retain "fondness and admiration" for your partner you can always salvage your relationship. Without it, there is more chance of disgust being expressed in arguments, and disgust is poison to a relationship.

According to Gottman, the purpose of marriage is "shared meaning." That is, each partner supports the other's dreams and hopes. A marriage is going in the wrong direction if one partner has to sacrifice what they want to make the other person happy. Genuine friendships are equal.

Related to this central issue of friendship are the following needs.

Have familiarity and interest in your spouse's world
Partners in strong relationships have good "love maps" of the other person— they're in touch with their partner's feelings and wants, and they know basic things like who their friends are. Without such knowledge, a major event such as the birth of a first child is likely to weaken the relationship, not strengthen it.

Turn toward your partner

Romance can stay alive even in the most humdrum conversations, Gottman points out. It is when you stop even acknowledging each other (turning away) that the relationship is on its way out. While some couples believe that romantic dinners or holidays can make a marriage happy, in fact it is the little daily attentions given to the other person (turning toward) that count.

Allow yourself to be influenced

Women are naturally open to the influence of their partners, but men find this more difficult. Yet the happier marriages are generally those in which the man listens to his wife and takes account of her views and feelings. Better, longer-lasting marriages are those in which the power is shared.

Final comments

Once you understand "what makes marriage tick" at a scientific level you are in a much better position to improve your relationship and protect it against failure. This, of course, applies to long-term relationships of any kind. Gottman also conducted a 12-year study of gay and lesbian couples, and found that their interactions were not that different to those of straight couples. Gays tend to take things a little less personally, use fewer hostile or controlling tactics, and generally employ more affection and humor when they bring up a disagreement, but the basic dynamics of conflict and conflict resolution are the same.

It is probable that in 50 years' time we will look back and be amazed how little knowledge the average person had on physiological and psychological responses to conflict, and on how to manage relationships overall. Paradoxically, hard science has much to teach us about the sort of things—love, romance, and friendship—that make life worth living.

John M. Gottman

Gottman is a professor emeritus at the University of Washington, where he was first appointed in 1986. He is the author of over 100 academic articles and many books, including A Couple's Guide to Communication *(1979),* What Predicts Divorce *(1993),* Raising an Emotionally Intelligent Child *(1996),* The Relationship Cure *(2001), and* The Mathematics of Marriage *(2003).*

The Gottman Institute, founded with his wife Julie Schwartz Gottman, provides training to professionals and families. Gottman's Family Research Lab, which received funding from the US National Institute for Mental Health for 15 years, is now part of an independent body, The Relationship Research Institute.

*Co-author **Nan Silver** is a contributing editor of* Parents *magazine.*

The Nature of Love

"The little we know about love does not transcend simple observation, and the little we write about it has been written better by poets and novelists. But of greater concern is the fact that psychologists tend to give progressively less attention to a motive which pervades our entire lives. Psychologists, at least psychologists who write textbooks, not only show no interest in the origin and development of love or affection, but they seem to be unaware of its very existence."

In a nutshell

Warm physical bonds in infancy are vital to our becoming healthy adults.

In a similar vein

Stanley Milgram *Obedience to Authority* (p 198)
Jean Piaget *The Language and Thought of the Child* (p 222)
Steven Pinker *The Blank Slate* (p 228)
B. F. Skinner *Beyond Freedom and Dignity* (p 266)

CHAPTER 25

Harry Harlow

I n 1958, primate researcher Harry Harlow was elected president of the American Psychological Association. In the same year he visited Washington DC, where the Association was having its annual meeting, to deliver a paper on his recent experiments with rhesus monkeys.

In the 1950s, American psychology was dominated by the behaviorists, whose endless experiments with lab rats aimed to show how easily the mammalian mind was shaped by its environment. Harlow and his wife Margaret went against the norm by studying monkeys, which they thought gave much better insights into human action. A straight talker, Harlow also refused to use terms like "proximity" when what he really meant was love. He told his audience:

"Love is a wondrous state, deep, tender, and rewarding. Because of its intimate and personal nature it is regarded by some as an improper topic for experimental research. But, whatever our personal feelings may be, our assigned mission as psychologists is to analyze all facets of human and animal behavior into their component variables. So far as love or affection is concerned, psychologists have failed in this mission."

The behavioral doctrine was that human beings were motivated according to their primary drives of hunger, thirst, elimination, pain, and sex. Other motives, including love and affection, were secondary to these. In child rearing, affection was downplayed in favour of the belief in "training," and there was little understanding of what we now know about the importance to babies of physical contact.

Harlow's paper "The nature of love" turned all this on its head. With his refusal to see love and affection as simply a "secondary drive," it became one of the most celebrated scientific papers ever written.

Food, water, and love
Harlow chose to work with young rhesus monkeys because they are more mature than human infants, and show little difference to human babies in how they nurse, cling, respond to affection, and even see and hear. The way they learn and even how they experience and express fear and frustration are also similar.

He noticed that, in the absence of contact with their mothers, these lab-raised monkeys became very attached to the cloth pads (actually diapers or nappies) that covered the hard floors of their cages. When they were periodi-cally removed in order to put new pads down, the baby monkeys had terrible tantrums. This reaction, Harlow noted, was just like the attachment that human babies develop to a certain pillow, blanket, or cuddly toy. Startlingly, his research found that baby monkeys raised in wire-mesh cages with no pads had very little chance of surviving for more than five days. It seemed that "soft things to cling to" were not merely a matter of comfort, but in the absence of their mothers were a primary factor in the monkeys' survival.

The behaviorist view was that babies—monkey or human—loved their mothers for the milk that they provided, since this satisfied a primary need. But what Harlow had seen with the cloth pads made him wonder whether babies might love their mothers not for their milk only, but because they provided warmth and affection. Perhaps love was as basic a need as food and water.

Cloth and wire moms

To test the idea further, Harlow and his team built a "surrogate mother" from wood covered with soft cloth, with a light bulb behind it providing warmth, and made another "mother" simply out of wire mesh. For four newborn monkeys, only the cloth mother provided milk and the wire mother did not; for four other newborns, the opposite was the case. The study showed that even when the wire mother was the one lactating, the monkeys vastly pre-ferred to be with and have physical contact with the soft-cloth mother.

This result overturned the conventional wisdom that babies become con-ditioned to love their mother because she provides milk and is therefore their ticket to survival. Clearly, the ability to nurse was not the main factor for the monkeys; what mattered was the bodily contact, or the "mother's love." Harlow went so far as to suggest that perhaps the main function of nursing was to ensure frequent physical contact between baby and mother, since the loving bond seemed so vital for survival. After all, he noted, long after the actual sustenance stops, it is the bond that remains.

Love is blind

As real babies flee to and cling to their mothers at any sign of fear or danger, Harlow wondered whether this would still apply to baby monkeys even with a cloth or wire mother. It did, with the monkeys running to the cloth mother irrespective of how much this mother had "nursed" them. The same happened when the monkeys were placed in an unfamiliar room with new visual stimuli, and were given the opportunity to return to the cloth mother.

Harlow also found that monkeys that were separated from the surrogate mother for long periods (five months) still responded immediately to it if given the chance. The bond, once initially formed, was highly resistant to being forgotten. Even monkeys reared without any mother figure at all, real or surrogate, after a bewildered and frightened day or two in the presence of a cloth mother would warm to her and forge a relationship. After a while these monkeys expressed similar behavior to those who had enjoyed a surrogate mother all along.

In another variation, some of the surrogate mothers were given a rocking motion and also made to feel warm. Baby monkeys became even more attached to these mothers, clinging to them for up to 18 hours a day.

Was it the face of the surrogate mother, with her big painted-on eyes and mouth, that especially kindled the love of the baby monkeys? Harlow's first surrogate-raised monkey only had a mother whose head was a ball of wood with no face, and she bonded with this surrogate over a period of six months. When later placed with two cloth mothers that had faces, the monkey actually turned the heads around so that she saw no face at all—just what she was used to in her mother! Again, Harlow's experiment showed that what matters most is the close connection we form with our mothers, irrespective of what they look like and even how indifferently they treat us. Harlow was not joking when he wrote, "Love is blind." He concluded that there was little difference in the quality of mothering provided by a surrogate or a real mother—it was apparent that the baby monkey needed only a very basic "mother figure" to grow up healthy and happy.

The truth emerges

This assessment, however, turned out to be premature. Harlow observed that when his baby monkeys grew up, they had many things wrong with them. Instead of the normal range of responses, they swung between clinging attachment and destructive aggression, often tearing at their body or shredding bits of cloth or paper. Even as adults they had to cling to soft, furry things, and did not seem to know the difference between living and inanimate objects. Though they could be affectionate to other monkeys, few were able to mate as adults, and those who did have offspring were not able to take care of them properly. Clearly, the lack of normal response from their fake mothers, and their isolation from other monkeys, had made them socially backward. They had no idea what was or wasn't appropriate behavior, no concept of the usual give and take of normal relationships.

What the Harlows discovered had actually been observed in the 1940s by Hungarian psychiatrist Rene Spitz. His well-known study compared babies raised in two institutional settings. The first was a foundling home that was very clean and orderly, but a little clinical; the second was a prison nursery, a rough-and-tumble sort of place where the children had lots of physical contact. Within a two-year period, over a third of the kids in the foundling home had died, whereas five years later all the prison nursery children were alive. Of the foundling home babies who did not die, many grew up with problems, with over 20 remaining institutionalized. What made all the difference was that the nursery kids' mothers were allowed to care for them, while the foundling home's children lived under a controlled regime run by professional nurses. Whether you define "death" as physical or psychological, it was the lack of physical affection and love that was the cause.

Final comments

Critics say that all Harlow did was prove scientifically what was common sense—that babies and young children need to form a close physical and emotional attachment to someone as much as they need oxygen. But the task of proving beyond any doubt what we already know seems to be the role of experimental psychology, and it took Harlow's experiments to change the way children's homes and social service agencies were run. What began as defiance of the prevailing view on child rearing has now become conventional wisdom. For instance, the suggestion often given to new mothers that they should hold their minutes-old newborn against their bare skin can be traced back to the devastating effects of not having such contact, discovered by Harlow.

His work with monkeys also elevated what we now believe about the intelligence and capacity for feeling in animals. B. F. Skinner (see p 266) believed that animals had no feelings, but Harlow's monkeys were creatures who thrived on curiosity and learning, and they had deep emotional needs.

Yet all this knowledge came at a price, for the great irony of the scientist who helped determine the "nature of love" was that his labs were often brutal places for the monkeys themselves. As he grew older, Harlow's experiments got more cruel, and with good reason he became a focus of the animal liberation movement. Many of those who helped in these later experiments found the experience devastating.

For a more personal account of Harlow—his divorce, the death of his second wife, remarriage, issues with alcohol, and the quality of his parenting— read Deborah Blum's *Love at Goon Park: Harry Harlow and the Science of Affection* (2003). The title comes from a nickname given to Harlow's lab at the University of Wisconsin, whose address was 600 N. Park, which could easily be read as "Goon Park." Many thought the name fitting, as with his antifeminist views, famous bluntness, and ruthless reputation as an experimenter, Harlow cut a frightening figure.

Harry Harlow

Born Harry Israel in Fairfield, Iowa in 1905, Harlow was an ambitious child whose intelligence gained him a place at Stanford University. He gained a BA and PhD, and when he was 25 was appointed to a position at the University of Wisconsin. About this time he changed his surname from Israel because, although he was Episcopalian, he was told that anti-Semitism would affect his career. Harlow soon established a primate psychology lab, and worked with IQ researcher Lewis Terman, and also Abraham Maslow.

Harlow stayed at the University of Wisconsin for most of his career, and was George Cary Comstock Research Professor of Psychology until 1974. He did a stint heading the Human Resources Research Branch with the US Army and lectured at Cornell and Northwestern universities among others. In 1972 he received a gold medal from the American Psychological Association, and in 1974 moved to Tucson to become an honorary professor at the University of Arizona.

His first wife Clara Mears worked with him on primate research, but they divorced in 1946. Harlow then married Margaret Kuenne (Marlow), and the year after her death in 1970, remarried Clara Mears. They had three sons and a daughter. Harlow died in 1981.

I'm OK–You're OK

"*The purpose of this book is not only the presentation of new data but also an answer to the question of why people do not live as good as they know how already. They may know that the experts have had a lot to say about human behavior, but this knowledge does not seem to have had the slightest effect on their hangover, their splintering marriage or their cranky children.*"

"*Once we understand positions and games, freedom of response begins to emerge as a real possibility.*"

In a nutshell

If we become more conscious of our ingrained reactions and behavior patterns, our life can begin to be genuinely free.

In a similar vein

Eric Berne *Games People Play* (p 26)
Anna Freud *The Ego and the Mechanisms of Defence* (p 104)
Karen Horney *Our Inner Conflicts* (p 156)

CHAPTER 26

Thomas A. Harris

Y ou know that a book has become a classic when you see it featured in sitcoms. In an episode of *Seinfeld*, Jerry Seinfeld opens the door of his apartment to find all-time hopeless case George Costanza spread out on the couch reading *I'm OK—You're OK*. For Jerry, reading a self-help book with a silly title is just one more piece of proof of his friend's loser status.

I'm OK—You're OK was indeed an icon of the pop psychology boom of the 1960s and 1970s. Demand for the book was tremendous, and today it sits comfortably in the pantheon of titles that have sold over 10 million copies. But what do sales figures indicate? A lot of tacky books sold by the truckload in that era. What is different about *I'm OK—You're OK* is that it is still read and used.

Your mental family: Parent, Adult, Child

To understand the success of Harris's book, we must look at the trail blazed by his mentor, Eric Berne, in *Games People Play* (see commentary on p 26). Harris used Berne's work as a basis for his own, but instead of analyzing the games people play, he focused on Berne's concept of the three internal voices that speak to us all the time in the form of archetypal characters: the Parent, the Adult, and the Child. All of us have Parent, Adult, or Child "data" guiding our thoughts and decisions, and Harris believed that transactional analysis would free up the Adult, the reasoning voice.

The Adult prevents us being hijacked by unthinking obedience (Child), or by ingrained habit or prejudice (Parent), leaving us a vestige of free will. The Adult represents the objectivity that inspired Socrates' statement, "The unexamined life is not worth living." It is the reasoning, moral voice that lets us grow, checking Child or Parent data to see if it is appropriate for a given situation. We might feel like throwing a tantrum when a hotel desk mixes up our booking, but instead we choose to accept it for the moment, figuring it is better to stay calm if we want a positive solution.

Harris includes many examples of conversations that display people caught up in Child or Parent patterns, showing how difficult it is to remove racism or any type of prejudice when one has no awareness of the patterns under which one is operating.

What it takes to be "OK"

What does the title phrase "I'm OK—You're OK" actually mean? Harris observed that children, by virtue of their inferior power in an adult world, learn that "I'm not OK, whereas you, being an adult, are OK." Every child learns this, even if they have a happy childhood, and many adults only over-turn this basic decision after their parents pass on, and then perpetuate it in reverse fashion with their own children. Yet the good news is that, once we are aware that it *was* a decision, we can decide to replace it with a relaxed, self-liking mode of being.

We do not drift into the "I'm OK—You're OK" position. We may experi-ence it on occasion, but for it to become more or less ingrained it has to be a conscious decision (not merely a feeling), based on faith in people in general. It is a little like the Christian concept of grace; that is, total acceptance of our-selves and of others. From this position we are also better able to see beyond another person's Parent or Child behavior, even if that behavior would nor-mally cause offense. We reach a level where we don't expect every transaction to make us happy, knowing that "I'm OK—You're OK" is true even when we don't see evidence of it.

Whether you name it the Superego, the Adult, or, in New Age parlance, the "Higher Self," a willingness to allow our grown-up internal voice to come to the fore is part of any human being's development. *I'm OK—You're OK* provides a key for letting us out of a mental prison that we may not even have known we inhabit. Often it is more satisfying, and certainly easier, to play games or be defensive or rest on prejudices, and in our society we can be con-sidered a success while essentially remaining in Child mode all our life; in doing so we consider other people as objects who will either help or stand in the way of our aims. Genuinely successful people, in contrast, assume that others are equals from whom they can learn valuable things.

Final comments

Though Berne's work on transactional analysis may be the better book, Harris's *I'm OK—You're OK* became a huge bestseller, and a major reason has to be his use of the easy-to-understand Parent, Adult, and Child frame-work. The terms may seem a little goofy, but in fact parallel Freud's original trinity of superego, ego, and id, the basic elements that Freud put forward for understanding human behavior. Although this is a work of popular psychol-ogy, Harris did not try to dumb it down to appeal to everyone. He freely quotes from the likes of Emerson, Whitman, Plato, and Freud, assuming that if readers do not know about such figures they certainly should.

Though it will never be a household term, transactional analysis does have real value in making us aware of our negative and normally unconscious behavior patterns. Given its "do-it-yourself" nature, the mainstream psychiatric profession never made much room for its way of seeing, but it has nevertheless become part of the tool bag of psychologists and counselors who need workable techniques to bring about change.

Transactional analysis has even found its way into fiction. James Redfield acknowledged Harris and Berne as crucial influences in writing one of the biggest-selling books of the 1990s, *The Celestine Prophecy*. The "control dramas" that his characters engage in, and seek to be free of, are squarely based on the games and positions of transactional analysis; the survival of the book's characters—and indeed the evolution of the human race—is made dependent on their ability to see beyond these automatic reactions.

Thomas A. Harris

Harris was born in Texas. He went to medical school at Temple University in Philadelphia, and in 1942 he began his psychiatry training in Washington DC at St Elizabeth Hospital. He was a US Navy psychiatrist for several years, and was at Pearl Harbor when it was attacked. He became chief of the Navy's Psychiatry Branch.

After the war Harris held a teaching post at the University of Arkansas, and for a period was a senior mental health bureaucrat. He entered private practice as a psychiatrist in Sacramento, California, in 1956, and was a director of the International Transactional Analysis Association.

The True Believer

"*A rising mass movement attracts and holds a following not by its doctrine and promises but by the refuge it offers from the anxieties, barrenness and meaninglessness of an individual existence.*"

"*Mass movements are usually accused of doping their followers with hope of the future while cheating them of the enjoyment of the present. Yet to the frustrated the present is irremediably spoiled. Comforts and pleasures cannot make it whole. No real content or comfort can ever arise in their minds but from hope.*"

In a nutshell

People allow themselves to be swept up in larger causes in order to be freed of responsibility for their lives, and to escape the banality or misery of the present.

In a similar vein

Nathaniel Branden *The Psychology of Self-Esteem* (p 42)
Viktor Frankl *The Will to Meaning* (p 100)

CHAPTER 27

Eric Hoffer

I f you have ever known someone who joined a cult, became a religious convert, or threw themselves into a political movement—and in the process seemed to lose their identity—this book may give you an insight into how that can happen. The work of an amateur—Hoffer's day job was loading and unloading cargo on San Francisco's docks—*The True Believer: Thoughts on the Nature of Mass Movements* is a compelling foray into mass movements and their power to shape minds, showing us how spiritual hunger leads people to jettison their old selves in order to become part of something apparently greater and more glorious.

The book had special meaning when published in the wake of the Second World War, given the havoc that a single movement—Nazism—wreaked across Europe, but Hoffer's work is timeless in its observations of the psychology of group identification and why people are so ready and willing to die for a cause. Virtually everything he wrote could be applied to the terrorists and suicide bombers of today. Although a half century old, *The True Believer* could therefore not be more relevant.

The wish for transformation

Why are mass movements so powerful? Because they are full of fervor, Hoffer suggested. Powerful political movements always have a religious fervor to them. The French Revolution was really a new religion, replacing all the dogma and rituals of the Church with similar ones devoted to the State. The same goes for the Bolshevik and Nazi revolutions: "The hammer and sickle and the swastika," Hoffer observed, "are in a class with the cross."

Those who make up the ranks of the early stages of a revolutionary movement are looking for some big and total change in their life. Leaders of mass movements know this, and therefore do all they can to "kindle and fan an extravagant hope." They do not promise gradual, incremental change but a total change in the believer's existence.

People normally join an organization for reasons of self-interest—to advance or benefit themselves in some way. Those who join a revolutionary mass movement, in contrast, do so "to be rid of an unwanted self." If we are not happy with who we are, in a mass movement this no longer matters, as the self is irrelevant in relation to the larger "holy cause" of the movement. Where before people experienced only frustration and meaninglessness in their individual existence, now they have pride, purpose, confidence, and hope.

"Faith in a holy cause is to a considerable extent a substitute for the lost faith in ourselves," Hoffer wrote. Yet this desire to lose a sense of individuality paradoxically brings enormous self-esteem and feelings of worthiness.

Other candidates

Who else is vulnerable to joining a mass movement? In his chapter on potential converts, Hoffer noted that the very poor are not good candidates. They are too satisfied with just surviving to be interested in some grand vision. It is, rather, those who have a bit more, who have had their eyes opened to greater things, who are more likely to get swept up. Hoffer observed: "Our frustration is greater when we have much and want more than when we have nothing and want some. We are less satisfied when we lack many things than when we seem to lack but one thing."

People join mass movements for a sense of belonging and camaraderie, a feeling so often lacking in an economically free and competitive society. They may simply be very bored. Hitler, Hoffer noted, was financed by the wives of some of Germany's great industrialists, whose regular amusements or enthusiasms no longer satisfied. The opportunity to get whipped up in a cause and its great leader is intoxicating, supplanting even reliable distractions such as family and work. Indeed, Hoffer remarked on the curious fact that it is often people with *unlimited* opportunities who are attracted to mass movements.

Finally, a movement will attract those who dislike having to be responsible for their lives. Young Nazis wished to free themselves from the burden of making decisions and slowly constructing an adult existence as their parents had done. Much more alluring were the simple promises of glory in the Third Reich. They were shocked when as losers of the war they were expected to feel responsibility for what had happened, because in their minds it was precisely responsibility that they had given up amid the pageantry of the new regime.

Why people die for a cause

A mass movement's promise of a dramatically better new world enables it to disregard normal moral inhibitions. The holy or glorious end justifies any means, and believers will do horrible things to other humans in the cause of creating their paradise. Hoffer warned us to be very careful "when hopes and dreams are loose in the streets." They usually precede some kind of disaster.

To the nonbeliever, the self-sacrifice of a martyr, a kamikaze pilot, or a suicide bomber seems totally irrational. However, if our present life is considered worthless, and our belief in the movement is so great, it will not be such a leap to die for it. Before people reach this watershed, Hoffer said, they will have stripped themselves of a sense of their own individuality. Absorbed fully into the collective body, they are no longer the person friends and family once knew, but only the representative of a people, a party, a tribe.

To the true believer, nonbelievers are weak, corrupt, without backbone, or decadent. The perception of their own purity of intent allows them to do anything in the name of that noble intention—including take their own lives. It is this close-mindedness, blindness even, of the true believer that provides their power. If the world is black and white, then action is clear. It is only the open-minded who have to deal with surprises or contradictions.

Final comments

One of Hoffer's insights was that "what is not" is always a more powerful motivating force than "what is." While to improve their lot the average person will work on what they already have, the true believer is not satisfied unless they are in the process of building a whole new world. Such a hatred of the present has done terrible damage, but on the other hand the overthrow of many kinds of tyrannies would not have been possible without those who dreamed and schemed for something better, who were willing to spark a bloody revolution in the cause of ideals such as liberty and equality. For better or worse, fanatics have made our world.

The True Believer is not just about mass movements. It is a work of philosophy with keen insights into human nature and contains almost no unnecessary words or sentences. The book is also a great example of why questions of human motivation and action should never be left to psychologists alone.

Eric Hoffer

Born in New York City in 1902, the son of an immigrant cabinetmaker, Hoffer grew up speaking German and English. At 7 he was blinded as the result of a head injury, and missed out on most of his schooling. At 15, without any surgery, he miraculously regained his sight.

Both his parents died while he was still in his teens. He inherited $300 and moved to California. Supporting himself as a traveling laborer and gold prospector, Hoffer spent his spare time reading everything from Montaigne to Hitler's Mein Kampf. *For many years he worked as a longshoreman (or stevedore) in San Francisco, and only ceased manual laboring in 1941.*

The True Believer brought Hoffer a measure of fame, and he devoted the second half of his life to writing. Other books include The Passionate State of Mind and Other Aphorisms *(1954),* The Ordeal of Change *(1963),* The Temper of Our Time *(1967),* Reflections on the Human Condition *(1973), and* In Our Time *(1976). He also published a journal of life on the waterfront, and an autobiography,* Truth Imagined, *was released after his death. In the year he died, 1983, Hoffer was awarded the Presidential Medal of Freedom by Ronald Reagan.*

Our Inner Conflicts

"*Living with unresolved conflicts involves primarily a devastating* waste of human energies, *occasioned not only by the conflicts themselves but by all the devious attempts to remove them.*"

"*Sometimes neurotic persons show a curious single-mindedness of purpose: men may sacrifice everything including their own dignity to their ambition; women may want nothing of life but love; parents may devote their entire interest to their children. Such persons give the impression of wholeheartedness. But, as we have shown, they are actually pursuing a mirage which appears to offer a solution of their conflicts. The apparent wholeheartedness is one of desperation rather than of integration.*"

In a nutshell

The neurotic tendencies we may have acquired in childhood are no longer necessary—if we leave them behind we can fulfill our potential.

In a similar vein

CHAPTER 28

Karen Horney

Karen Danielsen was in her mid-teens when Sigmund Freud wrote *The Interpretation of Dreams*. She would later be well-known for "feminizing" the male bastion of psychoanalysis, but it took her 35 years before she even published her first book. In between she married, had three children, and obtained a PhD.

Karen Horney (pronounced "Horn-eye"), as she became, broke away from Freud in some important ways. By refuting some of his ideas such as "penis envy" and generally downplaying the supremacy of sexual motivation, she arguably brought more sense to psychoanalysis. In addition, by showing how women were vulnerable to neuroses caused by unreal cultural expectations, she gained the deserved reputation of being the first feminist psychoanalyst.

Horney differed from Freudian dogma by saying that people did not always have to be prisoners of their unconscious minds or pasts. She wanted to find the root cause of psychological issues, but largely considered them a *present* problem that could be healed. Her delineations of neurotic types, so simple and elegant, have been a significant influence on modern therapeutic practice, and her interpersonal approach and emphasis on uncovering the "real self"—with its great potential—were important influences on the humanistic psychology of Carl Rogers and Abraham Maslow. Finally, Horney wished to make the process of analysis sufficiently understandable that people could analyze themselves. In this she presaged both cognitive therapy and the self-help movement.

Our Inner Conflicts: A Constructive Theory of Neurosis was conceived as a book for the layperson. While trained therapists should handle severe neuroses, Horney also believed that "with untiring effort we can go ourselves a long way towards disentangling our own conflicts." It is therefore a self-help book, but a very fine one based on 40 years of keen observation of the mind's defenses. You will be a remarkable person indeed if you don't see at least part of yourself in Horney's descriptions of the three neurotic tendencies.

Conflicts and inconsistencies

According to Horney, all neurotic symptoms (which are also called "rackets") indicate an unresolved deeper conflict. Though the symptoms cause difficulties for the person in real life, it is the conflict that actually produces depression, anxiety, inertia, indecision, undue detachment, overdependence, and so on. A conflict involves inconsistencies to which the person is generally blind. For example:

❖ Someone who is greatly affronted by a perceived slur, when in fact none was given.

❖ One who apparently values another's friendship, but nevertheless steals from them.

❖ A woman who claims devotion to her children, yet somehow forgets their birthdays.

❖ A girl whose chief desire is to marry, but avoids contact with men.

❖ A forgiving and tolerant person to others who is nevertheless very severe on themselves.

Thing that "don't add up" like this indicate a divided personality. In relation to the mother, Horney commented that perhaps she was "more devoted to her ideal of being a good mother than to the children themselves." Or perhaps she had an unconscious sadistic tendency to frustrate her children's enjoyment. The point is that an outward issue may often indicate a deeper conflict. Consider a marriage in which there are arguments over every little thing. Is it the subject of the arguments that is the real issue, or some underlying dynamic?

How conflicts develop

Freud believed that our inner conflicts were a matter of instinctual drives coming up against the "civilized" conscience, a situation that we could never change. But Horney felt that our inner turmoil came about through conflicting notions about what we actually wanted.

For instance, children growing up in a hostile family environment want love like everyone else, but feel forced to become aggressive in order to cope. When they become adults, these genuine needs conflict with the neurotic need to control situations and people. The person they feel neurotically driven to be, tragically, is the very personality that will never deliver them what they truly want. The behaviors they have taken on have effectively become their personality, but it is a divided personality.

Rather than being about "penis envy" or the "Oedipus complex," Horney felt that adult neuroses stemmed from more basic factors such as too little love, smothering love, lack of guidance, attention, or respect for the child, conditional love, inconsistent rules, isolation from other children, a hostile atmosphere, domination, and so on. All of these make children feel that they have to make up for their insecurity in some way, developing strategies or "neurotic trends" that they carry into adulthood. Taken to extremes, neuroticism ends up creating "Dr Jekyll and Mr Hyde" characters, divided within themselves yet tragically unaware of the division.

Horney identified three basic neurotic trends: moving toward people; moving against people; and moving away from people.

Moving toward people

This type of person experienced feelings of isolation or fear in childhood, and as a result attempted to win the affection of others in the family in order to feel safe. After several years of temper tantrums, they commonly became "nice" and docile—they found a strategy better suited to getting what they wanted.

As adults, their need for affection and approval manifests itself as a deep need for a friend, lover, husband, or wife who will "fulfill all expectations of life." The compulsive need to "secure" their chosen partner occurs irrespective of what that person feels about them. Other people seem "like strange and threatening animals" who must be won over. Through being submissive, caring, sensitive, and dependent (the other person may feel they are being "killed by kindness"), this type finds an effective way to create connections and therefore feel safe. The nature of the significant other does not actually interest them that much—deep down, they may not even like other people—the main thing is to be accepted, loved, guided by, and taken care of. Ultimately, though, the need for belonging leads to misjudgments about other people.

This type's taboo against being assertive or critical creates a "poor little me" feeling that progressively weakens them. Ironically, when they occasionally go out on a limb to be aggressive or detached, often they seem suddenly more likable. After all, their aggressive tendencies have not gone away, they have just been suppressed.

Moving against people

In childhood, such people had a hostile family environment, and chose to fight it through rebellion. They began to distrust the intentions and motivations of those around them.

Adults of this type assume the world to be basically hostile, but may have acquired "a veneer of suave politeness, fair-mindedness and good fellowship." They are benevolent as long as others submit to their command. As fearful and anxious as the compliant type, instead of choosing "belonging" as their defense against a feeling of helplessness, they choose the path of "every man for himself." They dislike weakness, particularly in themselves, and they are generally strivers for success, prestige, or recognition.

"Trust no one and never let down your guard" might be their motto. Such extreme self-interest may involve exploitation or control over others.

Moving away from people

Instead of wanting to belong or to fight, in childhood this type felt too close to those around them and tried to create distance between themselves and their family, retreating into a secret world of toys or books or wishes for the future.

As adults, they have a neurotic need for detachment from the world that is quite distinct from a genuine wish for solitude, or a wish not to get emotionally involved with anyone, whether in love or conflict. This group may get on well with other people superficially, as long as their "magic circle" is not penetrated, and may live very simply so as not to have to work hard for others and so lose control of their life. Able to live in "splendid isolation" because of a feeling of superiority over others and a belief in their uniqueness, they have a terror of being forced into joining a group, having to become gregarious, or engaging in common chit-chat at a party.

Together with these features comes a craving for privacy and independence, and a hatred of anything that involves coercion or obligation, such as marriage or financial debt. Such people are happiest when they are fully loved by someone, yet they have few obligations to that person. Their detached nature involves numbness to what they really feel about something, often leading to terrible indecision.

A healthy child or adult may express all of the tendencies above to some extent, harmoniously wanting to belong, fight, or be alone at appropriate times. It is when these are no longer choices but *compulsions* that the person becomes neurotic. This is the tragedy of neurosis—that it takes away free will, making people act out their tendency no matter how different the situation.

Tendency to dependency

The intense work of repression, externalization of feelings (avoiding self-examination), and idealization of a certain self-image takes a huge amount of energy, so that the individual actually "loses sight of himself." With this loss, other people paradoxically become more important and more powerful in the person's estimation; their opinion gains a "terrible power." In short, the extreme egocentrism of the neurotic person ironically leads to a loss of self and dependence on others.

The competitive spirit of modern civilization, Horney wrote, was fertile ground for neuroses, because the emphasis on success and achievement gave people who had a weak self-image the opportunity to greatly compensate by becoming "eminent." She noted, "blind rebellion, blind craving to excel, and a blind need to keep away from others are all forms of dependence." Psychologically healthy people are not driven in any of these ways. Rather, their motivation is to express their talents more fully, making a solid contribution to an area of work that deeply interests them, or to love more deeply. They are inspired by the possibility of integration, not fired by desperation.

Final comments

Horney's idea of the "wholehearted" person who is fully in touch with their genuine or real self is not that different to Abraham Maslow's "self-actualized" individual or Carl Rogers' notion of "becoming a person." To sum up her philosophy, Horney quotes psychologist John Macmurray: "What other significance can our existence have than to be ourselves fully and completely?" She believed that we are all powerful people. Our neurotic tendency is simply a mask we put on in order not to show our real self, but in nearly all cases it is no longer necessary. We can reclaim a compliant, aggressive, or detached self, giving up the compulsive behavior that we believed would protect us from imagined harm.

While she traced the origins of our inner conflicts to childhood, at the same time Horney made people accept the *present* dimensions of their neurotic tendency or complex, so that they could not hide behind an attitude of "this is how I am because of what happened to me." By confronting such truths she brought many readers to the *root cause* of their problems.

Our Inner Conflicts is well written, easy to understand, and contains many insights into human nature. Horney's optimism about the possibility of change is also quietly inspirational.

Karen Horney

Karen Danielson was born in Hamburg, Germany in 1885. Her father Berndt captained ships and was a strict Lutheran. Her parents divorced in 1904, and two years later the ambitious and intelligent Karen entered medical school at the University of Berlin. She soon married well-off PhD Oscar Horney, with whom she had three daughters.

From 1914 to 1918 she studied psychiatry and underwent psychoanalysis, including sessions with Karl Abraham. She began teaching at the Berlin Psychoanalytic Institute, of which she was a founding member, and was involved in all the major psychoanalysis congresses and debates. In 1923 her husband's business failed and he became ill. In the same year her beloved older brother died of an infection, events that plunged her into depression.

In 1932, separated from her husband, Horney moved to the United States with her daughters, taking up a post at the Psychoanalytic Institute in Chicago. Two years later she settled in New York, working at the New York Psychoanalytic Institute and enjoying the company of other European intellectuals, including psychologist Eric Fromm, with whom she had an affair. Her book New Ways in Psychoanalysis *(1939), which critiqued Freud, forced her resignation from the Institute, leading her to found her own American Institute for Psychoanalysis.*

Horney highlighted the social and cultural factors in psychology in her book The Neurotic Personality of Our Time *(1937). Other books included* Self-Analysis *(1942) and* Neurosis and Human Growth *(1950).*

Until her death in 1952, Horney continued to teach and work as a therapist. Feminine Psychology *(1967), a posthumous collection of essays, brought renewed interest in her work.*

The Principles of Psychology

"Consciousness, then, does not appear to itself chopped up in bits. Such words as 'chain' or 'train' do not describe it fitly as it presents itself in the first instance. It is nothing jointed; it flows. A 'river' or a 'stream' are the metaphors by which it is most naturally described. In talking of it hereafter, let us call it the stream of thought, of consciousness, or of subjective life."

"The only thing which psychology has a right to postulate at the outset is the fact of thinking itself."

"The most peculiar social self which one is apt to have is in the mind of the person one is in love with. The good or bad fortunes of this self cause the most intense elation and dejection... To his own consciousness he is not, so long as this particular social self fails to get recognition, and when it is recognized his contentment passes all bounds."

In a nutshell

Psychology is the science of mental life, which means the science of the self.

CHAPTER 29

William James

William James is widely regarded as America's greatest philosopher. He is also (with William Wundt) considered to be a father of modern psychology.

Psychology was once an area of study within philosophy, and James was for a number of years a philosophy professor. The distinction he made between the two fields was this: Psychology was the "science of mental life"; that is, of minds within a particular body, which exist in time and space, having thoughts and feelings in relation to the physical world they are in. On the other hand, explanations of thoughts as the product of some deeper force, such as the soul or ego, were really the realm of metaphysics or philosophy.

James considered this new subject a *natural* science that required analysis of feelings, desires, cognitions, reasoning, and decisions according to their own features and dynamics, in the same way that one would explain building a house by looking at its stones and bricks. His choice to look at the phenomena of psychology, rather than some theory behind them, advanced the subject considerably and achieved his aim of putting it on a firmer scientific footing.

James was often depressed or in frail physical health, and *The Principles of Psychology* took him all of 12 years to write. In his Preface he commented, "it has grown to a length which no one can regret more than the writer himself. The man must indeed be sanguine who, in this crowded age, can hope to have many readers for fourteen hundred continuous pages from his pen." This was the famous two-volume "long course," the full version of the book. But James also produced a condensed form, known as the "Jimmy" to college students, who are grateful not to have to tackle the real thing.

Given its size, it would be presumptuous to "sum up" James's masterpiece. However, we look at a few ideas that hopefully give a flavor of its contents.

Creatures of habit

"When we look at creatures from an outward point of view," James noted, "one of the first things that strike us is that they are bundles of habits."

What are habits exactly? In his research into the physiology of the brain and nervous system, James concluded that they boil down to being "discharges in the nerve centers" involving a pattern of reflex paths that are successively woken up. Once one of these paths is created, it becomes easier for the nerve current to pass along the same path again.

However, James noted a difference between the habitual behavior of animals and that of humans: While the actions of most animals are automatic, and relatively limited and simple, because of our wide variety of desires and wants, humans have to consciously form new habits if we are to achieve certain results. The problem is that creating new, good habits requires work and application. James wrote that the key to good habits is to act decisively on the resolutions you make. Actions create the motor effects in our nervous system that turn a wish into a habit; the brain has to "grow" to our wishes, and the path will not be made unless this repeated action takes place.

The key, James commented, was to make the nervous system our ally instead of our enemy: "As we become permanent drunkards by so many separate drinks, so we become saints in the moral, and authorities and experts in the practical and scientific spheres, by so many separate acts and hours of work." Though we don't think they matter that much at the time, our actions taken together account either for a powerful integrity or a damning failure.

This all seems very familiar to us now, but much of the emphasis on forging positive habitual behavior in today's psychology and personal development writing can be traced back to James's thinking on the subject.

Us and the rest

James's understanding of psychology revolved around the personal self. That is, general talk about "thought" and "feeling" as abstract concepts did not mean much next to the personal reality of "I think" and "I feel." He wrote that each person is separated from every other by a wall—that is, the skull enclosing the brain—and ventured that the world is neatly divided into two halves, with ourselves taking up one whole half, and the rest of the world, with everyone in it, the other:

> *One great splitting of the whole universe into two halves is made by each of us; and for each of us almost all of the interest attaches to one of the halves... When I say that we all call the two halves by the same names, and that those names are "me" and "not-me" respectively, it will at once be seen what I mean.*

This is a simple insight that, like so many of James's comments, borders on folk wisdom. However, it recognizes that people become interested in psychology not because they want to study broad principles regarding thought and emotion, but because they want to know why *they* think and feel the way they do.

A division of the world into "me" and "the rest" is a little confronting, especially for those who consider that they live for others, yet it is the very physiology of human beings, with one brain inside one body, always looking out at the rest of the world, that makes it a fact.

The stream of thought

Not only do we all see the world differently, but our own personal consciousness will not be the same from day to day, or even hour to hour. As James put this:

We feel things differently according as we are sleepy or awake, hungry or full, fresh or tired; differently at night and in the morning, differently in summer and in winter, and above all things differently in childhood, manhood, and old age... The difference of the sensibility is shown best by the difference of our emotion about the things from one age to another... What was bright and exciting becomes weary, flat, and unprofitable. The bird's song is tedious, the breeze is mournful, the sky is sad.

He observed that we can never have exactly the same thought more than once. We may be able to sustain an illusion of sameness, but the fact of a constantly changing world, and the need for our continually altering reactions to it, mean this is impossible:

Often we are ourselves struck at the strange differences in our successive views of the same thing. We wonder how we ever could have opined as we did last month about a certain matter. We have outgrown the possibility of that state of mind, we know not how. From one year to another we see things in new lights. And it is just as well, for this constant change, this perpetual movement and then return to equilibrium, is what makes us human.

James also famously observed that thought is continuous, like a stream. We use phrases like a "train of thought" or a "chain of thought," but the real nature of thought is flowing. He noted, "The transition between the thought of one object and the thought of another is no more a break in the thought than a joint in a bamboo is a break in the wood. It is a part of the consciousness as much as the joint is a part of the bamboo."

Since James, the science of psychology has parsed every thought, feeling, and emotion into thousands of categories, which indeed is the work of a science. But psychology would do well to remember that this is not how it *feels* to be conscious. Consciousness is not at all like the processing of a computer. Rather, to be alive is to experience a constantly flowing river of ideas, thoughts, and feelings.

The successful self

James admitted that he had sometimes fancied being a millionaire, an explorer, or a lady killer, but came back to the sad truth that he had to settle on one self. To be many things would be too contradictory. To be effective in life, we have to choose from many possible personages, and "stake our salvation" on that self. The downside is that if you stake your self on being, for instance, a great oarsman or a great psychologist, to fail at this ambition is a grievous hit to our self-esteem.

If there is little gap between our potentialities and our actualities, we regard ourselves well. James famously provided a formula for self-esteem:

$$Self\text{-}esteem = \frac{Success}{Pretensions}$$

He pointed to a "lightness of the heart" when we give up chasing certain potentialities or illusions that we will never achieve, such as being young, slim, musical, or a famous athlete. Each illusion, if discarded, is one less thing that will disappoint us, and one less thing that will hold us back from real success.

Final comments

James's focus on the self does not seem remarkable now, as we live in such an individualistic age. But at the time he was writing, the social fabric was much thicker and one's place in society was arguably of much greater import than what went on inside one's head. Yet when we consider the restrictions he placed on his own subject, James's thinking could not really have gone any other way. His definition of psychology as the science of mental life meant the life within individual brains, the thoughts and feelings of individual people— not the "human mind" in general.

While the twentieth-century psychologists who came after him got caught up in rather mechanical models of the mind and behavior, James described human consciousness as like the aurora borealis, the luminous northern lights, whose "whole internal equilibrium shifts with every pulse of change." Such a poetic gift for explanation did not endear James to the lab-rat-in-mazes brand of modern psychology, but it was precisely his artistic sensitivity, deep philosophical knowledge, and even openness to mystical ideas that allowed him to push out the boundaries of his field. Others would follow to do the laborious job of turning psychology into a science, but it needed a philosopher of his caliber to first paint a picture of the landscape.

Much has been made of James's elegant and lively prose, and it is this— plus a personal, familiar tone unusual for the times—that makes *The Principles of Psychology* readable today. James was often overshadowed by his novelist brother, but William James could easily have been a writer himself rather than a psychologist—it has been said that Henry James was the psychologist who wrote novels, and William the novelist who wrote psychology!

That said, *The Principles of Psychology* is no easy read, with the good parts lying amid many long passages that either are quite technical (involving the physiology of the brain and nervous system) or mull over difficult concepts. James himself suggested that readers skip around and read what interested them, rather than going through the whole work—from someone who helped establish a science, a typically humble suggestion.

William James

Born in New York City in 1842, the oldest son of Henry and Mary James, William James enjoyed a comfortable and cosmopolitan upbringing in a family of five children. His well-off father was deeply interested in theology and mysticism, particularly the writings of Emanuel Swedenborg. In 1855 the family moved to Europe, where James attended schools in France, Germany, and Switzerland; he learnt several languages and visited many of Europe's museums.

Returning to the United States in 1860, James spent a year and a half trying to become a painter under William Morris Hunt, but decided to enrol at Harvard University. He began studying chemistry but later changed to medicine. In 1865 he was offered the chance to go on a scientific expedition with the well-known naturalist Louis Agassiz, but suffered an array of health problems plus, away from his family for the first time, terrible homesickness and depression. In 1867 he went to Germany and studied physiology under Hermann von Helmholtz, and was exposed to thinkers and ideas in the new field of psychology. Two years later James returned to Harvard, where at 27 he finally received his medical degree.

Over the next three years he experienced an emotional breakdown, and was unable to study or work properly. In 1872, at the age of 30, he began his first job teaching physiology at Harvard. In 1875 he started giving courses in psychology, and also established the first experimental psychology laboratory in America. In the year he began work on The Principles of Psychology, *1878, he also married Alice Howe Gibbons, a Boston school teacher. They had five children.*

On their visits to America, James met both Sigmund Freud and Carl Jung. Among his famous students were educationalist John Dewey and psychologist Edward Thorndike. Landmark writings include The Will to Believe *(1897),* The Varieties of Religious Experience *(1902), and* Pragmatism *(1907).*

James died in 1910 at his summer home in New Hampshire.

The Archetypes and the Collective Unconscious

"*With the archetype of the anima we enter the realm of the gods… Everything the anima touches becomes numinous—unconditional, dangerous, taboo, magical. She is the serpent in the paradise of the harmless man with good resolutions and still better intentions. She affords the most convincing reason for not prying into the unconscious, an occupation that would break down our moral inhibitions and unleash forces that had better been left unconscious and undisturbed.*"

"*Whether he understands them or not, man must remain conscious of the world of the archetypes, because in it he is still a part of Nature and is connected with his own roots. A view of the world or a social order that cuts him off from the primordial images of life not only is no culture at all but, in increasing degree, is a prison or a stable.*"

In a nutshell

Our minds are connected to a deeper layer of consciousness that speaks in terms of imagery and myth.

In a similar vein

Isabel Briggs Myers *Gifts Differing* (p 46)
Anna Freud *The Ego and the Mechanisms of Defence* (p 104)
Sigmund Freud *The Interpretation of Dreams* (p 110)

CHAPTER 30

Carl Jung

W hy did primitive humans go to such lengths to describe and interpret happenings in the natural world, for example the rising and
setting of the sun, the phases of the moon, the seasons? Carl Jung
believed that the events of nature were not simply put into fairytales and
myths as a way of explaining them physically. Rather, the outer world was
used to make sense of the inner.

By his time, Jung noted, this rich well of symbols—art, religion, mythology—which for thousands of years helped people understand the mysteries
of life, had been filled in and replaced by the science of psychology. What
psychology lacked, ironically given its borrowing of the ancient Greek term,
was an understanding of the *psyche*, or the self in its broadest terms.

For Jung, the goal of life was the "individuation" of this self, a sort of
uniting of a person's conscious and unconscious minds so that their original
unique promise might be fulfilled. This larger conception of the self was also
based on the idea that humans are expressions of a deeper layer of *universal*
consciousness. To grasp the uniqueness of each person, paradoxically we had
to go beyond the personal self to understand the workings of this deeper collective wisdom.

The collective unconscious

Jung admitted that the idea of the collective unconscious "belongs to the class
of ideas that people at first find strange but soon come to possess and use as
familiar conceptions." He had to defend it against the charge of mysticism. Yet
he also noted that the idea of the unconscious on its own was thought fanciful
until Freud pointed to its existence, and it then became part of our understanding of why people think and act the way they do. Freud had assumed the
unconscious to be a personal thing contained within an individual. Jung, on the
other hand, saw the personal unconscious mind as sitting atop the *collective*
unconscious—the inherited part of the human psyche that was not developed
from personal experience.

The collective unconscious was expressed through "archetypes," universal thought forms or mental images that influenced an individual's feelings and action. The experience of archetypes often paid little heed to tradition or cultural rules, which suggests that they are innate projections. A newborn baby is not a blank slate but comes wired ready to perceive certain archetypal patterns and symbols. This is why children fantasize so much, Jung believed: They have not experienced enough of reality to cancel out their mind's enjoyment of archetypal imagery.

Archetypes have been expressed as myths and fairytales, and at a personal level in dreams and visions. In mythology they are called "motifs," in anthropology *représentations collectives*. German ethnologist Adolf Bastian referred to them as "elementary" or "primordial" thoughts that he saw expressed again and again in the cultures of tribal and folk peoples. But they are not simply of anthropological interest; usually without knowing it, archetypes shape the relationships that matter in our lives.

Archetypes and complexes

Jung highlighted a number of archetypes, including the anima, the mother, the shadow, the child, the wise old man, the spirits of fairytales, and the trickster figure found in myths and history. We look at two of these below.

The anima

Anima means soul with a female form. In mythology it is expressed as a siren, a mermaid, a wood-nymph, or any form that "infatuates young men and sucks the life out of them." In ancient times, the anima was represented either as a goddess or a witch; that is, aspects of the female that were out of men's control.

When a man "projects" the feminine aspect within his psyche onto an actual woman, that woman takes on magnified importance. The archetype makes itself present in a man's life either by infatuation, idealization, or fascination with women. The woman herself does not really justify these reactions, but acts as the target to which his anima is transferred. This is why the loss of a relationship can be so devastating to a man. It is the loss of a side of himself that he has kept external.

Every time there is an extreme love or fantasy or entanglement, the anima is at work in both sexes. She does not care for an orderly life, but wants intensity of experience—*life*, in whatever form. The anima, like all archetypes, may come upon us like fate. She can enter our life either as something wonderful or as something terrible—either way her aim is to wake us up. To recognize the anima means throwing away our rational ideas of how life should be lived, and instead admitting, as Jung puts it, that "Life is crazy and meaningful at once."

The mother

The mother archetype takes the form of a personal mother, grandmother, step-mother, mother in law, nurse, or governess. It can be fulfilled in figurative mothers such as Mary Mother of God, Sophia, or the mother who becomes a maiden again in the myth of Demeter and Kore. Other mother symbols include the Church, a country, the Earth, the woods, the sea, a garden, a plowed field, a spring, or a well. The positive aspect of the archetype is motherly love and warmth, so celebrated in art and poetry, which gives us our first identity in the world. Yet it can have negative meaning—it can be the loving mother or the terrible mother or goddess of fate. Jung considered the mother the most important archetype because it seemed to contain everything else.

When there is an imbalance of this archetype in someone, we see a mother "complex." In men, the complex may give rise to "Don Juanism," which can make a man fixated on pleasing all women. Yet a man with a mother complex may also have a revolutionary spirit: tough, persevering, extremely ambitious. In women, the complex can result in an exaggeration of the maternal instinct, with a woman living for her children, sacrificing her individuality. Her husband becomes just part of the furniture. Men may be initially attracted to women with a mother complex because they are the picture of femininity and inno-cence. Yet they are also screens onto which a man can project or externalize his anima, and he only later discovers the real woman he has married.

In other forms of the archetype, a woman will go to any lengths so that she is not like her biological mother. She may carve out a sphere of her own, for example becoming an intellectual to show up her mother's lack of educa-tion. A choice of marriage partner may be in order to antagonize and move away from the mother. Other women in the hold of the archetype may have an unconscious incestuous relationship with their biological father and jealousy of their mother. They may become interested in married men or in having roman-tic adventures.

Spiritual archetypes

Why is psychology as a science so young? Jung suggests that it is because for most of human history it simply wasn't necessary. The wonderful imagery and mythology of religions was able to express the eternal archetypes perfectly. People felt a need to dwell on ideas and images relating to rebirth and trans-formation, and religions supplied these in abundance for every aspect of the psyche. The Catholic Church's strange ideas of the virgin birth and the Trinity are not fanciful images but packed with meaning, Jung wrote, archetypes of protection and healing that administered to any ruptures in the minds of the faithful.

The Protestant Reformation reacted against all this. The rich Catholic imagery and dogma became nothing but "superstition," and in Jung's view this attitude made way for the barrenness of contemporary life. Genuine spirituality must engage both the unconscious and the conscious mind, he believed, the depths as well as the heights.

All humans have a religious instinct, whether it is a belief in God or in some secular faith like communism or atheism. "No one can escape the prejudice of being human," Jung observed.

Individuation

"Individuation" was Jung's term for the point at which someone is finally able to integrate the opposites within them—their conscious and unconscious minds. Individuation simply means becoming what you always were *in potentia*, fulfilling your unique promise. The result is an individual in the real sense of the word, a whole and indestructible self that can no longer be hijacked by splintered aspects or complexes.

But this reintegration does not happen by thinking about it rationally. It is a journey with unexpected twists and turns. Many myths show how we need to follow a path that transcends reason in order to fulfill ourselves in life.

Jung went to some lengths to define the self. He understood it to be something different from the ego; in fact the self incorporated the ego, "just as a large circle encloses a smaller one." While the ego relates to the conscious mind, the *self* belongs to the personal and collective unconscious.

The healing mandala

Jung included in *The Archetypes and the Collective Unconscious* many reproductions of mandalas, abstract patterned images whose name in Sanskrit means "circle." He believed that when a person draws or paints a mandala, unconscious leanings or wants are expressed in its patterns, symbols, and shapes.

In his therapeutic practice, Jung found mandalas to have a "magical" effect, reducing confusion in the psyche to order, and often affecting a person in ways that only became apparent later. They worked because the unconscious is allowed free reign; what has been swept under comes to the surface. Motifs such as egg shapes, a lotus flower, a star or sun, a snake, castles, cities, eyes, and so on are produced for no obvious reason, yet reflect or draw out processes that are going on deep below that person's conscious thinking. When someone became able to make a meaningful interpretation of the images, Jung observed that it was usually the beginning of psychological healing. It was one step taken in the individuation process.

Final comments

We think we are modern and civilized with all our technology and knowledge, but inside, Jung says, we are still "primitives." In Switzerland he once observed a local witch-doctor remove a spell from a stable—in the shadow of a railway line on which several trans-European expresses roared by.

Modernity does not do away with the need for us to attend to our unconscious minds. If we do neglect this side of ourselves, the archetypes simply look for new forms of expression, in the process derailing our carefully made plans. Usually the unconscious supports our conscious decisions, but when a gap appears the archetypes are expressed in strange and powerful ways; we can be ambushed by lack of self-knowledge.

The universe of ancient symbols we once used for deciphering life's changes and larger meaning has been replaced by a science—psychology—that was never designed to understand the soul and cater to it. About the scientific mindset in general, Jung wrote: "Heaven has become for us the cosmic space of the physicists... But 'the heart glows,' and a secret unrest gnaws at the roots of our being." Modern man or woman lives with a spiritual emptiness that was once easily filled by religion or mythology. Only a new type of psychology that actually recognized the depth of the psyche would be able to quell this secret unrest.

Carl Jung

Jung was born in Kesswil, Switzerland in 1875, the son of a Protestant minister. In 1895 he enrolled at the University of Basel to study medicine, and when his father died the following year had to borrow money to remain a student. He began to specialize in psychiatry, and from 1900 worked at the Burghölzli clinic in Zurich under the pioneering psychiatrist Eugen Bleuler. In 1903 he married Emma Rauschenbach, a wealthy Swiss heiress, and they built a large house in Kusnacht for their young family.

In 1905 Jung became a lecturer in psychiatry at the University of Zurich, and in subsequent years developed a successful private practice. In 1912 he broke with Freud, and two years later resigned from the International Psychoanalytic Society. Freud had considered Jung his heir in psychoanalytical theory, so the split was a major event. It enabled Jung to branch out and explore concepts such as synchronicity, individuation, and the theory of psychological types (see also the commentary on Isabel Briggs Myers, p 46).

Jung's other books include The Psychology of the Unconscious *(1911–12),* Symbols of Transformation *(1912),* Psychological Types *(1921),* Psychology and Religion *(1937),* Psychology and Alchemy *(1944), and* The Undiscovered Self *(1957). The Archetypes and the Collective Unconscious is Part I of the ninth volume of his* Collected Works.

After the Second World War Jung was accused of having Nazi sympathies, but there was no conclusive evidence. He spent time with native peoples in American and Africa, and had a strong interest in ethnology and anthropology. Jung died in 1961 in Switzerland.

Sexual Behavior in the Human Female

"*One may become conscious of an increase in temperature in his own or the sexual partner's body surfaces, partly due to this peripheral circulation of blood, and perhaps in part due to the neuromuscular tensions which develop when there is any sexual response. Even very cold feet may become warm during sexual activity. The identification of sexual arousal as a fever, a glow, a fire, heat, or warmth, testifies to the widespread understanding that there is this rise in surface temperatures.*"

"*Among the married females in the sample, about a quarter (26 per cent) had had extra-marital coitus by age forty. Between the ages of twenty-six and fifty, something between one in six and one in ten was having extra-marital coitus… Since the cover-up on any socially disapproved sexual activity may be greater than the cover-up on more accepted activities, it is possible that the incidences and frequencies of extra-marital coitus in the sample had been higher than our interviewing disclosed.*"

In a nutshell

There is a gap between the variety and extent of our sexual lives and what society or religion permits.

In a similar vein
Louann Brizendine *The Female Brain* (p 52)
Sigmund Freud *The Interpretation of Dreams* (p 110)
Harry Harlow *The Nature of Love* (p 142)
Jean Piaget *The Language and Thought of the Child* (p 222)

CHAPTER 31

Alfred Kinsey

The famous sex researcher Alfred Kinsey actually spent more than half his professional life as a zoologist studying gall wasps. He was known on Indiana University's Bloomington campus as a rather haughty middle-aged professor who knew more about bugs than people. How, then, did he go from this to being held partly responsible for ushering in the sexual revolution?

In the late 1930s, Indiana University's Association of Women Students made a petition for a course for married students or those contemplating marriage, and the job fell to Kinsey to run it. The students had questions such as: What would be the effect of premarital orgasm or sex on later married life? What is normal or abnormal in sexual activity? The little knowledge they did have had been shaped by religion, philosophy, or social mores, and Kinsey quickly found out that there was more scientific information on the behavior of small insects than there was on the sexual behavior of human beings.

The English physician Henry Havelock Ellis had produced the first dispassionate treatment of the subject, *Studies in the Psychology of Sex* (published in seven volumes between 1897 and 1928), but it was banned by the British government. And of course, Freud had made sex less of a forbidden subject, but had never conducted large-scale scientific research. So in 1938, Kinsey began collecting his own data.

Ten years later, Kinsey and his team published *Sexual Behavior in the Human Male*, which, although written for a university audience, became a surprise national bestseller (selling over half a million copies). He became a national figure, and the Kinsey Institute for Sex Research became famous. That book was followed five years later by the 800-page *Sexual Behavior in the Human Female* (written with Paul Gebhard, Wardell Pomeroy, and Clyde Martin). The two volumes, probably because their titles were embarrassing to ask for in a bookshop or library, became known simply as the "Kinsey reports." In the year of the second book's release, 1953, Kinsey appeared on the cover of *Time* magazine.

Getting the stories

The research that went into the Kinsey reports was one of the great scientific projects in history. Funding for it came from a combination of Indiana University and the National Research Council's Committee for Research in

Problems of Sex, guided by Robert Yerkes (known for his work in intelligence testing and animal behavior) and backed by the Rockefeller Foundation.

The study coincided with advances in research methods that allowed reasonably accurate sampling of large populations, instead of having to rely on a few case histories. But given the closed-door nature of sex, how was Kinsey going to get reliable information? The laws in different American states meant possible incrimination for people who submitted their stories. So his team had to develop a method of interviewing that would ensure people remained anonymous and secure in their confessions. They asked 350 questions on respondents' sexual history, and some of those interviewed provided diaries or calendars recording their sexual activity on a daily basis. All aspects of sexual behavior were investigated in reference to age, marital status, educational level, socioeconomic class, religious background, and status as a rural or urban dweller.

From 1938 to 1956, an incredible 17,000 people were studied, with Kinsey himself doing over 5,000 of the interviews. *Sexuality in the Human Female* was based mainly on the case histories of 5,940 white American females, and informed by the stories of 1,849 women who fell into other categories. The book includes a long list of the occupations of female subjects, everyone from army nurses to high-school students, dancers to factory workers, economists to gym instructors, movie directors to office clerks. The wider pool included women prisoners.

The results

Along with the huge amount of raw data, insights from the fields of psychology, biology, animal behavior, psychiatry, physiology, anthropology, statistics, and law made their way into *Sexual Behavior in the Human Female*, making it a more well-rounded work than the first Kinsey report, with more effort to look at sexual history through the ages. Despite the dry scientific language and endless pages of graphs and tables, it also seemed more shocking, since women's sexuality involves more taboos—and here was startlingly frank information on deep personal secrets.

The book covers a great array of subjects and presents thousands of findings. Among them we find the following.

Masturbation, orgasm, and dreams

❖ Children as young as two masturbate.
❖ More significant than genital stimulation in reaching orgasm, for both men and women, is rhythmic thrusting. The muscular tension involved in the sex act is a vital part of the overall physiological response.
❖ The vaginal walls have very few nerve endings. Female masturbation focuses on the clitoris, labia minora, and labia majora, more than actual penetration.
❖ Generally, men are more inclined to fantasize to achieve masturbatory orgasm,

while most women rely on physical sensations alone. However, 2 percent of women had experienced orgasm through fantasy alone.

❖ 36 percent of women reported having had no orgasm at all before getting married, and a substantial number never achieved it even during marriage.

❖ Women as well as men have orgasms during dreams: 65 percent of women had had sexy dreams, while 20 percent had experienced nocturnal dream orgasm.

❖ The common view was that women are slower than men in terms of sexual response and time needed to elapse before orgasm, but the evidence was that in masturbation, women reported an average time to achieve orgasm of 3–4 minutes—not much longer than a man usually takes.

❖ Despite a history of assertions going back thousands of years that masturbation damages your health, Kinsey found no evidence. The only damage that is done is psychological; that is, anxiety caused by guilt.

Noncoital sexual relations and petting

❖ Males are easily moved to an erotic state through petting, but a surprising number of women do not get "turned on" sexually by the activity. Generally, while a man cannot help being turned on if given the right physical stimulation, a woman's erotic feelings depend more on her feelings about the situation.

❖ Men's sexual feeling starts suddenly in puberty and rapidly climbs through the teenage years before leveling off in the 20s. A woman's sexual feeling is more like a slow climb, and her responses are more psychological.

❖ Of the 64 percent of married females who had experienced orgasm prior to marriage, only 17 percent of their orgasms had been experienced through actual penetrative sex. The rest occurred through petting, masturbation, dreams, or homosexual contact.

❖ Women are less aroused by breast stimulation than men are by giving the stimulation. Only 50 percent of women said they ever stimulated their own breasts as a form of sexual pleasure.

Premarital sex

❖ By the 1940s, much had been written alleging that premarital sex led to lasting regrets and psychological damage, particularly among women. Kinsey's research found that 77 percent of women who had engaged in unmarried sex did not, in fact, regret it.

❖ Those who had had unmarried sex with more than one man were even less likely to regret their experiences. Kinsey concluded that some degree of premarital experience—"promiscuity"—could actually bring a healthier relationship when the woman did marry, as she would have fewer of the usual hang-ups about sexuality. Interestingly, 83 percent of women who had become pregnant as a result of premarital sex did not regret what they had done either.

Extramarital sex

❖ By the age of 40, a quarter of all married women in Kinsey's surveys had had extramarital sex. Extramarital sex reached its zenith in the 30s and early 40s.

❖ Younger women's lower interest in sex outside marriage was put down to greater sexual interest in their partner, and their young husband's demand for sexual exclusivity in his wife.

❖ Despite the common perception that men like to have sexual affairs with younger women, many actually preferred them with older or similar-aged women, partly because they were more sexually experienced.

❖ Among women who had not had extramarital sex, 17 percent said they would consider it actively or at least not rule out the idea. But among those women who had already "strayed," 56 percent said they would probably do it again.

Other fascinating points

❖ The "missionary position" was simply a European and American cultural norm (why, Kinsey did not know). It was not so favored in other cultures, and was little used by other mammals. The Western world continued to favor this position, even though a woman is much more likely to experience orgasm if she is on top, because she is free to move as she wants.

❖ Men and women in a state of deep sexual engagement have exactly the same facial expression as people who are being tortured.

❖ As the sexual act reaches its climax, in both sexes the senses of touch and pain diminish and the vision narrows.

❖ Educated women generally had more sexual experience, possibly because they considered themselves more "enlightened" and less subject to taboos about female sexuality.

Final comments

If Kinsey was a biologist, why are *Sexual Behavior in the Human Female* and its brother volume considered classics in psychology? In 1950s America, psychology was equated more with behavior than with what went on in the mind, and his work was about human sexual behavior. His team wanted to show that humans could not escape their mammalian (read "animal") heritage; in relation to sex, we were bound by our physiology to have certain responses in relation to stimuli. Although we like to think of the sexual act as being about love, Kinsey aimed to show that it was less about the higher mind than we liked to believe.

Yet for a scientist, Kinsey made the fundamental mistake of blurring the line between his subjects—the people he was interviewing—and his private life. Those around him, including his wife and colleagues, found themselves in steamy and unorthodox situations in the name of "research." This less admirable aspect of the Kinsey phenomenon is shown to good effect in the film *Kinsey* (2004), starring Liam Neeson.

As well as a whole chapter on homosexuality and one on pre-adolescent sexual play, Kinsey also addressed such subjects as pornography (in the days before *Playboy*), sex graffiti, sado-masochism, erotic stimulation by animals, group sex, and voyeurism. The chapters on human sexual anatomy and on physiological response during sex and orgasm, in their explicit detail, did more to educate Americans about their own bodies than anything that had come before. Even today, it is a rare reader who does not learn something from these sections.

For conservatives, Kinsey's work was the beginning of a downhill slide for civilization, and they made much of his inclusion of sex offenders (1,300 were interviewed) in his studies. Yet Kinsey saw himself in the same light as Copernicus and Galileo, reporting what he saw in the physical world irrespective of theological or moral dogma. Given that the subject of his scrutiny was sex, his fame was perhaps inevitable.

Alfred Kinsey

Born in Hoboken, New Jersey in 1894, Kinsey was the oldest of three children. His father, who taught engineering at a local college, was a devout and domineering Methodist, and Kinsey grew up in an environment that outlawed any talk or experience of sexuality. He was an active Boy Scout, and loved camping and being outdoors.

Following school Kinsey obeyed his father and took engineering courses, but was desperate to study biology. After two years, and against his father's wishes, he enrolled at Bowdoin College in Maine, where he graduated magna cum laude *in biology and psychology. He received his doctorate in biology at Harvard in 1919, and the following year obtained a post as assistant professor of zoology at Indiana University.*

In the last years of his life Kinsey had to fight to continue his research. His goal was to interview 100,000 people, but in 1954 pressure from religious groups influenced the Rockefeller Foundation to cancel its annual funding.

Kinsey's other books include a widely-used school textbook, An Introduction to Biology *(1926),* The Gall Wasp Genus Cynips: A Study in the Origin of the Species *(1930), and* The Origin of Higher Categories in Cynips *(1935). He died in 1956.*

Envy and Gratitude

"The infant can only experience complete enjoyment if the capacity for love is sufficiently developed; and it is enjoyment that forms the basis for gratitude. Freud described the infant's bliss in being suckled as the prototype of sexual gratification. In my view these experiences constitute not only the basis of sexual gratification but of all later happiness, and make possible the feeling of unity with another person."

"An infant who has securely established the good object can also find compensations for loss and deprivation in adult life. All this is felt by the envious person as something he can never attain because he can never be satisfied, and therefore his envy is reinforced."

In a nutshell

How we cope with pain and pleasure as an infant can shape the basic life outlook we carry into adulthood.

In a similar vein

CHAPTER 32

Melanie Klein

Prior to Freud, people thought that childhood was a time of simple happiness. Children's rage, frustration, sadness, or lack of enthusiasm was explained away by physical factors, and their emotional lives were not taken seriously. But Freud showed that children experience significant conflicts, and that these shape us as we move into adulthood.

Taking up where Freud left off, Melanie Klein helped forge a whole subfield of psychoanalysis focusing on the earliest months of life. Other psycho-analysts including Anna Freud had focused on children, but Klein broke new ground in her emphasis on the mental life, including fantasies, defenses, and anxieties, of the infant. She believed that the way a baby comes to grips with its environment sets a pattern for adulthood, affecting the ability to love and the development of basic character traits such as envy and gratitude.

Klein never attended a university, and had three children before becoming a psychoanalyst. Yet this late starter attracted fanatical adherents, the "Kleinians," who waged intellectual war against other Freudians, including Anna Freud and her camp in the 1940s. For a long time Klein's detractors achieved their aim of sidelining her, but there has been a renewal of interest in her work, and her impact on child psychology cannot be denied.

Envy and Gratitude is a collection of writings covering the last 15 years of Klein's life. From these essays and articles we examine her well-known "paranoid/schizoid" and "depressive" positions in childhood, her practice of psychoanalyzing children while they played, and her controversial idea that in infancy people develop a basically envious or grateful view of the world.

The paranoid/schizoid position

To understand Klein, we must appreciate that her work was based on the Freudian idea of "object relations," in which emotions are always expressed toward an "object," usually a person but sometimes even a part of a person.

Klein believed that the first of a child's object relations is with the breast of the mother, which becomes the focus of all the baby's feelings. From babies' point of view, depending on whether they are satisfied, the breast seems to be either "good" or "bad," and all their latent feelings of love and hate are poured into this relationship with the breast. Babies either idealize the breast's source of love and sustenance, or feel persecuted by it if their needs are not instantly met. These split feelings are the first time that a human being experiences anxiety.

The splitting is what Klein called the "paranoid-schizoid" position. Whatever is good about the mother and her breast children "introject" or make part of themselves. Whatever is bad in themselves they "project" onto the mother. In short, the paranoid-schizoid position is babies' attempt to establish some kind of control over the external and internal world before they develop their own ego or sense of self.

According to Klein, Freud's "life instinct" and "death instinct" were evident even in infancy. These forces were what gave the early relationship to the "object" such intensity. There is both desperation to get what we need to survive, but also jealousy, anger, and aggression to destroy the object (observed in the baby's anguished screaming and "scooping out" of the breast) when it is not forthcoming with its love, attention, or food.

The depressive position

In the second half of babies' first year, however, Klein observed that the development of an ego means that the polarities of love and hate meld into one. The mother can now be seen to accommodate both, and children can take more responsibility for their feelings. This more realistic picture is helped along by the development of the superego—the socially conditioned self—which begins to take a major role in shaping children.

Freud believed that the superego developed over a number of years, but Klein found it displayed very early on, particularly in girls. She noted the sense of guilt regarding destructive feelings toward the mother, and the corresponding desire to make "reparation" or undo these negative feelings by being good or loving. The roots of schizophrenia, she theorized, were to be found in children's relations with their superego, which often involved a frightening or strict mother figure.

The depressive position comes as the result of a child's feelings of guilt that their own aggression, hatred, and greed will bring about the loss of the breast/mother. When a baby is weaned off breast milk, it is often the catalyst for the depressive position to occur, because the child may feel they have brought this loss on themselves.

A healthy ego

In the first two years of life children have obsessions or tendencies to do with eating, defecation, or the repetition of certain stories or movements. As adults we know these obsessions are neurotic, but understand them as part of the infant's desire to establish security. Children develop anxieties or psychotic tendencies, Klein wrote, only so that their still fragile ego can remain protected. The depressive position is actually the beginning of maturity, because babies now have greater sophistication in how they understand their own feelings and their world.

Normally, children's defenses or neuroses lessen as they develop and are able to adjust themselves better to reality. However, how we work through the depressive and schizoid positions also sets a template for how we deal with these feelings as adults. The early negative states can be reactivated in adult life at certain events. Mourning, for instance, is not only about the person lost, but about our internal losses. The development of a strong ego or sense of self in infancy, according to Klein, is therefore vital to adult mental health.

The envious and the grateful

If children can fully express love for their mother in infancy, this sets them up to be able to enjoy life and love fully in adulthood. However, some children, according to Klein, are more aggressive and greedy than others, and bear more of a grudge against their mother when they do not feel their needs are being met. Feelings of envy make children less able to enjoy and be grateful for the sustenance and attention they receive. Such babies, Klein asserted, become envious people as adults. In contrast, those infants who can internalize the good aspects of their parent(s) have a fundamentally positive and grateful view of life, and are capable of being loyal, possessing the courage of their convictions, and generally being of "good character."

Klein noted that a loving, supportive environment in infancy cannot prevent the love/hate split, but it does enable children eventually to grow out of it. In contrast, infants who do not get what they need may spend the rest of their lives chasing external things to make up for what they feel is missing inside, or have to express the anger they have never resolved.

Child's play

A couple took their son Peter to see Klein. Since Peter's brother was born Peter had become very aggressive with his toys, doing what he could to break them. Observing Peter smashing two toy horses into each other, Klein wondered out loud to him whether the horses represented people; he agreed. As the bumping together continued, she gleaned that Peter had seen his parents having sex and it had generated considerable jealousy and anxiety. The bumping together represented the sexual act. By bringing Peter's repressed feelings out into the open, Klein helped the boy to curb his aggression.

It may seem a stretch to believe that a child can make such interpretations, but Klein claimed that if you spoke in their language a child really could understand. She believed that the way children play is a window into their unconscious mind and what is troubling them. Given children's difficulty in articulating all their thoughts, play was the best way of healing any mental issues.

Final comments

The concept of "objects" in Freudian theory seems quite cold, but when we appreciate that in infancy we attach ourselves to a particular person (usually our biological mother) without giving much thought to who that person actually is—rather, we think only in terms of our own needs—the theory does make some sense. Arguably, this tendency carries over into adulthood, for in truth we are often less interested in who a person really is than in how they can satisfy some of our basic wants and wishes. It is only mature people who transcend "object relations" to really care about the worldview, interests, and aspirations of other people.

Whether or not you accept all Klein's ideas, it cannot be denied that most of our relationships with our parents and siblings—even if they are good—are complex, and we should not instantly dismiss the notion that many of our attitudes or hang-ups stem from the first few months of life. For Klein, this was the crucial time when the interaction between natural tendencies and environment sets us up to be a basically satisfied or unsatisfied person.

For some, Klein creates a rich world of ideas that explains our deepest needs and longings. For others, her books seem like mumbo-jumbo— Freudianism taken to its worst extremes. Her explanation of schizophrenia, manic depression, and depression as outgrowths of the paranoid-schizoid and depressive positions in infancy should be viewed critically; these days, such conditions are being increasingly fathomed by brain science rather than psychoanalysis.

Klein's style takes a while to get into, but for someone who was denied the chance to attend university she was clearly a profound thinker. Her own childhood clearly shaped her work, and her daughters provided a ready testing ground for her ideas. As with many children of psychoanalysts, this was not always appreciated.

Melanie Klein

Born in a middle-class suburb of Vienna in 1882, Klein was the youngest of four children. Her teenage ambition was to study medicine, but her marriage in 1903 to chemist Arthur Klein cut short her university experience.

The Kleins moved to Budapest in 1910 for Arthur's work, where Klein discovered Sigmund Freud's writings and first underwent psychoanalysis with Sandor Ferenczi. She met Freud at the 1918 Psycho-Analytic Congress in Budapest.

Splitting from her husband, Klein took her three children to Berlin, where she gained a mentor in psychoanalyst Karl Abraham. In 1926 she moved to London, where she remained for the rest of her life.

Klein's personal tragedies included the death of her much-loved brother Emmanuel and sister Sidonie, both while they were young, and that of her son Hans in 1935. Her daughter Melitta, who also became a psychoanalyst, was one of her most vocal opponents. Klein also suffered from depression and anxiety for much of her life.

Klein's writings include The Psychoanalysis of Children *(1932),* Contributions to Psychoanalysis *(1948), and* Narrative of a Child Analysis *(1961).* Love, Guilt, and Reparation: And Other Works 1921–1945 *is a companion volume to* Envy and Gratitude.

Klein died in 1980.

The Divided Self

"*The paranoic has specific persecutors. Someone is against him. There is a plot on foot to steal his brains. A machine is concealed in the wall of his bedroom which emits mind rays to soften his brain, or to send electric shocks through him while he is asleep. The person I am describing feels at this phase persecuted by reality itself. The world as it is, and other people as they are, are the dangers.*"

"*Everyone is subject to a certain extent at one time or another to such moods of futility, meaningless and purposelessness, but in schizoid individuals these moods are particularly insistent. These moods arise from the fact that the doors of perception and/or the gates of action are not in the command of the self but are being lived and operated by a false self.*"

In a nutshell

We take a strong sense of self for granted, but if we don't have this, life can be torture.

In a similar vein

CHAPTER 33

R. D. Laing

W hen Scottish psychiatrist R. D. Laing sat down to write *The Divided Self: A Study of Sanity and Madness* in the late 1950s, the conventional view in psychiatry was that the mind of an unbalanced person was just a soup of meaningless fantasies or obsessions. Patients were examined for the official symptoms of mental illness, and treated accordingly.

However, with his first book, written at the age of 28, Laing helped change the way we look at psychoses. His aim was "to make madness, and the process of going mad, comprehensible," and he achieved this by showing how psychosis—specifically, that relating to schizophrenia—actually makes sense to the person suffering it. Therefore the psychiatrist's role should be to get into the sufferer's mind.

Laing was at pains to point out that *The Divided Self* was not a medically researched theory of schizophrenia, but rather a set of observations—colored by existentialist philosophy—about the nature of schizoid and schizophrenic people. The science of schizoid conditions has moved on considerably since his day, toward a biological and neurological explanation, but his descriptions of what it feels like to live with a divided self, go "mad," or have a breakdown remain some of the best written.

Beware psychiatry

In the first few pages, Laing expressed a view common in the 1960s and 1970s that it is not the people who are locked up in asylums who are truly mad, but the politicians and generals who are ready to destroy the human race at the push of a button. He felt it was somewhat arrogant of psychiatry to class some people as "psychotic," as if they had ceased to be part of the human race. For Laing, the psychiatrist's labels said more about the profession of psychiatry and the culture that created it than they did about anyone's real state of mind.

Mainstream psychiatry had got it wrong in dealing with schizophrenics. The salient point about schizoid individuals, Laing noted, was their hypersensitivity to what is going on in their mind, as well as extreme protectiveness of the self hidden behind layers of false personality. A doctor looking only for "schizophrenic symptoms," as if the person were an object, would be resisted at every turn. Such patients did not want to be examined but to be *heard*; the real question was what had led them to experience the world in such a way.

The schizoid's unique anxieties

"I've been sort of dead in a way. I cut myself off from other people and became shut up in myself... You have to live in the world with other people. If you don't something dies inside."

Peter, one of Laing's patients

Laing defined "schizoid" people as those who live with a split, either within themselves, or between themselves and the world. They do not experience themselves as "together" and feel a painful isolation from the rest of humanity. His distinction between the schizoid person and the schizophrenic was this: While a schizoid can remain troubled but sane, the schizophrenic's split mind has crossed a line into psychosis.

Most people take for granted a level of certainty about themselves. They are essentially comfortable with who they are and their relationship to the world. Schizoid people, in contrast, have what Laing called an "ontological insecurity," a basic, existential, and deep-rooted doubt about their identity and their place in the scheme of things.

Schizoid people's unique forms of anxiety include:

❖ The terrifying nature of interactions with others. They may even dread being loved, because being known by someone so clearly means being exposed. To avoid being absorbed into another person through love, the schizoid may go to the other extreme and choose isolation, or even prefer to be hated, as this involves less chance of being "engulfed." A common feeling is that, with such a fragile sense of self, they are drowning or being burned up.

❖ "Impingement," the feeling that at any moment the world may crash into their mind and destroy their identity. Such an apprehension can only come from a great feeling of emptiness in the first place—if someone has little sense of self to begin with, the world can seem like a persecuting force.

❖ "Petrification" and "depersonalization," the feeling that they may turn to stone, which has a corresponding effect of wishing to deny other people their feelings of reality so that they become an "it" that does not have to be dealt with.

While Laing noted that "hysterics" will do what they can to forget or repress themselves, schizoids are fixated on themselves. Yet the fixation is the opposite of narcissism, as there is no self-love involved, only a coldly objective, relentless inspecting and prodding of the self to see what, if anything, is inside.

A problem with the self

Laing commented that many people experience a mental schism as a way of dealing with horrible situations from which there is no physical or mental escape (for example, someone in a concentration camp). If they can't accept what is happening, they may withdraw into themselves or fantasize about being elsewhere. This "temporary dissociation" is not an unhealthy way of dealing with life.

The schizoid personality, however, feels that the dissociation is permanent. Their experience is *life, without feeling alive*. Invoking a literary allusion, Laing observed that Shakespeare's characters are often flawed types with significant personal conflicts, yet they still remain in the flow of life and in possession of themselves. The characters in Kafka's novels and Samuel Beckett's plays, on the other hand, lack this basic existential security and therefore recall the schizoid type. They cannot simply "question their own motives," since they do not even have a solid, cohesive sense of self to question. Life becomes a daily battle to preserve themselves against threats from the outside world.

Because schizoid people do not have self-certainty, they often try to impersonate the sort of person they think the world expects them to be, blending into their environment to a morbid extent. A patient of Laing's, a 12-year-old girl, had to walk across a park every night and was afraid of being attacked. To cope with the situation, she developed the belief that she could make herself disappear and therefore be safe. Such a defensive fantasy, he wrote, could only be contemplated by someone with a vacuum inside where we would normally find a self.

The split mind

Laing made a distinction between embodied people—who have "a sense of being flesh and bones," feel normal desires, and seek to satisfy them—and unembodied people, who experience a gap between their mind and body.

Schizoid people live such an internal, mental life that their body does not represent their true self. They set up a "false self system" through which they encounter the world, but in doing so their real self becomes more hidden. They have a great fear of being "uncovered" and so try to control every inter-action with other people. This elaborate internal world enables them to feel protected, but because it is no replacement for real-world relations their inte-rior life becomes impoverished. Ironically, their eventual collapse or break-down does not come from the others they feared, "but by the devastation caused by the inner defensive maneuvers themselves."

For the schizoid, everything is experienced as desperately personal, yet inside it feels as if there is a vacuum. The only relationship they experience is with the self, yet it is a relationship in turmoil—hence their extreme anguish and despair.

Pushed over the edge

What makes someone with schizoid tendencies actually cross the line into psychosis?

Living with a system of false selves that are presented to the world, schizoid people are able to live an imaginary inner life. In the place of normal, creative relationships are attachments to things, trains of thought, memories, and fantasies. Anything becomes possible. Schizoids feel free and omnipotent, but as this happens they are whirling themselves further away from the center of objective truth. If their fantasies are destructive, these are likely actually to result in destructive acts, since without access to a real self there can be no guilt or reparation.

This is why schizophrenic people can apparently seem normal one week and psychotic the next, declaring that a parent or husband or wife is trying to kill them, or that someone is trying to steal their mind or their soul. The veil of the false self or selves that made them seem relatively normal is suddenly lifted, revealing the secret, tortured self that has been hidden from the world's view for so long.

Final comments

The Divided Self also presented Laing's controversial belief that if a child has a genetic predisposition to schizophrenia, there may be certain ways that a mother (or larger family) acts that will either encourage or prevent the condition from being expressed. Unsurprisingly, this angered parents of schizophrenics.

The more lasting effect of the book was to help lift the taboo around mental illness and create a better understanding about the schizoid mind. It was also important in its idea that psychology should be about achieving personal growth and freedom instead of mimicking the disease/symptom/cure paradigm of conventional medicine. Exploring who you were, even if the explorations were risky adventures, Laing saw as vital; the other route was to try to make yourself fit into society's regimented molds, with all the related anxieties of such a compromise.

Because of such ideas Laing became famous in the 1960s, attractive to anyone who felt marginalized by their families or cultures, or who wanted to be a part of the "self-realization" mindset of the human potential movement.

Drug use, alcohol addiction, depression, and an interest in unorthodox subjects such as shamanism and reincarnation all contributed to a lowering of Laing's professional reputation, and he was forced to resign from the UK's medical register in 1987.

Despite critics' attempts to devalue his work, his twin aims of changing attitudes to mental illness and helping to recast the ultimate aim of psychology were realized. Laing remains one of the major figures of twentieth-century psychology.

R. D. Laing

Born an only child in 1927 in Glasgow to middle-class Presbyterian parents, Ronald David Laing later wrote of a lonely and often frightening childhood. He excelled at school, reading Voltaire, Marx, Nietzsche, and Freud by the time he was 15, and went on to study medicine at the University of Glasgow.

He worked as a psychiatrist with the British Army, and in 1953 took up a post at the Gartnavel Psychiatric Hospital in Glasgow. In the late 1950s, he began a program of psychoanalytical training at the Tavistock Clinic in London.

In 1960s London, Laing counted among his friends writer Doris Lessing and rock band Pink Floyd's Roger Waters. In 1965 he established a psychiatric community, Kingsley Hall, in which patients were not coerced into particular behaviors or drug regimes, and were treated as equals by the staff.

Laing's The Politics of Experience *(1967), which criticized the family and political institutions of the West, sold millions of copies. Other books include* Sanity, Madness and the Family *(1964), and his autobiography,* Wisdom, Madness and Folly *(1985). His critical view of standard psychiatric practice has been echoed in the writings of Thomas Szasz (*The Myth of Mental Illness*) and William Glasser (*Reality Therapy*).*

Laing has been the subject of at least five biographies. He died of a heart attack in 1989 in St Tropez while playing tennis.

1971

The Farther Reaches of Human Nature

"*On the whole I think it fair to say that human history is a record of the ways in which human nature has been sold short. The highest possibilities of human nature have practically always been underrated.*"

"*People selected as self-actualizing subjects, people who fit the criteria, go about it in these little ways: They listen to their own voices; they take responsibility; they are honest; and they work hard. They find out who they are, not only in terms of their mission in life, but also in terms of the way their feet hurt when they wear such and such a pair of shoes and whether they do or do not like eggplant or stay up all night if they drink too much beer. All this is what the real self means. They find their own biological natures, their congenital natures, which are irreversible or difficult to change.*"

In a nutshell

Our view of human nature must expand to incorporate the features of the most advanced and fulfilled people among us.

In a similar vein

Mihaly Csikszentmihalyi *Creativity* (p 68)
Viktor Frankl *The Will to Meaning* (p 100)
Carl Rogers *On Becoming a Person* (p 238)
Martin Seligman *Authentic Happiness* (p 254)

CHAPTER 34

Abraham Maslow

Though the term "self-actualized" was coined by another psychologist, Kurt Goldstein, it was Maslow who made the concept well known. It described those seemingly rare individuals who had achieved "full humanness," a blend of psychological health and devotion to their work that made them highly effective. If there were many more such people, Maslow reasoned, our world would be transformed. Instead of putting all our energies into dreaming up faster and better things, we should be trying to create societies that produced more self-actualized people.

Before Maslow, psychology was divided into two camps—the "scientific" behaviorists and positivists, who felt that no idea in psychology was valid unless it had been proven, and the Freudian psychoanalysts. Maslow originated a "third force," humanistic psychology, which refused to see human beings as machines operating "in response to environment" or as the pawns of subconscious forces. In his approach human beings became *people* again, creative, free-willed, and wanting to fulfill their potential. In addition, Maslow's studies of "peak experiences," those transcendent moments in which everything makes sense and we experience a unity in ourselves and with the world, helped to lay the ground for transpersonal psychology. This "fourth force" lent a more scientific framework to the study of religious or mystical experience, and made Maslow a celebrated figure in the milieu of West Coast America in the 1960s.

Published after his death, *The Farther Reaches of Human Nature* is really a collection of articles rather than an integrated work. The first half is the more inspiring, and provides an excellent introduction to the thoughts of this psychological adventurer.

The self-actualizer

Maslow's study of self-actualizing people began with his admiration for his teachers, anthropologist Ruth Benedict and psychologist Max Wertheimer. Though not perfect, they struck him as fully evolved in every aspect, and he recalled his excitement that it was possible to generalize about such people.

What marked out these individuals from the rest? First, they had a devotion to something greater than themselves, a vocation. They devoted their lives to what Maslow called "being" values, such as truth, beauty, goodness, and simplicity. Yet these "B-Values" are not simply nice attributes that the self-actualizer wishes for—they are *needs* that must be fulfilled. "In certain definable and empirical ways," Maslow observed, "it is necessary for man to live in beauty rather than ugliness, as it is necessary for him to have food for his aching belly or rest for his weary body." We all know we must eat, drink, and sleep, but Maslow argued that once these basic needs are met, we develop "metaneeds" regarding the higher B-values that also have to be fulfilled. This was his famous "hierarchy of needs," which began with oxygen and water and finished with the need for spiritual and psychological fulfillment.

Nearly all psychological problems, Maslow believed, stemmed from "sicknesses of the soul," which involved lack of meaning or anxiety about these needs not being met. Most people cannot articulate that they even have these needs, yet their pursuit is vital to being fully human.

Achieving full humanness

To make self-actualization a less esoteric concept, Maslow was keen to show what it meant on a daily basis, from moment to moment. For him it was not a case of "one great moment" like a religious experience. Rather, it involved:

❖ Experiencing with full absorption. Engagement with something that makes us forget our defenses and poses and shyness. We regain "the guilelessness of childhood" in these moments.
❖ Awareness of life as a series of choices—one way advances us toward personal growth, the other involves a regression.
❖ Being aware that you have a self and listening to its voice, rather than the voice of a parent or society.
❖ Deciding to be honest, and as a result taking responsibility for what you think and feel. The willingness to say "No, I don't like such and such," even if it makes you unpopular.
❖ Willingness to work and apply yourself in order make the most of your abilities. In whatever field you are in, to be among the best.
❖ Real desire to uncover your psychological defenses and give them up.
❖ Being willing to see other people in their best light, "under the aspect of eternity."

What were the implications of studying only healthy, creative, fully realized people? Not surprisingly, Maslow concluded, "You get a different view of mankind."

It is hard to see now what a revolution Maslow sparked in deciding on this focus, but remember that it occurred within a medical paradigm framed only on psychological illness. Maslow felt that psychology should rather be focused on "full humanness." In this context, a neurotic person becomes simply a person who is "not yet fully actualized." This may seem like a semantic difference, but it actually represented a sea change in psychology.

The Jonah complex

Why is it that we are all born with limitless potential, yet few people fulfill those possibilities? One of the reasons Maslow put forward is what he called the "Jonah complex." The Biblical Jonah was a timid merchant who tried to resist God's call for him to go on an important mission. Maslow's complex refers to the "fear of one's greatness," or avoiding our true destiny or calling.

Maslow observed that we fear our best as much as our worst. Perhaps it seems too frightening to have a mission in life, so instead we take on a series of jobs for survival's sake. We all have perfect moments in which we glimpse what we are truly capable of, when we know ourselves to be great. "And yet," Maslow noted, "we simultaneously shiver with weakness, awe and fear before these very same possibilities."

He liked to ask his students questions such as "Which of you intends to become President?" or "Which of you will become an inspirational moral leader, like Albert Schweitzer?" When they would squirm or blush, he then posed the question, "If not you, then who else?" These were all people who were training to be psychologists, but Maslow asked them what the point was of learning to be a mediocre psychologist. Doing only as much as necessary to be competent, he told them, was a recipe for deep unhappiness in life. They would be evading their own capacities and possibilities. Maslow recalled Nietzsche's idea of the law of eternal recurrence; that is, that the life we lead has to be lived over and over again into eternity, like in the movie *Groundhog Day*. If we lived with this law in mind, we would only ever do what was really important.

Some people avoid seeking to be great because they fear being seen as grandiose, as wanting too much. Yet this can just become an excuse not to try. Instead, we adopt mock humility and set low aims for ourselves. The possibility of becoming remarkable shoots a thunderbolt of fear into many unremarkable people. They suddenly realize that they will attract attention. The Jonah complex is partly a fear of losing control, of the possibility that we might undergo a total transformation from the old person we were.

Maslow's suggestion was this: We need to balance grand aims with having our feet on the ground. Most people have too much of one and not enough of the other. If you study successful and self-realized people, you find that they have a blend of both; that is, they shoot for the sky, yet are also grounded in reality.

Work and creativity

As an academic psychologist, Maslow was surprised when, in the 1960s, big business came knocking on his door. In a time of increasing competition to produce better products, companies sensed that work environments in which people were more creative and fulfilled would also be more productive. Maslow had written about "Eupsychia," which was "the culture that would be generated by 1,000 self-actualizing people on some sheltered island where they would not be interfered with." While this was a utopia, his real-world solution of Eupsychian management aimed to achieve the psychological health and fulfillment of everyone in the workplace.

Over a quarter of *The Farther Reaches of Human Nature* is devoted to the question of creativity, for this lay at the heart of Maslow's idea of the self-actualizing person. He distinguished between primary creativity—the flash of inspiration that "sees" a final product before it has been created—and secondary creativity—working out and developing the inspiration, seeing it through.

Maslow noted that because we live in a world that changes much more quickly than it did in the past, it is not enough to do things the way they have always been done. The best people will be willing to give up the past, and instead to study a problem as it is, without baggage. This feature, which he called "innocence," was common in self-actualized people. Of this trait Maslow wrote: "The most mature people are the ones that can have the most fun... These are people who can regress at will, who can become childish and play with children and be close to them."

He was keenly aware that such people are often the unconventional ones or troublemakers in an organization, and was frank in telling businesses that they had to somehow accommodate and value these individuals. Organizations are by nature conservative, but to survive and prosper they also needed to indulge in the creative flights of fancy that may foresee the need for, or produce, great new products or concepts. The ideal workplace would be like a reflection of the self-actualized person's creative nature—a childlike inspiration to create something truly new; and the maturity to see a vision through to reality.

Final comments

As with many trailblazers, Maslow was not at all sure of his ground in terms of research methodology (he wrote, "Knowledge of low reliability is also a part of knowledge"), but his ideas breathed new life into psychology. As Henry Geiger points out in an introduction to *The Farther Reaches of Human Nature*, as well as being highly respected academically Maslow's writings also sold in big numbers to the general public. They responded to the fact that, rather than being a crazy notion, self-actualization was actually a goal within most people's reach. It was not just for the "saints and the sages" and the great figures of history, but was everyone's birthright.

It is no surprise, therefore, that Maslow's ideas have been adapted for the world of work. While on the one hand the concept of self-actualization inspires us always to seek meaningful work above other rewards, being reminded of the Jonah complex can urge us to live up to our potential and think really big.

Abraham Maslow

Born in 1908 in a poor part of Brooklyn, New York, Maslow was the oldest of seven children. Although his parents were uneducated Russian-Jewish immigrants, his father became a prosperous businessman who was eager for his shy but fiercely intelligent son to become a lawyer. Abraham did initially study law at City College of New York, but in 1928 transferred to the University of Wisconsin where his interested in psychology was awakened, and where he worked with the primate researcher Harry Harlow (see p 142). In the same year Maslow married Bertha Goodman, his cousin.

In 1934 Maslow obtained his PhD in psychology, but returned to New York to do controversial work on the sex lives of college women with Edward Thorndike at Columbia University, where he also found a mentor in Alfred Adler (see p 14). He began a 14-year teaching post at Brooklyn College, where his mentors included European emigrés such as psychologist Eric Fromm, Karen Horney (see p 156), and anthropologist Margaret Mead. Maslow's Principles of Abnormal Psychology *was published in 1941, and in 1943 came his famous journal article in* Psychological Review, *"A Theory of Motivation," which introduced the concept of a hierarchy of needs.*

From 1951 to 1969 Maslow headed the psychology department at Brandeis University, where he wrote Motivation and Personality *(1954) and* Towards a Psychology of Being *(1968). In 1962 he held a visiting fellowship at a Californian high-tech company, which helped him relate the idea of self-actualization to a business setting.*

In 1968 he was elected president of the American Psychological Association, and at the time of his death in 1970 he was a fellow with the Laughlin Foundation.

1974

Obedience to Authority

"*Gas chambers were built, death camps were guarded, daily quotas of corpses were produced with the same efficiency as the manufacture of appliances. These inhuman policies may have originated in the mind of a single person, but they could only have been carried out on a massive scale if a very large number of people obeyed orders.*"

"*Men do become angry; they do act hatefully and explode in rage against others. But not here. Something far more dangerous is revealed: the capacity for man to abandon his humanity, indeed, the inevitability that he does so, as he merges his unique personality into larger institutional structures.*"

In a nutshell

Awareness of our natural tendency to obey authority may lessen the chance of blindly following orders that go against our conscience.

In a similar vein
Robert Cialdini *Influence* (p 62)
Eric Hoffer *The True Believer* (p 152)

CHAPTER 35

Stanley Milgram

I n 1961 and 1962, a series of experiments were carried out at Yale University. Volunteers were paid a small sum to participate in what they understood would be "a study of memory and learning." In most cases, a white-coated experimenter took charge of two of the volunteers, one of whom was given the role of "teacher" and the other "learner." The learner was strapped into a chair and told he had to remember lists of word pairs. If he couldn't recall them, the teacher was asked to give him a small electric shock. With each incorrect answer the voltage rose, and the teacher was forced to watch as the learner moved from small grunts of discomfort to screams of agony.

What the teacher didn't know was that there was actually no current running between his control box and the learner's chair, and that the volunteer "learner" was in fact an actor who was only *pretending* to get painful shocks. The real focus of the experiment was not the "victim," but the reactions of the teacher pressing the buttons. How would he cope with administering greater and greater pain to a defenseless human being?

The experiment, described in *Obedience to Authority: An Experimental View*, is one of the most famous in psychology. Here, we take a look at what actually happened and why the results are important.

Expectations and reality

Most people would expect that at the first sign of genuine pain on the part of the person being shocked, the experiment would be halted. After all, it was only an experiment. This is the response that Milgram received when, outside the actual experiments, he surveyed a range of people on how they believed subjects would react in these circumstances. Most predicted that the teachers would not give shocks beyond the point where the learners asked to be freed. These expectations were entirely in line with Milgram's own. But what actually happened?

Most subjects asked to act as teachers were very stressed by the experiment, and protested to the experimenter that the person in the chair should not have to take any more pain. The logical next step would then have been to demand that the experiment be terminated. In reality, this rarely happened.

Despite their reservations, *most people* continued to follow the orders of the experimenter and inflict progressively greater shocks. Indeed, as Milgram noted, "a substantial proportion continued to the last shock on the generator." That was even when they could hear the cries of the learner, and even when that person pleaded to be let out of the experiment.

How we cope with a bad conscience

Milgram's experiments have caused controversy over the years; many people are simply unwilling to accept that normal human beings would act like this. Many scientists have tried to find holes in the methodology, but the experiment has been replicated around the world with similar outcomes. As Milgram noted, the results astonish people. They want to believe that the subjects who volunteered were sadistic monsters. However, he made sure that they came from a range of social classes and professions, and that they were normal people put in unusual circumstances.

Why don't the subjects administering the "shocks" feel guilty and just opt out of the experiment? Milgram was careful to point out that most of his subjects knew that what they were doing was not right. They hated giving the shocks, especially when the victim was objecting to them. Yet even though they thought that the experiment was cruel or senseless, most were not able to extract themselves from it. Instead, they developed coping mechanisms to justify what they were doing. These included:

❖ Getting absorbed in the technical side of the experiment. People have a strong desire to be competent in their work. The experiment and its successful implementation became more important than the welfare of the people involved.

❖ Transferring moral responsibility for the experiment to its leader. This is the common "I was just following orders" defense found in any war crimes trial. The moral sense or conscience of the subject is not lost, but is transformed into a wish to please the boss or leader.

❖ Choosing to believe that their actions needed to be done as part of a larger, worthy cause. Where in the past wars have been waged over religion or political ideology, in this case the cause was science.

❖ Devaluing the person receiving the shocks: "If they are dumb enough not to remember the word pairs, they *deserve* to be punished." Such impugning of intelligence or character is commonly used by tyrants to encourage followers to get rid of whole groups of people. They are not worth much, the thinking goes, so who really cares if they are eliminated? The world will be a better place.

Perhaps the most surprising result was Milgram's observation that the subject's sense of morality did not disappear, but was *reoriented*, so that they felt duty and loyalty not to those they were harming but to the person giving the orders. The subject was not able to extract themselves from the situation because—amazingly—it would have been *impolite* to go against the wishes of the experimenter. The subject felt they had agreed to do the experiment, so to pull out would make them appear a promise-breaker.

The desire to please authority was seemingly more powerful than the moral force of the other volunteer's cries. When the subject did voice opposition to what was going on, he or she typically couched it in the most deferential terms. As Milgram described one subject: "He thinks he is killing someone, yet he uses the language of the tea table."

From individual to "agent"

Why are we like this? Milgram observed that humans' tendency to obey authority evolved for simple survival purposes. There had to be leaders and followers and hierarchies in order to get things done. Man is a communal animal, and does not want to rock the boat. Worse even than the bad conscience of harming others who are defenseless, it seems, is the fear of being isolated.

Most of us are inculcated from a very young age with the idea that it is wrong to hurt others needlessly, yet we spend the first 20 years of our life being told what to do, so we get used to obeying authority. Milgram's experiments threw subjects right into the middle of this conundrum. Should they "be good" in the sense of not harming, or "be good" in the sense of doing what they're told? Most subjects chose the latter—suggesting that our brain is hardwired to accept authority above all else.

The natural impulse not to harm others is dramatically altered when a person is put into a hierarchical structure. On our own we take full responsibility for what we do and consider ourselves autonomous, but once in a system or hierarchy we are more than willing to give over that responsibility to someone else. We stop being ourselves, and instead become an "agent" for some other person or thing.

How it becomes easy to kill

Milgram was influenced by the story of Adolf Eichmann, whose job it was to engineer the death of six million Jews under Hitler. Hannah Arendt's book *Eichmann in Jerusalem* argued that Eichmann was not really a psychopath, but an obedient bureaucrat whose distance from the actual death camps allowed him to order the atrocities in the name of some higher goal. Milgram's experiments confirmed the truth of Arendt's idea of the "banality of evil." That is, humans are not inherently cruel, but become so when cruelty is demanded by authority. This was the main lesson of his study:

Ordinary people, simply doing their jobs, and without any particular hostility on their part, can become agents in a terrible destructive process.

Obedience to Authority can make for painful reading, especially the transcript of an interview with an American soldier who participated in the Mai Lai massacre in Vietnam. Milgram concluded that there was such a thing as inherent psychopathy, or "evil," but that it was statistically not common. His alarm was more about how an average person (his experiments included women too, who showed almost no difference in obedience to men), if put into the right conditions, can do terrible things to other people—and not feel too bad about it.

This, Milgram noted, is the purpose of military training. Trainee soldiers are put into an environment separate from normal society and its moral niceties and instead are made to think in terms of "the enemy." They are instilled with a love of "duty"; the belief that they are fighting for a great cause; and a tremendous fear of disobeying orders: "Although its ostensible purpose is to provide the recruit with military skills, its fundamental aim is to break down any residues of individuality and selfhood." Trainee soldiers are made to become agents for a cause, rather than freethinking individuals, and herein lies their vulnerability to dreadful actions. Other people stop being human beings, and become "collateral damage."

The ability to disobey
What makes one person able to disobey authority, while the rest cannot? Disobedience is difficult. Milgram's subjects generally felt that their allegiance was to the experiment and the experimenter; only a few were able to break this feeling and put the person suffering in the chair above the authority system. There was a big gap, Milgram noticed, between protesting that harm was being done (which nearly all subjects did), and actually refusing to go on with the experiment. Yet this is the leap made by those few who do disobey authority on ethical or moral grounds. They assert their individual beliefs *despite* the situation, whereas most of us bend *to* the situation. That is the difference between a hero who is willing to risk their own life to save others, and an Eichmann.

Culture has taught us how to obey authority, Milgram remarked, but not how to disobey authority that is morally reprehensible.

Final comments
Obedience to Authority seems to offer little comfort about human nature. Because we evolved in clear social hierarchies over thousands of years, part of our brain wiring makes us want to obey people who are "above" us. Yet it is only through knowledge of this strong tendency that we can avoid getting ourselves into situations in which we might perpetrate evil.

Every ideology requires a number of obedient people to act in its name, and in the case of Milgram's experiment, the ideology that awed subjects was not religion or communism or a charismatic ruler. Apparently, people will do things in the name of Science just as Spanish Inquisitors tortured people in the name of God. Have a big enough "cause," and it is easy to see how giving pain to another living thing can be justified without too much difficulty.

That our need to be obedient frequently overrides previous education or conditioning toward compassion, ethics, or moral precepts suggests that the cherished idea of human free will is a myth. On the other hand, Milgram's descriptions of people who did manage to refuse to give further shocks should provide us all with hope for how we might act in a similar situation. It may be part of our heritage to obey authority mindlessly, but it is also in our nature to set aside ideology if it means causing pain, and to be willing to put a person above a system.

Milgram's experiments might have been less well known were it not for the fact that *Obedience to Authority* is a gripping work of scientific literature. This is a book that anyone interested in how the mind works should have in their library. The genocide in Rwanda, the massacre at Srebrenica, and the affronts to human dignity at Abu Ghraib prison are all illuminated and partly explained by its insights.

Stanley Milgram

Born in New York City in 1933, Milgram graduated from high school in 1950 and earned a bachelor's degree from Queens College in 1954. He majored in political science, but decided he was more interested in psychology and took summer courses in the subject in order to be accepted into a doctoral program at Harvard. His PhD was taken under the supervision of eminent psychologist Gordon Allport, on the subject of why people conform. Milgram worked with Solomon Asch at Princeton University, who developed famous experiments in social conformity.

Other areas of research included why people are willing to give up their seats on public transport, the idea of "six degrees of separation," and aggression and nonverbal communication. Milgram also made documentary films, including Obedience, *on the Yale experiments, and* The City and the Self, *on the impact of city living on behavior. For more information, read Thomas Blass's* The Man Who Shocked the World: The Life and Legacy of Stanley Milgram *(2004)*

Milgram died in New York in 1984.

Brainsex

"*The sexes are different because their brains are different. The brain, the chief administrative and emotional organ of life, is differently constructed in men and in women; it processes information in a different way, which results in different perceptions, priorities and behaviour.*"

"*There has seldom been a greater divide between what intelligent, enlightened opinion presumes—that men and women have the same brain—and what science knows—that they do not.*"

In a nutshell

By the time we emerge from the womb, most of the differences between males and females are already formed.

In a similar vein
Louann Brizendine *The Female Brain* (p 52)
John M. Gottman *The Seven Principles for Making Marriage Work* (p 136)
Alfred Kinsey *Sexual Behavior in the Human Female* (p 174)
Steven Pinker *The Blank Slate* (p 228)

CHAPTER 36

Anne Moir &
David Jessel

For thousands of years, everyone treated men and women as quite different; people were assigned roles based on skills, aptitudes, perceptions,
and behavior, and it was taken as given that these things depended on
what gender you were. In the sexual revolution of the 1960s, however, these
role definitions were dismissed as a male conspiracy to maintain social and
economic domination over women. Educational policies were reframed to
remove gender bias in how children were taught, and the Israeli kibbutz,
which threw out the traditional demarcations of "male" and "female" jobs,
was thought to be a great model. In this new world, never again would a
woman simply fall into a role assigned to her by society.

Just one thing got in the way of this brave new world of equality: science.
While we were being taught to believe that there were no differences between
men and women that mattered, advances in brain science and empirical behavior studies were coming up with contrary findings. The sexes were not just different in a physical way, but worlds apart in life priorities, ways of
communication, and sexual needs. According to Anne Moir and David Jessel,
the idea of equality was "a biological and scientific lie."

Brainsex: The Real Difference Between Men and Women was a bestseller
and one of the first popular books on gender differences, long before John
Gray wrote *Men Are From Mars, Women Are From Venus*. Superbly written
and often amusing, it remains a great example of "myth busting." Moir is a
geneticist and the book is based on plenty of scientific references—there is a
lot of information in fewer than 200 pages—yet despite being over 15 years
old it does not seem dated. Readers seeking the latest information on the link
between gender, neurology, and behavior should read Brizendine's *The Female
Brain*; however *Brainsex* is still an excellent all-round treatment of the subject.

Sexed in the womb

Children are not born a blank slate, comment Moir and Jessel, ready to be
conditioned. At six or seven weeks in the womb a baby literally "makes up
its mind" with the help of hormones, and is configured into a male or a
female patterned brain. Sex differences in the brain originate with the chro-
mosomes (generally "xx" for female, "xy" for male), but the foetus will only

become a boy if male hormones are present; if they are absent it will become a female.

It is the concentration, timing, and appropriateness of hormonal action on a fetus that organize the neural network into its definite male or female pattern—and these patterns are very resistant to change after birth. Moir and Jessel note that mammal brains generally are "dimorphic"; that is, they are either male patterned or female patterned. As mammals, therefore, it would have been a freak of nature if the human brain had defied this neural sex patterning.

Boys will be boys
Even at a few hours old, before external conditioning can influence them, babies exhibit definite tendencies. A girl baby gazes at people's faces, while boys seem more interested in objects. Girl babies respond better to soothing sounds and are more frightened by noise, reflecting a keener sense of hearing.

When babies turn into toddlers, the way they see and experience the world is through the lens of their gender's brain chemistry. Boys are more adventurous in their play and roam more widely. They work to improve their spatial skills, while girls work harder at their interpersonal skills. Girls talk on average a year earlier than boys (Einstein, Moir and Jessel note, was five before he could speak). The difference continues at the pre-school stage, boys preferring vigorous play over a large area, while girls tending to more sedentary play and orderly activity. Girls treat newcomers with friendliness and curiosity, boys show nothing but indifference.

Hormones and the brain
At puberty, the brain, which has already been "pre-wired" by the hormones in the fetal stage, responds to the gush of hormones with massive physical and psychological changes. Teenage boys have a testosterone level 20 times that of girls, and as an anabolic steroid, testosterone bulks up body mass and makes boys think about sex all the time.

Whereas the male hormonal system remains in steady balance, working like a thermostat, in women the system generates cycles of highs and lows corresponding to the menstrual cycle. In the premenstrual period the flow of progesterone, which helps to create a feeling of wellbeing, stops; the effect can be like coming off a drug. The authors note the rise in crime committed by premenstrual women; in the French penal code, premenstrual tension is included in the category of "temporary insanity," and elsewhere has been used successfully in judicial defenses.

Overall, Moir and Jessel conclude, male hormones increase aggression, competition, self-assertion, self-confidence, and self-reliance; these traits are reduced in the presence of female hormones. However, as they age, men's level of testosterone declines and they tend to mellow out; in contrast, changes to their hormonal chemistry see women become more assertive.

Intelligence and emotion

Men's brains are more specialized and compartmentalized, with their spatial and language skills located in specific centers, while women's brain functions are generally more diffused, with these skills controlled by centers in both sides. The more focused organization of the male brain may account for male single-mindedness, and men's famous ability to read maps can be attributed to stronger spatial capacity. Women, on the other hand, have greater overall awareness of a situation and are much more successful at picking up small facial cues that men don't see; this helps them to be better judges of character, and may account for "women's intuition." Women also have more effective peripheral vision and generally better senses all round.

Men's brains give them an action orientation and a preference for things over people. They are disturbed when women cry, and wonder why it happens so often. Moir and Jessel explain: "Women... see, hear, and feel more, and what they see, hear and feel means more to them. Women cry more often than men because they have more to cry about—they are receiving more emotional input, reacting more strongly to it, and expressing it with greater force." When a man cries, on the other hand, there must be something seriously wrong.

Sex

When it comes to sex, men and women's brains and hormones are so configured that the experience is totally different.

Men are easily aroused by visual sexual stimuli: They are happy for the light to be left on so they can "see the action," and they enjoy seeing images of breasts and genitalia. Women are aroused when they feel secure and intimate, and their keener sense of touch and hearing gives them a preference for making love in the dark.

Men can easily treat sex as an isolated event and women as objects. A man is probably being truthful when he says, after a fling, "It didn't mean anything." But the event will be a disaster for the woman because for her, sex is inseparable from intimacy and love. Moir and Jessel quote a psychologist's summing up of the differences: "Women want a lot of sex with the man they love, while men want a lot of sex."

Love and marriage

Men and women enter into a marriage under the misconception that they are essentially the same; they seem "compatible." They are not.

Women crave emotional intimacy, interdependence, and verbal affirmation in their daily life with their partner, while men assume that financial security and a good sex life form the basis of a successful marriage. The man does not properly appreciate just how much a woman's biology makes her vulnerable to changes in mood, while the woman will not know that her man's tendency to "blow up" at her is in large part attributed to a biologically lower threshold for anger and frustration.

Women perennially complain that men do not communicate, yet men's brains are not structured to make them want to talk frequently about their deepest feelings—the parts of their brain relating to feelings and to conveying thoughts are literally in separate places.

Brainsex refers to a number of surveys on men's and women's priorities. These indicate that what men value most in life are power, profit, and independence, while women value personal relationships and security. Men are happier in marriage when their wives look good and provide "services," while women seem happier if their husband was affectionate on the day they answered the questionnaire!

Given men's inclination to "roam," the success of marriage as an institution, Moir and Jessel suggest, is a triumph of the female brain: "Power, in any state, depends on the possession of information. In the married state, women have more of it." Marriage works not because women become subservient, but because women's social intelligence enables the relationship to be well managed.

Men and women at work

The priority that women give to personal relationships tends to rule out the egocentricity, obsession with success, ruthlessness, and "suspension of personal values" that can characterize a man's approach to his career. A woman's brain is programmed to find fulfillment in whatever role she does above and beyond some external perception of status, achievement, or success. Men, on the other hand, move into occupations where success can be easily measured. They have historically avoided fields where there is a high concentration of women.

On the other hand, there are many success stories of women who have managed to carry their institutions to the pinnacle of success without necessarily copying "male" styles of management. Psychologists note that women and men have a "preferred cognitive strategy" or way of dealing with the world based on the way their brain is wired. A culture with advanced working practices, Moir and Jessel observe, will try to allow both to exist for the greater productive good.

Final comments

We think we are free-willed beings who are not determined by our sex, but our brains are so constructed that it is difficult to be objective about which feelings, thoughts, and actions are ours as an individual and which are simply driven by our gender's natural instincts and hormones. Though not determined by our "brain sex," we are strongly shaped by it, and awareness of these shaping forces cannot be a bad thing.

Brainsex quotes American sociologist Alice Rossi: "Diversity is a biological fact, while equality is a political, ethical, and social precept." Equality is a fine idea, and of course girls and boys should have all the same chances in life, but if they don't go into the same careers, Moir and Jessel note, it does not mean there is something wrong. While being sympathetic to feminist aims, they comment that women become more powerful not when they try to be like men, but, on the contrary, when they maximize and celebrate their differences. This may sound like "reverse feminism," yet it is the only approach that reflects the biological truth.

Instead of trying to deny the differences for some politically correct reason, perhaps we should be marveling at the skills, creations, and particular attitudes to life that each gender contributes. Civilization could not have been created by either males or females exclusively; it needed many different forms of intelligence that only the two sexes in combination can supply.

Anne Moir & David Jessel

Anne Moir has a PhD in genetics and runs a UK television production company. With her husband Bill she wrote Why Men Don't Iron: The Fascinating and Unalterable Differences Between Men and Women *(2000)*

David Jessel is a UK journalist well known for presenting television programs relating to the criminal justice system. He and Moir are also co-authors of A Mind to Crime: The Controversial Link Between the Mind and Criminal Behaviour *(1997).*

Conditioned Reflexes

"Conditioned reflexes are phenomena of common and widespread occurrence: their establishment is an integral function in everyday life. We recognize them in ourselves and in other people under such names as 'education,' habits,' and 'training'; and all of these are really nothing more than the results of an establishment of new nervous connections during the post-natal existence of the organism."

"If the animal were not in exact correspondence with its environment it would, sooner or later, cease to exist... To give a biological example: if, instead of being attracted to food, the animal were repelled by it, or if instead of running from fire the animal threw itself into the fire, then it would quickly perish. The animal must respond to changes in the environment in such a manner that its responsive activity is directed towards the preservation of its existence."

In a nutshell

In the way that our minds are conditioned, we are less autonomous than we think.

In a similar vein

William James *The Principles of Psychology* (p 162)
V. S. Ramachandran *Phantoms in the Brain* (p 232)
B. F. Skinner *Beyond Freedom and Dignity* (p 266)

CHAPTER 37

Ivan Pavlov

You have probably heard of Pavlov and his famous dogs, but who was he and what was his contribution to psychology? Born in 1849 in central Russia, he was expected to follow in his father's footsteps and become a priest in the Eastern Orthodox church, but, inspired by reading Darwin, he escaped the local seminary and went to study chemistry and physics in St. Petersburg.

At university Pavlov became passionate about physiology, and worked in the labs of several eminent professors. In time he became well known for his work as a specialist in digestion and the nervous system. As a physiologist Pavlov did not think much of the new science of psychology, yet it was this work that would lead him to insights on "conditioning," or the way in which animals (including humans) develop new reflexes in order to respond to their environment.

Conditioned Reflexes: An Investigation of the Physiological Activity of the Cerebral Cortex, translated from the Russian, is a collection of lectures first given by Pavlov at the Military Medical Academy in St. Petersburg in 1924. In mind-numbing detail, it summarizes the 25 years of research carried out by his team that ultimately led to a Nobel Prize. Here, we look at what Pavlov actually discovered and its implications for human psychology.

Animals as machines

Pavlov began *Conditioned Reflexes* by noting the lack of knowledge about the brain that existed at the time. He regretted that the brain had become the domain of psychology, when it should have been the preserve of physiologists who could determine the facts about its physics and chemistry.

He paid tribute to philosopher René Descartes, who three centuries earlier had described animals as machines who reacted predictably according to stimuli in their environment in order to achieve a certain equilibrium with it. These reactions were part of the nervous system and occurred along set nerve pathways. One of these reflex reactions is the creation of saliva, and it was the action of the digestive glands in dogs that Pavlov initially investigated. He wanted to chemically analyze the differences in saliva produced in response to food under different conditions.

But in his early experiments Pavlov noticed something strange. There was a psychological element to the dogs' saliva reflex; that is, they would begin to salivate simply when they thought they were *about* to get food. Descartes' idea of the automatic reaction was clearly not so simple; Pavlov wanted to investigate further.

Creating reflexes

He decided to try out a range of stimuli on the dogs to see what exactly would provoke their saliva secretion, if it was not just a simple automatic reflex. In order that his experiments would be in real time, he had to perform a minor operation so that some of the dog's saliva passed through a hole to the outside of the cheek and into a pouch where the amounts produced could be measured.

Pavlov gave the dogs various stimuli such as the beat of a metronome, buzzers, bells, bubbling and crackling sounds, plus showing a black square, heat, touching the dog in various places, and intermittent flashes of a lamp. Each of these occurred just prior to giving food, so when the dog heard, saw, or felt a certain stimulus another time, he started to salivate even if the food had not appeared. Merely the sound of a beating metronome produced saliva even if no food was to be seen; physiologically there was no difference between the dog's reaction when he heard the metronome and what happened when he actually saw food. For the dog, the metronome—rather than a bowl of meat—came to "mean" food.

Pavlov realized that there were two types of reflexes or responses of an animal to its environment:

❖ the natural or *unconditioned* reflex (e.g., a dog's salivation when it begins to eat, to aid its digestion); and
❖ the acquired or *conditioned* reflex, which arises through unconscious learning (e.g., when a dog begins to salivate at the sound of a bell, because the sound "equates" to food).

The fact that reflexes could be instilled so that they became part of the animal's natural functioning made Pavlov aware that if an animal was really a machine responding to its environment, then it was a very complex machine. He showed that the cerebral cortex, the most advanced part of the brain, was very malleable, as were the nervous pathways linking to it. So-called instincts could be *learnt*—and unlearnt, since he was also able to demonstrate that reflexes could also be inhibited or *extinguished* by associating food with something the dog didn't like.

Yet Pavlov also noted limits to the creation of conditioned reflexes. They either wore off over time, or the dogs sometimes did not bother to respond and just fell asleep. He concluded that the cerebral cortex cannot be overworked or changed too much. It seemed that a dog's survival and proper functioning required it to retain a certain amount of stability in its brain wiring.

Advanced environment-responding machines

Pavlov observed two levels in the way in which the animal responded to its environment. There was first a "neuro-analysis," in which it used its senses to work out what things were, then a "neuro-synthesis" to establish how something fitted into its existing reactions and knowledge. In order to survive, for instance, a dog must be able to quickly determine if something is a threat to it or not.

Some of Pavlov's experiments involved removing a dog's whole cerebral cortex. This turned the dog into little more than a reflex machine. It retained its unconditioned reflexes that were hardwired into its brain and nervous system, but was not able to respond to its environment properly—it could still walk, but if it came to even a small obstacle like the leg of a table it did not know what to do. In contrast, with a normal dog even if there is a minute change in environmental stimulus or something new, an "investigatory reflex" will cause the animal to prick up its ears or sniff the stimulus. A dog may spend a lot of time simply "investigating" in order that its reflexes to its environment are fully up to date.

Pavlov knew that the results of his experiments did not just apply to dogs. The more advanced the organism, he said, the greater its ability "to multiply the complexity of its contacts with the external world and to achieve a more and more varied and exact adaptation to external conditions." "Culture" and "society" could be understood as a complex system of the management of reflexes, with humans only different to dogs to the extent that conditioned reflexes had surpassed the natural ones. While dogs could develop advanced social and territorial knowledge as their optimal response to their environment, human beings had responded by creating "civilization."

Man and dog: The similarities

The final chapter of *Conditioned Reflexes* concerns the applications of Pavlov's work to humans. Given that a human has a much more complex cerebral cortex than a dog, Pavlov was wary of reading too much into his own work. However, he noted the following parallels:

❖ The way human beings are trained, disciplined, and encultured is not that different to how dogs are taught to do things. We know that the best way to learn something is to do it in stages, in the same way that the dogs' conditioned reflexes were effected in steps. And as he found with dogs, humans have to unlearn things as well as learning them.

❖ Pavlov had a special soundproofed building created for his experiments because he found that external stimuli affected the ability to condition reflexes. In the same way, most of us cannot study a book if a movie is showing at the same time; and we find it hard to "get back into things" after a holiday or some break from routine. As with the dogs, neuroses and psychoses occur as the result of extreme stimulation that cannot be properly incorporated into existing thinking and reactions.

❖ The reactions of the dogs could not be predicted. Pavlov recalled that when one of Petrograd's famous floods swept through the experimental quarters, some dogs grew excited, others frightened, some withdrew. In the same way, he noted, we can never predict how a person will react emotionally to, for instance, a strong insult or the loss of a loved one. These reactions seemed to mirror the two common psychological reactions to shock recognized in both dogs and humans—neurasthenia (fatigue, withdrawing, immobilization) and hysteria (neurotic excitation).

With the last point, Pavlov's implication was that evolution has ensured that we cannot *not* react to a major event—we must take account of it some way. To eventually return to a state of stability, we have to incorporate what we have experienced. The phenomenon of "fight or flight" in the face of a challenge is the nervous system's manner of self-protection in the short term. In the longer term, the fact that we have had a reaction ensures that we can eventually return to a state of equilibrium with our environment.

Final comments

Pavlov saw the cerebral cortex as a complicated switchboard in which groups of cells were responsible for different reflexes. There was always room for more reflexes to be created, but also capacity for existing ones to be altered. His dogs did have "automatic" characteristics, but at the same time their reflexes and reactions were changeable. The implication for humans? Although we live for the most part through habit or enculturation, we are in a position to change our behavior patterns. We are as susceptible to conditioning as any animal, yet at the same time we also have the ability to break our own patterns if they ultimately prove not to be in our interests. Via feedback from our environment we learn what are effective responses to life and what are not.

Pavlov's research had a major impact on the behavioral school of psychology, which holds that humans are little different to dogs in that we have predictable reactions to stimuli and can be conditioned into certain ways of behavior. For the hard-core behaviorist, the idea of free will is a myth—whatever inputs are made into a person will yield certain outputs in terms of attitudes or behaviors. Yet Pavlov's own observations seem to contradict this. For instance, he noted that that many of the dogs' reactions were *not* predictable. Even when conditioning had occurred, there was still room for canine personalities to be expressed. Given our much larger cerebral cortexes, how much more room for varied expression—or "responses to environment"—must we enjoy?

Conditioned Reflexes has a very plodding, scientific style. Reflecting his love of empirical fact, order, and discipline, Pavlov did not allow much of his personality to come through. Yet he was a fascinating figure. Although critical of communism, he flourished after the Bolshevik revolution, with Lenin handing down a decree that Pavlov's work was "of enormous significance to the working classes of the whole world."

Given his distrust of the claims of the subject, it is ironic that the name Pavlov has come to be associated with psychology. His focus on measurable physiological reaction alone was almost the opposite approach of the Freudian immersion in "inner drives and wishes," yet that focus enabled psychology to come to rest on harder scientific ground.

Ivan Pavlov

Ivan Petrovich Pavlov was born in 1849 in Ryazan in central Russia, the oldest of 11 children, and his father was the village priest. His time at the University of St. Petersburg produced acclaimed work on the pancreatic nerves, and on receiving his degree in 1875 he continued his studies at the Imperial Medical Academy. There he gained a fellowship and later a position as professor of physiology. His doctorate concerned the centrifugal nerves of the heart.

In 1890 Pavlov set up the physiology department of the Institute of Experimental Sciences in St. Petersburg, where he did most of his work on digestion and conditioned reflexes. He was in charge of a large team of mostly young scientists.

His many honors included membership of the Russian Academy of Sciences, winning the 1904 Nobel Prize for medicine, and in 1915 being awarded France's Order of the Legion of Honor. His marriage to Seraphima (Sara) Vasilievna Karchevskaya, a teacher, in 1881 produced four children who lived past infancy, one of whom went on to become a physicist.

Pavlov was still working in his laboratories when he died in 1936, at the age of 87.

Gestalt Therapy

"*Much of the constant effort you supposed to hold yourself together is actually unnecessary. You do not fall apart, go to pieces, or 'act crazy,' if you let up on your deliberate holding back, forcing attention, constant 'thinking' and active interference with the trends of your behavior. Instead, your experience begins to cohere and to organize into more meaningful wholes.*"

"*Some of us have no heart or no intuition, some have no legs to stand on, no genitals, no confidence, no eyes or ears.*"

In a nutshell

Be alive every minute in your physical world. Listen to your body; don't live in abstractions.

In a similar vein

Milton Erickson *My Voice Will Go With You* (p 78)
Karen Horney *Our Inner Conflicts* (p 156)
R. D. Laing *The Divided Self* (p 186)
Abraham Maslow *The Farther Reaches of Human Nature* (p 192)
Carl Rogers *On Becoming a Person* (p 238)

CHAPTER 38

Fritz Perls

T he Esalen Institute on the Californian coast at Big Sur was an epicenter of the 1960s social revolution. Literally "on the edge," perched on steep hills high above the Pacific ocean, it attracted people who wanted to push the boundaries of the self and break free of society's constraints. Fritz Perls, a psychologist, arrived at Esalen in 1964. Having grown up in avant-garde Berlin and fled from Hitler's Germany to the United States, Esalen must have seemed like a spiritual home, and he spent much time there until his death in 1970.

Charismatic and sometimes cantankerous, Perls was one of the early West Coast personal development gurus. His philosophy was that the modern man or woman thinks too much, when they should be experiencing, feeling, doing; and his slogan "Lose your mind and come to your senses" chimed perfectly with the counter-culture.

Gestalt Therapy: Excitement and Growth in the Human Personality, written with the brilliant radical Paul Goodman and a college professor and patient of Perls, Ralph Hefferline, became the manifesto of a new type of psychotherapy. Though he had trained in Freudian psychoanalysis, Perls had long since dispensed with the couch, instead finding that confrontational group sessions were often the best way of piercing a person's psychological "body armor" and letting their true, vibrant self out.

For a book about excited feeling, *Gestalt Therapy* can be a tedious read requiring a fair amount of concentration. Its purpose, however, was to lay out the theoretical basis for Gestalt therapy ideas. Its theme of shaking off the straitjackets of normal societal roles to live in the "here and now" made it a very confronting work. It is easy to forget how novel it would have seemed in 1950s America.

Gestalt = wholeness

Have you ever seen those pictures where if you look one way you see a beautiful woman, but then from the same drawing an old hag appears? If so, you have had a gestalt or "aha!" experience. There is no exact English translation, but the German word *Gestalt* roughly means "shape" or "form," or the wholeness of something. The Gestalt school of psychology (associated with figures such as Max Wertheimer, Wolfgang Köhler, Kurt Lewin, Kurt Goldstein,

Lancelot Law Whyte, and Alfred Korzybski) showed that in experiments to do with visual perception, the brain always tries to "complete the picture" when incomplete images are put before it. We are programmed to find a "figure" against a "ground" or background; that is, to give attention to one thing at the expense of another and find meaning amid a chaos of color and shape.

Perls took ideas from Gestalt psychology and fashioned from it his own form of therapy. He wanted to apply the idea of wholeness to personal well-being, and borrowed the notion that a person is always being shaped by a certain dominant need—the figure—and when this need is satisfied it drops back into the background—the ground—making way for another need. In this way all organisms regulate themselves, getting what they require for their survival.

The issue with human beings, however, is that our complexity can muddy the waters of the simple need-satisfaction equation. We can repress some needs and overemphasize others; or our idea of survival can get warped, so we believe we must maintain ourselves in a certain way, even if to an outsider what we are doing is stupid. Our dominant need becomes connected totally with our sense of self, but it is a self that it is no longer fluid or elastic, a neurotic self. It has stopped being aware.

In traditional Freudian analysis, the "doctor" tries to "understand" such a person by trying to delve into their mind, by treating them as an object. The Gestalt therapist, in contrast, appreciates the person as part of their environment. The mind, the body, the environment are all part of one consideration. Instead of psychology's tendency to break things down into pieces, Gestalt therapy apprehends the whole. In Perls' words: "[The] Gestalt outlook is the original, undistorted, natural approach to life; that is, to man's thinking, acting, feeling. The average person, having been raised in an atmosphere full of splits, has lost his Wholeness, his Integrity."

Contact and confluence

Smell, touch, taste, hearing, and seeing are our "contact boundary" with the world. When someone has begun to think of themselves as an isolated object, they have ceased to be a sensing, contacting, excited being. Perls recognized how modern life, sitting in air-conditioned offices, anesthetizes us. We purposefully reduce our level of awareness to create a more ordered existence with no surprises. But what do people say on their deathbed? Not "I wish I had sought more security or earned more money," but "I wish I had taken chances, done more things"—that is, had more contact with life.

Someone in genuine contact with their environment, Perls noted, is in a state of excitement. They are feeling, one way or another, all the time. Neurotics, in contrast, instead of risking real contact with the world, withdraw into the inner world they know, and do not grow. Healthy people engage with life: "eating and food-getting, loving and making love, aggressing, conflicting, communicating, perceiving, learning," and so on.

The opposite of contact is "confluence," acting out of what you have been taught to do, out of habit, or seeing things as you "should" be seeing them. Perls gives the example of someone standing in a gallery looking at a work of modern art. He feels he is directly perceiving the work, when in fact "he is actually in contact with the art critic of his favorite journal." People grow into the world with heavy expectations to change their basic nature into something they are not, and this gap between our biological nature and society leads to holes in the personality: "Some of us have no heart or no intuition, some have no legs to stand on, no genitals, no confidence, no eyes or ears," Perls would rather shockingly tell his groups. In Gestalt therapy, people claimed their missing parts, and in the process got back lost aggression or sensitivity.

Awareness of body and emotion

Perls saw a clear difference between introspection and awareness. Awareness was the "spontaneous sensing of what arises in you—of what you are doing, feeling, planning." Introspection, on the other hand, was considering the same activities in an "evaluating, correcting, controlling, interfering way." The distinction is important, because traditionally psychology involves the assumption that we can analyze ourselves as if we are somehow separate to our brain and body. But such analysis only makes us neurotic; what brings us back to sanity and puts us in happy balance with the world is reconnection with our *senses*.

Gestalt Therapy contains many experiments Perls used to get people to increase awareness, such as telling them to "Feel your body!" By lying still and feeling every part of your body, you find some areas feel "dead"; in other parts you may experience pain or imbalance. Just the simple act of giving attention to certain areas of muscle or joints may lead you to conclusions as to why your neck is stiff or there is pain in your stomach. Perls noted: "The neurotic personality *creates* its symptoms by *unaware manipulation of muscles*." Often, the experiments resulted in someone having the realization that they are either "a nagger or a person nagged at."

In another experiment, Perls asked people to tell themselves what they were seeing and doing in each moment; that is, "I am now sitting in this chair, this afternoon, looking at the table in front of me. This moment there is the sound of a car in the street and I now feel the sun on my face through the window." He then asked them what difficulties they were experiencing while they were doing this. They invariably answered, "What difficulties?" The discovery was that as long as you are fully in the present, noticing and feeling the environment around you, you are trouble free. Abstract worries and anxieties reenter only when you "leave" your environment. Some people found the experience to cause impatience, boredom, or anxiety, which according to Perls indicated how much their normal consciousness lacked "actuality."

What is hidden can't be transformed

The goal of Gestalt is to stop living life as if you are on automatic. Many people find that they truly live in actuality only a small amount of the time; when they consciously do it more, this can be a breakthrough. Full awareness and attention resolves an issue, Perls taught, not rationalizing about it.

Most of us find that the parts of ourselves we try to throttle into non-existence always come back. Yet purposeful reduction of awareness, or repression, means that we can never change or resolve the issue. If something terrible happened in the past, Perls taught that we have to bring it fully into the present, even act it out again, in order to "own" it. Trying to ignore it only gives it more energy.

Earnestness vs responsibility

Perls believed that healthy adults should not throw out completely the ways of children. Spontaneity, imagination, curiosity, and wonder are things we should keep—as all great artists and scientists do—and we should not be deadened by "responsibility" and always having to make sense.

Children are superior to adults in their earnestness, even when they are involved in play. They may leave an activity on a whim, but when they are doing it nothing else matters. Gifted people retain this very direct awareness, but the average adult is usually not interested enough in what they are doing.

Perls points out that what we think of as being "responsible" a lot of the time is simply closing ourselves off to living life intensely. As he put it: "habitual deliberateness, factuality, non-commitment, and excessive responsibility, traits of most adults, are neurotic; whereas spontaneity, imagination, earnestness and playfulness, and direct expression of feeling, traits of children, are healthy."

Final comments

Perls's philosophy of doing what you feel instead of doing what you ought to do ensured his place in many hearts and minds. His famous "Gestalt Prayer" summed up the spirit of the 1960s:

"I do my thing, and you do your thing.
I am not in this world to live up to your expectations
And you are not in this world to live up to mine.
You are you and I am I,
And if by chance we find each other, it's beautiful.
If not, it can't be helped."

Sometimes the last line was left off the posters, as it didn't seem to gel with the flower-power ethos. But then, Perls often made fun of the seekers of "joy," "ecstasy," and "highs," and made a point of noting the hard work involved in his therapy. It was frequently unpleasant and raw and could reduce people to tears. No one wanted to have their privacy invaded and be told about the holes in their personality. Yet Perls pointed out that we can only move on after we admit we are stuck.

Like Milton Erickson, Perls was a master at reading body language. In group sessions, he was often less interested in what someone said than in the tone of their voice and how they were sitting. People were not allowed to discuss anyone not in the room, reinforcing the "here and now" intensity of Gestalt therapy. He considered himself a good "shit detector" in people, a skill vital in life that was a long way from the hazy "love and peace" mantra of the times.

Perls also liked to talk about aggression. He believed that holding in anger denied that humans are essentially animals. We stifle tiredness or boredom, but we should be like cats, yawning and stretching to put ourselves back into action again. What the body wants we should give it, in order to stay in equilibrium. Is there a part of yourself that you have cut off because it was antisocial or not worthy of a nice person? To come alive again, reclaim it.

Fritz Perls

Born in 1893 in Berlin, Frederick Salomon Perls gained his medical degree in 1926. On graduating he worked at the Institute for Brain Damaged Soldiers in Frankfurt, where he was influenced by Gestalt psychologists, existential philosophy, and the neo-Freudians Karen Horney and Wilhelm Reich.

In the early 1930s, with Germany becoming unsafe for Jews, Perls and his wife Laura moved to the Netherlands and then South Africa. There they established their own psychoanalytic practices and the South African Institute for Psychoanalysis. But they became critical of Freudian concepts, and slowly developed the Gestalt method of practice, articulated in Ego, Hunger and Aggression: A Revision of Freud's Theory and Method *(1947). In 1946 the couple moved to New York, setting up an Institute of Gestalt Therapy in 1952. After separating, Fritz moved to California and Laura stayed in New York with their children. He went to Esalen in 1964.*

The year before he died, Perls published Gestalt Therapy Verbatim *(1969), which chronicles sessions held at Esalen, and his autobiography,* In and Out of the Garbage Pail.

The Language and Thought of the Child

"Child logic is a subject of infinite complexity, bristling with problems at every point—problems of functional and structural psychology, problems of logic and even of epistemology. It is no easy matter to hold fast to the thread of consistency throughout this labyrinth, and to achieve a systematic exclusion of all problems not connected with psychology."

"The child… seems to talk far more than the adult. Almost everything he does is to the tune of remarks such as 'I'm drawing a hat,' 'I'm doing it better than you,' etc. Child thought, therefore, seems more social, less capable of sustained and solitary research. This is true only in appearance. The child has less verbal continence simply because he does not know what it is to keep a thing to himself. Although he talks almost incessantly to his neighbours, he rarely places himself at their point of view."

In a nutshell

Children are not simply little adults, thinking less efficiently—they think differently.

In a similar vein

Edward de Bono *Lateral Thinking* (p 38)
Alfred Kinsey *Sexual Behavior in the Human Female* (p 174)
Stephen Pinker *The Blank Slate* (p 228)

CHAPTER 39

Jean Piaget

In the same way that Alfred Kinsey spent years collecting specimens of and writing about the gall wasp before he launched himself on the study of human sexuality, Jean Piaget was a master of natural-world observation before he turned his mind to human matters. As a child and teenager he wandered the hills, streams, and mountains of western Switzerland collecting snails, and later wrote his doctoral thesis on the mollusks of the Valais mountains.

What he learnt in these years—to observe first and classify later—set him up well for examining the subject of child thought, which had attracted plenty of theories but not a great deal of solid scientific observation of actual children. Entering the field, Piaget's main wish was that his conclusions be drawn from the facts, however difficult or paradoxical they seemed. Added to his methodical skills was—for a scientist—an unusually good grasp of philosophy. Child psychology was a tangle of epistemological questions, yet he decided to focus on very down-to-earth issues such as: "Why does a child talk, and who is she talking to?" and "Why does she ask so many questions?"

If there were answers, he knew they could benefit teachers greatly, and it was for educators mainly that he wrote *The Language and Thought of the Child*. Most explorers of the child mind had focused on the quantitative nature of child psychology—children were thought to be how they are because they have fewer mental abilities than adults and commit more errors. But Piaget believed that it was not a matter of children having less or more of something, they are fundamentally *different* in the way they think. Communication problems exist between adults and children not because of gaps in information, but due to the quite different ways they have of seeing themselves within their worlds.

Why a child talks

In the opening pages, Piaget asked what he admitted was a strange question: "What are the needs which a child tends to satisfy when he talks?" Any sane person would say that the purpose of language is to communicate with others, but if this were the case, he wondered why children talk when there is no one around, and why even adults talk to themselves, whether internally or muttering aloud. It was clear that language could not be reduced to the one function of simply communicating thought.

Piaget conducted his research at the Rousseau Institute in Geneva, opened in 1912 for the study of the child and teacher training. There he observed children of four and six, taking down everything they said while they worked and played, and the book includes transcripts of their "conversations."

What Piaget quickly discovered—and what every parent can confirm—is that when children speak, a lot of the time they are not talking to anyone in particular. They are thinking aloud. He identified two types of speech, egocentric and socialized. Within the egocentric type were three patterns:

❖ Repetition—speech not directed to people, saying words for the simple pleasure of it.
❖ Monologue—whole commentaries that follow the child's actions or play.
❖ Collective monologue—when children are talking apparently together, yet are not really taking account of what the others are saying. (A room of 10 children seated at different tables may be noisy with talk, but in fact are all really talking to themselves.)

He noted that until a certain age (seven, he thought), children have no "verbal continence," but must say anything that comes into their head. A kindergarten or nursery, he wrote, "is a society in which, strictly speaking, individual and social life are not differentiated." Because children believe themselves to be the center of the universe, there is no need for the idea of privacy or withholding views out of sensitivity to others. Adults, in contrast, because of their comparative lack of egocentricity, have adapted to a fully socialized speech pattern in which many things are left unsaid. Only madmen and children, as it were, say whatever they think, because only *they* really matter. It is for this reason that children are able to talk all the time in the presence of their friends, but are never able to see things from the friends' point of view.

Part of the reason for the egocentricity of children is that a significant part of their language involves gestures, movements, and sounds. As these are not words, they cannot express everything, so children must remain partly a prisoner of their own mind. We can understand this when we appreciate that the greater an adult's mastery of language, the more likely they are to be able to understand, or at least be aware of, the views of others. Language, in fact, takes people beyond themselves, which is why human culture puts such stress on teaching it to children—it enables them to eventually move out of egocentric thinking.

Different thinking, different worlds

Piaget borrowed a distinction from psychoanalysis between two types of thought:

❖ *Directed or intelligent thought,* which has an aim, adapts that aim to reality, and can communicate it in language. This thinking is based on experience and logic.

❖ *Undirected or autistic thought,* which involves aims that are not conscious and not adapted to reality, based on satisfaction of desires rather than establishing truth. The language of this sort of thinking is images, myths, and symbols.

For the directed mind, water has certain properties and obeys certain laws. It is conceived of conceptually as well as materially. To the autistic mind, water is only relevant in relation to desires or needs—it is something that can be drunk or seen or enjoyed.

This distinction helped Piaget appreciate the development of children's thought up to the age of 11. From 3–7 children are largely egocentric and have elements of autistic thought, but from 7 to 11 egocentric logic makes way for perceptual intelligence.

Piaget set up experiments in which children were asked to relate a story they had been told or to explain something, such as the workings of a tap, that had been shown to them. Before they were 7, the children did not really care if the people they were talking to understood the story or the mechanism. They could describe, but not analyze. But from 7–8 onwards, the children did not assume that the other person would know what they meant and attempted to give a faithful account—to be objective. Until that age, their egocentrism does not allow them to be objective. What they can't explain or don't know they make up. But after the age of 7–8 children know what it means to give a correct rendering of the truth; that is, the difference between invention and reality.

Piaget noticed that children think in terms of "schemas," which allow them to focus on the whole of a message without having to make sense of every detail. When they hear something they don't understand, children don't try to analyze the sentence structure or words, but attempt to grasp or create an overall meaning. He noted that the trend in mental development is always from the syncretic to the analytical—to see the whole first, before gaining the ability to break things down into parts or categorize. Prior to age 7 or 8, the child's mind is largely syncretic, but it later develops powers of analysis that mark the shift from the juvenile to the adult mind.

Child logic

Piaget wondered why children, particularly those under 7, fantasize and dream and use their imagination so much. He observed that because they do not engage in deductive or analytical thought, there is no reason to make a firm demarcation between "the real" and "the not real." As their minds do not work in terms of causality and evidence, everything seems possible.

When a child asks "What would happen if I were an angel?" to an adult the question is not worth pursuing because we know it can't be real. But for a child anything is not only possible, it is explainable, since no objective logic is required. To satisfy their mind, all that is required is motivation—for example, the ball wanted to roll down the hill, so it did. At age 6, a boy might feel that a river flows down a hill because it wants to. A year later, he will explain it in terms of "water always flows downhill, so that is why the river is flowing down this hill here."

Why do many young children incessantly ask "Why?" Because they want to know the intention of everyone and everything, even if it is inanimate, not realizing that only some things have intentions. Later, when children can appreciate that most things are *caused* rather than intended, their questions become about causality. The time before they understand cause and effect—precausality—coincides with the time of egocentrism.

The "world of make believe," as we tag it in our superior way, has the feel of cold, hard reality to younger children, because within it everything makes sense according to their own intentions and motivations. In fact, as Piaget wryly observed, a child's world seems to work so well that, according to their understanding, logic is not required to support it.

Adults often find it difficult to understand children because they have forgotten that logic plays no role in a child's mind. We cannot make children think in the same way as us before they reach a certain age. At each age, children gain a particular equilibrium in relation to their environment. That is, the way they think and perceive at age 5 perfectly explains their world. But that same way does not work when they are 8.

In later writings, Piaget explored the final stage of mental development, beginning at age 11 or 12. Teenagers' abilities to reason, think abstractly, make judgments, and consider future possibilities make them essentially the same as adults. From this point on it is a matter of increases in ability rather than qualitative changes.

Final comments

Despite some questions about the precise timings, Piaget's stages of child development have largely stood the test of time, and his impact on pre-school and school education has been great.

Yet Piaget never considered himself a child psychologist, and was more accurately a scientist focused on theories of knowledge. His observation of children led to broader theories on communication and cognition, because what he learnt about the child's mind threw the adult's into clearer view. For instance, it was not only children who used schemas to make sense of the world—adults also have to accommodate and assimilate new information by making it conform to what we know already.

Piaget invented the field of "genetic epistemology," which means how theories of knowledge evolve or change in relation to new information. He saw the mind as a relatively arbitrary creation, formed in such a way that reality can be explained according to that person's own model of the world. Education has to take account of these models rather than simply shoving facts down people's throats, otherwise information will not be assimilated. Such a method of education results in dull conformists who are uncomfortable with change, and Piaget was ahead of his time in suggesting that we should educate people to be innovative and inventive thinkers who are aware of the subjectivity of their own minds, yet mature enough to accommodate new facts. His initial experiments observing the language and thought of the child, therefore, led to great insights into how adults process knowledge and create new understanding.

Jean Piaget

Born in 1896 in Neuchâtel, western Switzerland, Piaget was the son of a professor of medieval literature at the local university. His strong interest in biology resulted in the publication of several scientific articles before he had even left school, and in 1917 he published a philosophical novel, Recherché.

After gaining his PhD, Piaget began studying child linguistic development, and in 1921 he became director of the Institut Jean-Jacques Rousseau in Geneva. From 1925–29 he was professor of psychology, sociology, and the philosophy of science at the University of Neuchâtel, after which he returned to the University of Geneva to be its professor of scientific thought for the next decade. He simultaneously held posts with the Swiss education authorities. In 1952 Piaget became professor of genetic psychology at the Sorbonne in Paris, and until his death in 1980 directed the International Center for Genetic Epistemology in Geneva.

Key books include The Child's Conception of the World *(1928),* The Moral Judgment of the Child *(1932),* The Origins of Intelligence in Children *(1953),* Biology and Knowledge *(1971), and* The Grasp of Consciousness *(1977).*

The Blank Slate

"*To acknowledge human nature, many think, is to endorse racism, sexism, war, greed, genocide, nihilism, reactionary politics, and neglect of children and the disadvantaged. Any claim that the mind has an innate organization strikes people not as a hypothesis that might be correct but as a thought it is immoral to think.*"

"*Everyone has a theory of human nature. Everyone has to anticipate the behavior of others, and that means we all need theories about what makes people tick. A tacit theory of human nature—that behavior is caused by thoughts and feelings—is embedded in the very way we think about people.*"

In a nutshell

Genetic science and evolutionary psychology show that human nature is not simply a result of socialization by our environment.

In a similar vein

Louann Brizendine *The Female Brain* (p 52)
Hans Eysenck *Dimensions of Personality* (p 90)
William James *The Principles of Psychology* (p 162)
Anne Moir & David Jessel *Brainsex* (p 204)
V. S. Ramachandran *Phantoms in the Brain* (p 232)

CHAPTER 40

Steven Pinker

The well-worn debate about "nature vs nurture" concerns whether we come into the world already wired to have certain traits or talents, or are totally molded by our culture and environment. In the 1960s and 1970s, parents took on board the expert advice of behavioral psychologists, anthropologists, and sociologists that environment was everything. They did their bit in creating a more peaceful, less sexist world by not letting their boys play with toy guns and giving them dolls instead. Anyone who has had children, however, knows that from day one each child is innately different to their siblings. Leading experimental and cognitive psychologist Steven Pinker wrote *The Blank Slate: The Modern Denial of Human Nature* to correct many wild claims about how malleable the human mind is, and to expose the myth that all our behaviors are the result of socialization.

Pinker likens our unwillingness to admit the fact of biologically determined human nature to the Victorians not wanting to discuss sex, and adds that it distorts public policies, scientific research, and even how we see each other. Yet he does not simply take the position that "genes are everything and culture is nothing." Rather, his intention is to reveal the facts about how much human nature is shaped by patterns already in the brain, compared to the extent to which we are shaped by culture and environment.

History of an idea

Enlightenment philosopher John Stuart Mill pointed out the importance of experience and the malleability of the human mind, picturing it as a sheet of paper ready to be written on, an idea that became known as the "blank slate." Pinker defines this concept as implying "that the human mind has no inherent structure and can be inscribed at will by society or ourselves." This contains the logical assumption that everyone is equal, and today we rightly accept that, barring severe mental or physical handicap, anyone can reach any station in life.

However, this acceptance also brought with it the view that the forces of biology play no role in accounting for how people are. In a famous passage from *Behaviorism* (1924), John B. Watson boasted that if he was given a dozen healthy infants he could shape them into anything he wanted as adults, whether doctor, artist, beggar, or thief.

Even though behaviorism is no longer psychological orthodoxy, its idea of a perfectly blank mental slate has stubbornly remained. It has become "the secular religion of modern intellectual life," Pinker says. Quite understandably, we don't want to go back to a time in which biological differences between people are highlighted, because this seemingly allows for racial, gender, or class discrimination and prejudice. However, the irony is that the vacuum the blank slate idea creates has allowed it to be used and abused by totalitarian regimes, which believe they can fashion the masses into anything they want. Pinker asks: How many more "human reengineering" projects do we need to go through before the blank slate idea is finally laid to rest?

We are what we are

Pinker points out that the human mind could never have been blank because it was forged through Darwinian competition over thousands of years. People whose brains made them cunning problem solvers with acute senses naturally triumphed over others and their genes lived on. Minds that were too malleable were "selected out" of existence.

Evolutionary biologists and some enlightened anthropologists have shown that a range of "socially constructed" factors such as emotions, kinship, and differences between the sexes are in fact to a large extent biologically pro-grammed. Donald Brown mapped out what he calls "human universals," traits or behaviors found in societies around the globe, regardless of level of development. These include conflict, rape, jealousy, and dominance, but also, as we would expect, conflict resolution, a sense of morality, kindness, and love. Human beings can be brutish *and* smart *and* loving because we have inherited the neurological makeup of people who engaged in skirmishes and battles and survived, yet who were also able to live in close community and be peace-makers. "Love, will and conscience," Pinker concludes, "are 'biological' too— that is, evolutionary adaptations implemented in the circuitry of the brain."

Wired at birth

A variety of research by neuroscientists has found just how minutely set our brains are when we are born. For example:

❖ Gay men usually have a part of the brain (the third interstitial nucleus in the anterior hypothalamus) that is smaller than normal. This part of the brain is recognized as playing a role in sex differences.

❖ Einstein's brain had large and unusually shaped inferior parietal lobules, which are important in spatial and numbering intelligence. In contrast, studies on the brains of convicted murderers found their brains to have a smaller than average prefrontal cortex, which governs decision making and inhibits our impulses.

❖ Identical twins separated at birth have been found to have very similar levels of general intelligence, verbal and mathematical skills, plus personality traits such as introversion or extroversion, agreeableness, and general life satisfaction. They even have the same personality quirks and behaviors such as gambling and television watching. This can be attributed not only to having exactly the same genetic material, but to the fact that the actual physiology of their brains (the valleys and folds and size of certain parts) is almost exactly the same.

❖ Many conditions once thought caused by a person's environment alone have now been found to have genetic roots. These include schizophrenia, depression, autism, dyslexia, bipolar illness, and language impairment. Such conditions run in families and cannot be predicted easily from environmental factors.

❖ Psychologists are able to divide personality into five main dimensions: introverted or extraverted; neurotic or stable; incurious or open to new things; agreeable or antagonistic; and conscientious or undirected. All five dimensions can be inherited, with 40–50 percent of our personality related to these genetic tendencies.

Pinker acknowledges our fear that if genes affects the mind, then we are completely controlled by genes in our thinking and behavior. However, genes only entail a certain *probability*—they determine nothing.

Final comments

Pinker compares the belief in a blank slate to the cosmology of Galileo's time, when people believed that the physical universe rested on a moral framework. In the same way, today's moral and political sensitivities have meant that scientific fact—the biological basis of human nature—has been swept aside in favor of ideology. We are afraid that these facts will lead to a "meltdown of values" and a loss of control over the sort of society we want to live in.

In response, Pinker recalls a line from Chekhov: "Man will become better when you show him what he is like." Only by sticking to the facts about who and what we are, supplied by biology, genetic science, and evolutionary psychology, can we move forward. There may be many aspects of human nature we don't like to admit, but denying them does not make them go away.

The Blank Slate is a big, fat book that will take you a while to read and fully understand. It is an intellectual *tour de force*, and may well shatter some of your cherished opinions or shift them to firmer scientific ground. It is easy to see why Pinker is in the top echelon of popular science writers today—his work combines scientific gravitas with a highly enjoyable style.

Steven Pinker

Born in 1954 in Montreal, Canada, Steven Pinker has degrees from McGill University and Harvard, where he obtained his PhD in experimental psychology. He is best known for his research into language and cognition.

Other books include The Language Instinct *(1994),* How the Mind Works *(1997),* Visual Cognition *(1985),* Lexical and Conceptual Semantics *(1992), and* Words and Rules: The Ingredients of Language *(1999). Until 2003 Pinker was a professor of psychology at Massachusetts Institute of Technology and director of its Center for Cognitive Neuroscience. He is currently the Johnstone Family Professor of Psychology at Harvard University.*

Phantoms in the Brain

"*There is something uniquely odd about a hairless neotenous primate that has evolved into a species that can look back over its own shoulder and ask questions about its origins. And odder still, the brain cannot only discover how other brains work but also ask questions about its own existence: Who am I? What happens after death? Does my mind arise exclusively from neurons in my brain? And if so, what scope is there for free will? It is the peculiar recursive quality of these questions—as the brain struggles to understand itself—that makes neurology fascinating.*"

In a nutshell

Unraveling the weirder cases in neurology can provide insights into how we perceive ourselves.

In a similar vein

CHAPTER 41

V. S. Ramachandran

What is consciousness? What is the "self"? Such big questions have been the preserve of philosophers for thousands of years. Now, with our increasingly advanced knowledge of the brain itself, science is entering the debate. V. S. Ramachandran, one of the world's top neuroscientists, says that the study of the brain is still too young to be knitted into some grand theory of consciousness in the way that Einstein came up with the theory of relativity, but that perhaps we are at the early stages of such an understanding.

Phantoms of the Brain: Probing the Mysteries of the Human Mind (written with Sandra Blakeslee) is Ramachandran's bestselling foray into the "mysteries of the mind," and it is a revelation. After reading this book you will never again be able to lift your arm or grab a cup and take it for granted. While scientists are apt to develop theories and then find the evidence to support them, Ramachandran does the opposite, purposely embracing the medical anomalies that current science cannot easily explain away. For readers with an interest in psychiatry, perhaps the standout message of the book is that many cases previously diagnosed as "madness" are now better understood as malfunctions in brain circuitry. Seemingly crazy behaviors may not mean that a person is insane.

As well getting us abreast of basic cranial anatomy, the book is also entertaining. Sherlock Holmes-loving Ramachandran admits he is not your average scientist, and includes quotations from Shakespeare and holistic healing guru Deepak Chopra, as well as references to Freud and Indian religion. Instead of counting off his academic accomplishments, he reveals his intellectual debt to popular science books. Such broad-mindedness makes *Phantoms of the Mind* a pleasure to read even if you have never heard of a thalamus or a frontal lobe. Though it can ramble a little, Ramachandran's informal style conveys his wonder and amazement at how a mass of wet gray cells can create self-awareness and consciousness.

The bits of the brain

Ramachandran notes an astounding fact: "A piece of your brain the size of a grain of sand would contain one hundred thousand neurons, two million axons and one billion synapses, all 'talking' to each other." He details the various parts, including the four lobes—frontal, temporal, parietal, and occipital—which form the "two halves of the walnut." Each of these hemispheres controls movement on the opposite side of the body—the left half controls movement on our right side, and vice versa. The left hemisphere tends to be that part of the brain that "talks" all the time, whether in thought or speech—the rational aspect of consciousness. The right relates more to our emotions and a holistic awareness of life. The frontal lobes are often considered the most "human" part of the brain, where the facilities of wisdom, planning, and judgment are based.

Other features include:

* The corpus callosum, a band of fibers that connects the two halves.
* The medulla oblongata at the top of the spinal cord, which regulates blood pressure, heart rate, and breathing.
* The thalamus, which sits at the center of the brain, and through which all the senses except smell are relayed; thought to be a primitive part of the brain.
* Underneath is the hypothalamus, related to "drives" such as aggression, sex, and fear, and also to hormonal and metabolic functions.

Despite this basic knowledge, Ramachandran notes, we are still not really sure how memory and perception occur. For example, are memories housed in particular parts of the brain, or is memory more holistic, involving the whole brain? The author suggests that both explanations may be true, in that while particular parts of the brain have certain jobs, it is in understanding how they interact that we begin to get closer to comprehending what makes up "human nature."

Phantom limbs

What does the title *Phantoms in the Brain* refer to? Ramachandran is best known for his work with people who experience phantom limbs. After an amputation or paralysis, a person will have all the normal sensations of the limb. The worst part is that people can actually experience a lot of *pain* in their phantom limbs. Ramachandran wondered how and where these phantoms were generated in the nervous system. Why does the sensation of having a limb remain "frozen" in the brain after amputation? Through experiments and work with patients, he explains phantom limb sensation thus: Essentially, the brain has a body image, a representation of itself that includes the arms and legs. When a limb is lost, it may take a while for the brain to catch up to this fact.

The conventional view is that, in shock over the loss of an arm or leg, the person engages in wishful thinking that the limb is still there, or goes into denial that it is lost. But Ramachandran points out that most of the people he sees are not neurotic. Indeed, he treated a woman, Mirabelle, who was born without arms and yet has vivid sensations of their use. This suggests that the brain is hard wired for limb coordination, and wants to enjoy that use even when sensory information tells it there is nothing there to move. He mentions another case where a girl frequently used her fingers to do simple calculations in arithmetic—except that she was born without forearms. What usually happens when a person loses a limb is that their brain keeps sending signals to use it, but in time the feedback that there is no limb is enough for the sensations to stop. Unlike amputees, however, people actually born without arms have never received the sensory feedback from their stumps that anything has changed, so their brain can keep on believing that they have arms to use.

Denial of limb paralysis

Anasognosia is a syndrome in which a patient, obviously sane in most respects, denies that their arm or leg has become paralyzed, but the denial happens only if it is their *left* arm or leg. What causes this disorder? Is it simply wishful thinking, and why only left limbs?

Ramachandran's explanation involves the division of labor between the two brain hemispheres. The left hemisphere works to create belief systems or models of reality. It is conformist in nature and "always tries to cling tenaciously to the way things were." Therefore when it has new information that does not fit into the model, it employs defense mechanisms of denial or repression in order to preserve the status quo. The job of the right hemisphere, conversely, is to challenge the status quo, and look for inconsistencies and any sign of change. When the right hemisphere is damaged, the left hemisphere is free to pursue its "denials and confabulations." Without the right's reality check, the mind wanders down a path of self-delusion.

Preserving the self at all costs

Ramachandran's work with people living with anasognosia seems to prove the Freudian idea of defense mechanisms; that is, thoughts and behaviors whose purpose is to protect the idea we have of ourselves. Neurology's task is to discover why people rationalize and avoid reality, only it involves considerations of brain wiring instead of the psyche. Patients in denial mode are the best way to research this because their defense mechanisms are concentrated and amplified.

The brain will do anything to preserve a sense of self. This evolved perhaps because the brain and nervous system involve so many different systems and a grand illusion is necessary to tie them all together. To survive, to be social, to mate, we need to have the experience of being an autonomous being who is in charge. However, the part of us that is in charge is in fact only a small part of our whole being; the rest carries on automatically, zombie like.

Weird and wonderful cases

Ramachandran refers to Thomas Kuhn and his landmark book *The Structure of Scientific Revolutions*, which noted that science tends to sweep the unusual cases under the carpet until they can be fitted into established theories. But Ramachandran's view turns this on its head: We can get closer to generalities by solving the strange cases. Consider just three he discusses:

❖ Hemi-neglect patients are indifferent to objects and events in the left side of the world, sometimes even indifferent to the left side of their own bodies. Ellen doesn't eat the food on the left of her plate, doesn't put makeup on the left side of her face, and doesn't even brush the teeth on the left side of her mouth. Though alarming to the people living with her, the condition is not uncommon and often follows strokes in the right brain, especially in the right parietal lobe.

❖ Capgras' delusion is a rare neurological condition in which the patient comes to regard their own parents, children, spouse, or sibling as imposters. The patient can identify these people, but does not experience any emotions when looking at their faces, which leads the brain to create the assumption that they must be imposters. In neurological terms, there is a disconnection between the face recognition area (in the temporal cortex) and the amygdala (a gateway to the limbic system), which helps generate emotional responses to particular faces.

❖ Cotard's syndrome is a bizarre condition where people believe themselves to be dead. They claim to smell their rotting flesh and see worms crawling in and out of their carcass. Ramachandran suggests this comes about through a connection failure between the sensory areas of the brain and the limbic system, which deals with emotions. Patients literally no longer feel any kind of emotion and therefore disengage from life. The only way their brain can deal with the situation is to presume that they are no longer alive.

What is consciousness?

Such bizarre cases, because they are easier to form experiments around, can reveal how the normal mind works. We take our representation of the world for granted, yet if our wiring goes slightly wrong, our whole conception of what is real and what is not can fail us. We begin to understand that our sense of reality is really more like an elaborate illusion designed to allow us to make our way in the world and survive. If we had to deal with the act of pure perception every second, we would never accomplish anything. We need to take for granted a basic amount of reality perception, and normally the brain delivers this brilliantly. It is only when things go wrong that we see how finely balanced consciousness is.

The amygdala and the temporal lobes play a vital role in consciousness. Without these, Ramachandran says, we would effectively be robots, unable to sense the meaning of what we are doing. We not only have circuitry in the brain that tells us how to do things, we also have pathways that tell us *why* we do them. He devotes a whole chapter to the link between increased religious feeling and temporal lobe epilepsy; when this part of the brain has a seizure, the person can suddenly see everything in an intense spiritual way. Establishing the different meanings of things, including the ability to discuss the fact that we are conscious, is what separates humans from all other animals, but if this facility is damaged or altered it is possible for people to experience *too much* meaning.

Final comments

Ramachandran says that the greatest revolution in the history of the human race will be when we really begin to understand *ourselves*. He has called for more funding of research into the brain, not simply to satisfy our curiosities, but because this is where "all the nasty stuff"—war, violence, terrorism—originates.

Neurology provides knowledge of the brain's anatomy and circuitry, and we need this as a starter. But the larger task is to understand the relationship between a mass of gray cells and the sense we have of being free-willed individuals. Even if, as Ramachandran suggests, the sense of self is an elaborate illusion created by our brain to ensure that our bodies survive, it is also how we interact with the universe at a philosophical or spiritual level. This is unique in the animal world, therefore we should treat it as precious and deserving of much further study.

V. S. Ramachandran

Vilayanur Ramachandran grew up in India and obtained his MD at Stanley Medical College in Chennai (Madras) and his PhD at Cambridge University. He is currently director of the Center for Brain and Cognition, University of California, San Diego, and adjunct professor in biology at the Salk Institute for Biological Studies. Awards include the Ariens-Kappers Medal from the Netherlands, a Gold Medal from the Australian National University, and a fellowship from All Souls College, Oxford.

Ramachandran has presented major lecture series around the world, including the 2003 Reith lectures in Britain and the Decade of the Brain lecture for the US National Institute for Mental Health. Phantoms in the Brain *was made into a two-part documentary shown on Channel Four in the UK and PBS in the US. Other books include* Encyclopaedia of the Human Brain *(2002),* The Emerging Mind *(2003), and* A Brief Tour of Human Consciousness *(2005).*

*Co-author **Sandra Blakeslee** is a science writer for* The New York Times, *specializing in cognitive neuroscience.*

On Becoming a Person

"If I can provide a certain type of relationship, the other person will discover within himself the capacity to use that relationship for growth, and change and personal development will occur."

"It seems that gradually, painfully, the individual explores what is behind the masks he presents to the world, and even behind the masks with which he has been deceiving himself... Thus to an increasing degree he becomes himself—not a façade of conformity to others, not a cynical denial of all feeling, nor a front of intellectual rationality, but a living, breathing, feeling, fluctuating process—in short, he becomes a person."

In a nutshell

A genuine relationship or interaction is one in which you are comfortable to be yourself, and in which the other person clearly sees your potential.

In a similar vein

Robert Bolton *People Skills* (p 32)
Milton Erickson *My Voice Will Go With You* (p 78)
Abraham Maslow *The Farther Reaches of Human Nature* (p 192)
Fritz Perls *Gestalt Therapy* (p 216)
Douglas Stone, Bruce Patton, & Sheila Heen *Difficult Conversations* (p 272)

CHAPTER 42

Carl Rogers

H ave you ever felt "healed" by a long conversation with someone? Has a particular relationship made you feel normal or good about yourself again? Chances are that these interactions happened in an environment that was trusting, open, and frank, and in which you were given full attention and really listened to without judgment.

Carl Rogers took these features of a good relationship and applied them to his work as a psychologist and counselor. The result was a revolutionary overturning of the traditional psychologist–patient model, which has had broader implications for successful human interaction.

Rogers came to his profession with the assumption that he would be the superior practitioner "solving" the problems of whoever came to see him. But he began to realize that this model was rarely effective, and that progress depended more on the depth of understanding and openness between the two people sitting in the consulting room. He was strongly influenced by existential philosopher Martin Buber and his notion of "confirming the other." This meant fully affirming a person's potential, the ability to see what he or she "has been created to become." Such a shift in emphasis toward the possible (as opposed to merely the problematic) made Rogers, along with Abraham Maslow, a major figure in the new humanistic psychology, with its notions that we take for granted today about personal growth and human potential.

On Becoming a Person: A Therapist's View of Psychotherapy is not a single piece of writing but a collection of pieces that Rogers wrote over a decade. It is the accumulated wisdom of a career in psychotherapy spanning over 30 years, and while not an easy read, once you get to grips with the ideas it can be very inspiring.

Letting everyone be themselves

In his training as a psychologist, Rogers naturally absorbed the idea that he controlled the relationship with the client, and that it was his job to analyze and treat patients as if they were objects. But he came to the conclusion that it was more effective to let patients (or clients) guide the direction of the process. This was the beginning of his famous *client*-centered (or person-centered) form of therapy.

Rather than trying to "fix" clients, Rogers felt it was much more important to listen absolutely to what they were saying, even if it seemed wrong, weak, strange, stupid, or bad. This stance allowed people to be accepting of all their thoughts, and after a number of sessions they would heal themselves. Rogers summed up his philosophy as "simply to be myself and to let another person be himself." As this was a time when the study of psychology revolved around the behavior of rats in laboratories, his belief in letting "crazy" patients set the direction was a big challenge to the profession, and many denounced his ideas.

If this were not enough, Rogers also shattered the idea of the calm and collected therapist who objectively listened to clients' issues. He asserted the right of therapists to have a personality, to express emotions themselves. If, for instance, in the course of the session he felt hostile or annoyed, he would not pretend to be a pleasant, detached doctor. If he did not have an answer, he would not claim he did. If the psychologist–client relationship was to rest on truth, he felt, it had to include the moods and feelings of the practitioner.

At the heart of Rogers' work was the view that life is a flowing process. The fulfilled person, he believed, should come to accept themselves "as a stream of becoming, not a finished product." The mistake people made was to try to control all aspects of their experience, with the result that their personality was not grounded in reality.

Becoming a real person

Rogers observed that when people first came to see a counselor for treatment, they usually gave a reason, such as issues with a wife or husband, or an employer, or their own uncontrollable behavior. Invariably, these "reasons" were not the real problem. There was in fact just *one* problem with all the people he saw: They were desperate to become their real selves, to be allowed to drop the false roles or masks with which they had approached life to date. They were usually very concerned with what others thought of them and what they *ought* to be doing in given situations. Therapy brought them back to their immediate experience of life and situations. They became a *person*, not just a reflection of society.

One aspect of this transformation was that people began to "own" all aspects of their selves, to allow totally contradictory feelings (one client admitted that she both loved and hated her parents). Rogers' dictum was "the facts are always friendly" when it comes to sorting out one's emotions and feelings; the real danger is in denying what we feel. As each feeling we are ashamed of comes to the surface, we realize it will not kill us to allow it to exist.

Final comments

Rogers' impact was felt way beyond his own field of counseling psychology. His emphasis on people needing to see themselves more as a fluid process of creation rather than a fixed entity was part of the climate of ideas that led to the 1960s counter-cultural revolution, and it is easy to see his influence on today's self-help writers. For instance, one of Stephen Covey's "7 habits of highly effective people" is *Seek first to understand, then to be understood,* a very Rogerian notion that progress in relationships is never made unless the people within them feel safe to speak their mind and be heard. And the rallying cry to "live your passion" can also in part be traced back to Rogers' focus on living a life that expresses who we truly are.

Rogers felt that psychologists had the most important job in the world, because ultimately it was not the physical sciences that would save us, but better interactions between human beings. The climate of openness and transparency he created in his sessions, if replicated within the family, the corporation, or in politics, would result in less angst and more constructive outcomes. But the key was a desire to really feel what the other person or party wanted and felt. Such a willingness, although never easy, could transform those involved.

Carl Rogers

Born in 1902 in Chicago into a strict religious household, Rogers was the fourth of six children. At the University of Wisconsin he studied agriculture, then history, but his aim was to enter the Christian ministry. In 1924 he enrolled at the liberal Union Theological Seminary in New York City, but after two years felt hemmed in by doctrinal beliefs and began taking courses in psychology at Columbia University's Teachers College. There he obtained his MA in 1928 and his PhD in 1931.

With doctoral work in child psychology, Rogers obtained a post as a psychologist at the Society for the Prevention of Cruelty to Children in Rochester, New York, working with troubled or delinquent children. Though not academically prestigious, the post enabled him to support his young family, and he stayed there for 12 years. In 1940, on the strength of his book Clinical Treatment of the Problem Child, *he was offered a professorship at Ohio State University. His influential* Counselling and Psychotherapy *was published in 1942, and in 1945 he began a 12-year posting at the University of Chicago, where he established a counseling center.*

Client-Centered Therapy *(1951) further heightened Rogers' profile, and in 1954 he received the American Psychological Association's first Distinguished Scientific Achievement Award. In 1964 he moved to La Jolla, California, for a position at the Western Behavioral Studies Institute, and remained in California until his death in 1987. He was also well known for his work on encounter groups, for his contribution to theories of experiential learning for adults, and for his impact in the area of conflict resolution.*

The Man Who Mistook His Wife for a Hat

"*Neurology and psychology, curiously, although they talk of everything else, almost never talk of 'judgment'—and yet it is precisely the downfall of judgment... which constitutes the essence of so many neuropsychological disorders.*"

"*The super-Touretter, then, is compelled to fight, as no one else is, simply to survive—to become an individual, and survive as one, in face of constant impulse... The miracle is that, in most cases, he succeeds—for the powers of survival, the will to survive, and to survive as a unique inalienable individual are, absolutely, the strongest in our being; stronger than any impulses, stronger than disease. Health, health militant, is usually the victor.*"

In a nutshell

The genius of the human brain is its continual creation of a sense of self, which persists even in the face of terrible neurological disease.

In a similar vein

Viktor Frankl *The Will to Meaning* (p 100)
William James *The Principles of Psychology* (p 162)
V. S. Ramachandran *Phantoms in the Brain* (p 232)

CHAPTER 43

Oliver Sacks

As neurologist Oliver Sacks notes at the beginning of *The Man Who Mistook His Wife for a Hat: And Other Clinical Tales*, which was a massive bestseller around the world and made him famous, he has always been equally interested in diseases and people. A lifetime's work convinced him that it is often less a matter of "what disease does this person have" than "what person has the disease." You can't examine a patient as if they are an insect—you are talking about a *self*.

This is all the more important in neurology, which involves a physical dysfunction of the brain that often affects a person's sense of who they are. Sacks' book aims to show that even when people's normal faculties desert them, they retain an unmistakable uniqueness. For Sacks, who has seen many strange cases, how people adapt or reinvent themselves in the face of mental or physical setbacks is amazing.

The book's 24 chapters detail a myriad of strange and interesting cases that give it the page-turning quality of a novel. Part One is titled "Losses" and it relates to people who have battled to return to a sense of normal self after suffering some debilitating loss of mental faculty.

Jimmie's lost decades

Without memories, is it possible to have a self? Sacks tells us about Jimmie G, a 49 year old admitted to the old people's home where Sacks was working in 1975.

Jimmie was a handsome, healthy man and very genial. He had been drafted into the US Navy on his graduation from school, and became a radio operator on a submarine. But while talking about his personal history and family life, Sacks noticed that Jimmie was talking in the present tense. He asked Jimmie what year it was, and received a reply to the effect of "1945 of course!" For Jimmie, the war was won, Truman was President, and he was looking forward to going to college on the GI Bill. He believed he was 19.

Sacks went out of the consulting room, and when he returned two minutes later Jimmie seemed to have no idea who he was. It was as if their session had never happened. Jimmie was apparently living in a permanent present, his longer-term memory stopping dead in 1945. With his ability in science he had no trouble solving complex problems in tests, but was disturbed by what seemed like major changes in the world around him. He could not deny that the man in the mirror was in his late 40s, but was not able to explain it. Sacks wrote in his notes that his patient was "without a past (or future), stuck in a constantly changing, meaningless moment." He diagnosed the condition as Korsakov's syndrome, damage to the mamillary bodies in the brain caused by alcohol. This affects memory, although the rest of the brain experiences no change.

Sacks located Jimmie's brother, who noted that Jimmy had left the navy in 1965 and without the structure it provided began drinking heavily. For some reason he had experienced retrograde amnesia, going back to 1945.

Sacks asked Jimmie to keep a diary so that he knew what he had done the day before, but this did nothing to give him a sense of continuity as it was as if the events he read about had happened to someone else. Jimmie seemed to have been "de-souled," something was missing in terms of a self.

Sacks asked the religious Sisters in the old people's home whether they thought Jimmie had indeed lost his "soul." Somewhat affronted, they responded by telling him to watch Jimmie when he was in chapel. When Sacks went to observe him there, it was a different Jimmie. He seemed lost in the act of worship and the ritual of the mass, somehow more "together" than before. The level of spiritual meaning was obviously enough to overcome his normal mental chaos. Sacks writes: "Memory, mental activity, mind alone, could not hold him; but moral attention and action could hold him completely." The same was true if Jimmie was in the garden or looking at art or listening to music.

Thus, although Jimmie was dead to the normal experience of memory that we feel gives us a sense of self, at other times he was evidently a fully alive person, gaining meaning from experience. Through a careful regimen of like activity he was able to maintain a sense of calm; there was still some part of him, whether a "soul" or a "self," that had found a way to exist despite the disease.

The self vs Tourette's

Part Two of *The Man Who Mistook His Wife for a Hat* is titled "Excesses." The cases looked at involve not a loss but a *superabundance* of certain functions: flights of fancy, exaggerated perception, irrational exuberance, manias. These "hyper-states" actually give the people involved a heightened sense of life that normality does not. While they are technically ill, such conditions give subjects a feeling of great wellbeing and zest for life (although in the back of their mind there is the feeling that it cannot last). The functions meld with the person's identity, so that some may not want to be cured.

One example of neurological excess is a syndrome first described in 1885. Gilles de la Tourette was a pupil of the pioneering neurologist Charcot (as was

Freud) and recorded a condition of tics, extravagant motions, cursing, funny noises, mad humor, and strange compulsions. There were varying degrees of the syndrome and it was manifested differently in each sufferer, from benign to violent. Because of its inexplicable strangeness and relative rarity, Tourette's was largely forgotten about by the medical world.

However, the condition never went away, and by the 1970s there was a Tourette's Syndrome Association that grew to have thousands of members. Research confirmed Gilles de la Tourette's initial belief that it was a brain disorder, centered in the "old brain" (the most primitive part of the human brain) involving the thalamus, hypothalamus, limbic system, and amygdala, the instinctual areas that together form the basic personality. Touretters were found to have more than the usual amount of excitor transmitters in their brains, particularly the transmitter dopamine (people with Parkinson's have a lack of dopamine). They can be treated with the drug haldol, which counteracts the excess.

But Tourette's is not simply a matter of brain chemistry, for there are times—such as when singing, dancing, or acting—that Touretters lose their normal tics and behaviors. In such cases, Sacks observes, the "I" of the person seems to overcome the "It" of their condition. Normal people assume that they *own* their perceptions, reactions, and movements, so it is easy to have a strong sense of self. Touretters are so constantly bombarded with uncontrollable impulses that it is amazing if their ego can manage to keep a sense of self. Some people, Sacks notes, are able to "take" Tourette's and incorporate it into their personality, even making use of the way it increases their rate of thinking; others are simply possessed by it.

Ray, 24, came to Sacks with a rather extreme version of Tourette's. Every few seconds he went into a convulsive tic, which frightened everyone except those who knew him well. With high intelligence, wit, humor, and sound character, Ray had got through school and college, and even married. He had obtained jobs but had been fired from each for his behavior, which was pugnacious and included blurting out swear words. His Tourette's was a "sudden intruder" that he did his best to incorporate into his weekend role as a jazz drummer, producing sometimes wild drum solos. The only time he was free of his condition was while asleep, just after sex, or when deeply engaged in some task.

Ray was willing to try haldol, but was worried what would be left of him if his tics went away. He had, after all, been like this since he was 4. When the drug began to work, Ray had to deal with himself as a different person. During the week, when at work, the drug made him a sober, tic-free—even dull—individual, but as he missed his old intense, convulsive, wise-cracking self (the only self he had ever known), he chose not to take the drug at the weekend so he could be "witty, ticcy Ray," as he called himself.

In this case, which was Ray's real self? Sacks does not offer an answer, but points to the story as an example of "resilience of spirit"—there is always some "I" inside us that seeks to assert itself, even in the face of an extreme "It" that can take us over.

The enchanted loom

Sacks notes that our current model for understanding the brain is based on the computer. But he asks: Could algorithms and programs account for the rich way we experience reality, in terms of the dramatic, the artistic, the musical? How do we reconcile the idea of memories being held in the back of the brain's computer, and *reminiscence* of the type expressed by Proust and other great writers in works of literature? Surely a human is not just a "thinking machine" but a being who lives through the meaningfulness of experience, having an "iconic" representation of reality that takes account of the vivid sense of things, their wholeness.

English physiologist Charles Sherrington imagined the brain as an "enchanted loom," constantly weaving patterns of meaning. This analogy, Sacks suggests, is surely better than the computer in explaining the very personal nature of experience and the way meaning is gained over time. His own analogy for understanding the brain is in terms of "scripts and scores." Our lives are akin to a script that makes sense of them as we go along, or perhaps a musical score that does the same. Ultimately, then, the prism through we which we grasp our lives should not be scientific or mathematical—this would do for the left brain's functioning, perhaps—but artistic. For the right brain, which is so deeply involved with the creation of this thing we feel to be the "self," meaning must be gained from "the artful scenery and melody of experience and action."

From one angle humans may look like advanced robots responding to their environment via a neurological computer, but to form a "self" requires something more. Sacks notes, "empirical science... takes no account of the soul, no account of what constitutes and determines personal being." It is this something that his patients were striving to get back or retain in the face of an invader.

Final comments

It is only when something goes neurologically wrong that we realize how much we take for granted the effort that goes into keeping up the feeling of being an autonomous being, always in control. We are a "miracle of integration," Sacks says, and often underestimate just how strong the will of the self is to assert itself in the face of the forces of disintegration such as neurological damage or disease.

Were the brain merely like a computer it could not bring itself back from the edge of chaos to reestablish a sense of meaning and independence. Rather than simply efficient operation, the human mind strives for wholeness; it seeks to create meaning out of random sensation and experience.

A painting or a symphony is not just oil paint or musical sounds—it is meaning. In the same way, over a lifetime human beings become something greater than the sum of their parts. When people die we mourn them not because they were "good bodies" but because they represented a certain meaning. This is what Sacks writes about: the undefined, meaningful, precious self.

Oliver Sacks

Born in London in 1933 to physician parents, Sacks gained his medical degree at Oxford University. Moving to the United States in the 1960s, he did an internship in San Francisco and a residency at the University of California, Los Angeles.

He settled in New York in 1965, and his work in the 1960s dealing with victims of "sleepy sickness" at the Beth Abraham Hospital in the Bronx is well known. He treated them with a then-experimental drug, L-dopa, which enabled many to come back to normal life. The experiments became the subject of his book Awakenings (1973), *which inspired the Harold Pinter play* A Kind of Alaska *and the Hollywood movie* Awakenings *starring Robert De Niro and Robin Williams.*

In addition to having a private practice, Sacks is a clinical professor of neurology at the Albert Einstein College of Medicine and an adjunct professor of neurology at the New York University School of Medicine. He is also a consultant neurologist to the Little Sisters of the Poor religious order. He has received many honorary doctorates.

Other books include Seeing Voices: A Journey into the World of the Deaf *(1990),* An Anthropologist on Mars *(1995),* The Island of the Colorblind *(1996), and* Uncle Tungsten: Memories of a Chemical Boyhood *(2001).*

The Paradox of Choice

"*Unlike other negative emotions—anger, sadness, disappointment, even grief—what is so difficult about regret is the feeling that the regrettable state of affairs could have been avoided and that it could have been avoided by you, if only you had chosen differently.*"

"*After millions of years of survival based on simple distinctions, it may simply be that we are biologically unprepared for the number of choices we face in the modern world.*"

In a nutshell

Paradoxically, happiness may lie in limiting our choices rather than increasing them.

In a similar vein

Daniel Gilbert *Stumbling on Happiness* (p 120)
Martin Seligman *Authentic Happiness* (p 254)

CHAPTER 44

Barry Schwartz

I s it good or bad to have choice? Based on the findings of psychologists, economists, market researchers, and experts working in the field of decision making, *The Paradox of Choice: Why More Is Less* begins with psychologist Barry Schwartz reeling off facts and figures on how many brands of cereal he can buy in his local supermarket, how many types of television set there are to choose from, and how the sales assistant doesn't know what he means when he asks for "regular" jeans in a clothing store, because with today's infinite variety there is no such thing as regular.

Schwartz cites a study in which two groups of college students were asked to rate boxes of chocolates. The first group was given only a small box of six chocolates to taste and rate, the second was given a box of thirty. The result: Those offered the smaller array were more satisfied with the chocolates they were given (they literally "tasted better") than those given the greater choice; they even opted to be paid for their time in the form of chocolates rather than cash.

This is a surprising result, since we would assume that greater choice makes us feel better about the choices available—it is a form of power. In fact, when offered less choice, we seem to be more satisfied with what we are given. Schwartz says that this indicates a particular type of anxiety found in rich, developed nations; that is, too much choice can adversely affect our happiness, since it does not necessarily mean greater quality of life or more freedom.

The rising cost of decisions

Schwartz skillfully points out the rising costs of having to make more and more decisions.

Technology was meant to save us time. Instead, he notes, it has brought us back to foraging behavior, as we now have to sift through thousands of options to find what we really need. Once, for instance, people had little or no choice in who provided their phone or utility services. Now the options are often so bewildering that we end up sticking with our old provider, just to avoid the hassle of considering all the various deals on offer.

In the world of work, while our parents may have spent their whole career with one company, today's generation routinely change jobs every two to five years. We are always on the lookout for something better, even if we are relatively happy in our current position.

In our romantic lives, again the choices are legion. Even when we have settled on "the one," we have to decide: Whose family should we live near? If both of us are working, whose job will determine where we live? If we have children, which one will stay at home with the kids?

Even with religion, Schwartz observes, we now follow the faith of our choosing, not the one our parents gave us. We can choose our identities, the very stuff of who we are. Although we are all born with a certain ethnicity, family, and class, such things are now seen as nothing more than "baggage." They used to tell others a lot about who we are, but now we can assume nothing.

With so many factors that were once out of our hands now choices, something else is brought into play—the human mind's susceptibility to error, which Schwartz goes to some lengths to illustrate. Given this susceptibility, the chances of making a "correct" decision most of the time are pretty low. The consequences of some mistakes may not be great, but others are; choosing a marriage partner, for instance, or which college to attend, will shape our lives. The more options we have, the more is at stake if we make the wrong decision. Our reasoning becomes, "If there was so much choice, how did we get it so badly wrong?"

Schwartz highlights three effects of the mushrooming in our choices and options:

❖ Each decision requires more effort.
❖ Mistakes are more likely.
❖ The psychological consequences of those mistakes are greater.

When "only the best" may not do

Given that we often make wrong decisions, and given the sheer number of decisions we need to make, surely it would make more sense to seek what is "good enough" rather than always seeking "the best"? Schwartz is fascinating in his division of people into "maximizers" and "satisficers."

Maximizers are people who are not happy unless they have obtained "the best," in whatever circumstance. This requires them to look at every option before coming to a decision, whether they are trying on 15 sweaters or 10 potential partners.

Satisficers are those who are willing to settle for what is merely good enough without needing to make sure there is some better option. Satisficers have certain criteria or standards that if met will make their decision for them. They don't have an ideological need to obtain "the best."

The concept of satisficing was introduced by economist Herbert Simon in the 1950s. Simon's fascinating conclusion was that, if you take into account the time required to make decisions, satisficing is actually the best strategy.

Schwartz wondered: Given the effort they put into choosing, do maximizers actually make better decisions? He found that objectively the answer was yes, but subjectively it was no. By this he means that maximizers may arrive at what they believe is the best available choice, but the choice will not necessarily make them happy. They may get a slightly better job with slightly higher wages, but they are unlikely to be satisfied with their position.

Being a maximizer can exact a bitter toll on our life. If everything we do has to be just right, we lay ourselves open for hefty self-criticism. We crucify ourselves for choices we made that didn't turn out right, and wonder why we never explored other options. The phrase "shoulda, coulda, woulda" sums up the state of many a maximizer in a tangle over their decisions, and Schwartz sums up their lot with a cartoon of a downcast freshman sporting a college sweater emblazoned with "BROWN, but my first choice was Yale."

In contrast, satisficers are more forgiving of themselves for mistakes, thinking, "I did what I did based on the choices before me." Satisficers don't believe they can create a perfect world for themselves, and so are less bothered when—as is normally the case—the world is imperfect.

Studies show that maximizers are generally less happy, less optimistic, and more prone to depression than their satisficing cousins. If you want more peace of mind and life satisfaction, be a satisficer.

Happy within limits

In the last four decades, Schwartz notes, Americans' per capita income (with inflation taken into account) has doubled. The number of homes with dishwashers has gone from 9 to 50 percent, and the number of those with air conditioning has increased from 15 to 73 percent. Yet there has been no measurable increase in happiness in the same period.

What does provide happiness is close relationships with family and friends, and there is the paradox: Close social ties actually *decrease* our choices and autonomy in life. Marriage, for instance, lessens our freedom to have more than one romantic or sexual partner. If this is so, it follows that happiness must be linked to having less, not more, freedom and autonomy. "Then can it be," Schwartz asks, "that freedom of choice is not all it's cracked up to be?" After all, the time we spend having to deal with our thousands of choices is time that we might have invested in our precious relationships. Choices may not only not improve the quality of our life, but may actually lessen it. In this equation, some level of constraint may be liberating.

Schwartz notes a study in which 65 percent of people said if they got cancer, they would want to control what treatment they received. But among people who actually have cancer, a full 88 percent did *not* want to choose. We think we want choice, but when we actually have it, it becomes less attractive—too much choice actually causes us distress.

Why everything suffers from comparison

Schwartz points to studies suggesting that the need to consider tradeoffs in choices makes people both indecisive and less happy. When confronted with two attractive options to buy, for instance, we are in fact not likely to buy either.

Perhaps the key to understanding why more choices do not make us more happy is that they increase our level of responsibility. In this context, there is significant research showing that we are happier when we know our decisions are not reversible. This is because when we make a decision that we know can't be changed, we work to justify that decision in our mind and put all our psychological weight behind it. Flexibility in our attitude to marriage, for example, will naturally weaken the marriage.

Once, if you lived and worked in a blue-collar neighborhood with all your friends in the same boat, you may have been pretty happy with your lot. But with the advent of television, the internet, and so on, we have an enormous pool of other people to whom we can compare ourselves. Even if we are relatively well off, there are always others who are richer. These are what Schwartz calls "upward comparisons," and they tend to make us jealous, hostile, and stressed, and to lower our self-esteem.

The "downward comparison," in contrast, involves us noting how fortunate we are compared to those who have little. Such comparisons boost mood and self-esteem and lower anxiety. Simply saying to ourselves every morning and evening "I have a lot of things to be grateful for" and thinking about them brings us closer to reality and increases our happiness. Grateful people are healthier, happier, and more optimistic than people who are not.

Because more choices bring more opportunities for comparison, the recipe for happiness is simple and twofold:

❖ make your decisions irreversible; and
❖ constantly appreciate the life you do have.

Final comments

An abundance of choice is one of the main sources of psychological pain, since it involves the anxiety of missed opportunities and the regret of paths not taken. Yet this peculiar sort of misery, which was once experienced by a relative few, has been turned into almost an epidemic with rising wealth and increased choice. In a global village, we can't help but wonder why we are not as famous as Madonna or as rich as Bill Gates, and how banal or restricted our own life seems by comparison.

If you are a maximizer, *The Paradox of Choice* could be a life-changing book. If you have put yourself into agonies over "if only," it could make you see that how satisfied you are with life depends not on the actual quality of your experiences, but whether or not you perceive a gap between how things are and how they might be.

Schwartz includes a couple of seven-question surveys so you can determine whether you are a maximizer or a satisficer. He admits that he is a satisficer, and it shows in his writing. *The Paradox of Choice* is clearly not the result of years of toil to get every line and phrase just right so that it would be the "best possible book" about choice and decision making—yet it succeeds because Schwartz has spent decades thinking about these issues and the impact they can have on our happiness.

Barry Schwartz

Schwartz received a BA from New York University in 1968, and a PhD from the University of Pennsylvania in 1971. In line with his own theory about limiting the number of choices in life, Schwartz has taught and researched at the one university for the last 35 years. In 1971 he became an Assistant Professor at Swarthmore College, Pennsylvania, and is currently its psychology department's Dorwin Cartwright Professor of Social Theory and Social Action. He also married young and has stayed married.

Schwartz has published many journal articles in the fields of learning, motivation, values, and decision making. Other books include The Battle For Human Nature: Science, Morality and Modern Life *(1986),* The Cost of Living: How Market Freedom Erodes the Best Things in Life *(2001), and* Psychology of Learning and Memory *(5th edn, 2001), with E. Wasserman and S. Robbins.*

Authentic Happiness

"This was an epiphany for me. In terms of my own life, Nikki hit the nail right on the head. I was a grouch. I had spent fifty years enduring mostly wet weather in my soul, and the last ten years as a walking nimbus cloud in a household radiant with sunshine. Any good fortune I had was probably not due to being grumpy, but in spite of it. In that moment, I resolved to change."

"[Very] happy people differ markedly from both average and unhappy people in that they all lead a rich and fulfilling social life. The very happy people spend the least time alone and the most time socializing, and they are rated highest on good relationships by themselves and also by their friends."

In a nutshell

Happiness has little to do with pleasure, and much to do with developing personal strengths and character.

In a similar vein

David D. Burns *Feeling Good* (p 58)
Mihaly Csiksentmihalyi *Creativity* (p 68)
Daniel Gilbert *Stumbling on Happiness* (p 120)
Daniel Goleman *Working with Emotional Intelligence* (p 130)
Barry Schwartz *The Paradox of Choice* (p 248)

CHAPTER 45

Martin Seligman

For every 100 scientific journal articles on sadness, there is only one for happiness. The science of psychology has always been about what is wrong with people, Martin Seligman notes, and in the last 50 years it has become pretty successful at diagnosing and treating mental illness. But this focus has meant that much less attention has been given to finding out what makes people happy or fulfilled.

For the first 30 years of his working life, Seligman himself worked in the field of abnormal psychology, but his work on feelings of helplessness and pessimism led him to research optimism and positive emotion, and how their presence could be increased in our life. This work caused him to rethink the larger purpose of psychology, and he is now known as the founder of the "positive psychology" movement. While his 1991 book *Learned Optimism* is an acknowledged classic, *Authentic Happiness: Using the New Positive Psychology to Realize Your Potential for Lasting Fulfilment* has also had a significant impact as a sort of manifesto for positive psychology, and has much to teach us about leading a good and meaningful life.

What causes happiness?

Collating hundreds of research findings, Seligman makes the following points about some of the factors conventionally thought to bring happiness.

Money

Purchasing power in the last 50 years has more than doubled in rich nations like the United States, Japan, and France, but overall life satisfaction has not changed at all. Very poor people have a lower level of happiness, but once a certain basic income and purchasing power has been reached ("barely comfortable"), beyond this point there are no increases in happiness on a par with extra wealth. Seligman notes: "How important money is to you, more than money itself, influences your happiness." Materialistic people are not happy.

Marriage

In a huge survey looking at 35,000 Americans over the last 30 years, the National Opinion Research Center found that 40 percent of married people said that they were "very happy." Only 24 percent of divorced, separated, and widowed people were "very happy." This statistic has been borne out in other surveys. Marriage seems to increase happiness levels independent of income or age, and that is true for both men and women. In one of Seligman's own studies, he found that nearly all very happy people are in a romantic relationship.

Sociability

Nearly all those who consider themselves very happy lead a "rich and fulfilling social life." They spend the least time alone among their peers. People who spend a lot of time alone generally report a much lower level of happiness.

Gender

Women experience twice as much depression as men, and tend to have more negative emotions. However, they also experience many more positive emotions than men. That is, women are both sadder and happier than men.

Religion

Religious people are consistently shown to be happier and more satisfied with life than the nonreligious, have lower rates of depression, and are more resilient to setbacks and tragedy. One study found that the more fundamentalist the adherents of a religion are, the more optimistic they are. Orthodox Jews are more hopeful for the future, for instance, than Reform Jews. The sermons in Evangelical Christian churches are rosier than those heard in regular Protestant congregations. This strong "hope for the future," as Seligman terms it, makes people feel really good about themselves and the world.

Illness

Illness does not affect life satisfaction or happiness nearly as much as we would think. Good health on its own is taken for granted, and only severe or multiple illnesses actually lower people's normal level of positive feeling.

Climate

Climate has no effect on happiness levels. Seligman remarks: "People suffering through a Nebraska winter believe people in California are happier, but they are wrong; we adapt to good weather completely and very quickly."

Finally, intelligence and a high education level have no appreciable effect on happiness. Neither does race, although some groups, such as black Americans and Hispanics, record lower levels of depression.

Character and happiness

All the above factors have traditionally been seen as the chief factors causing happiness, but the research indicates that together they account for only 8–15 percent of your happiness. Considering that the factors relate to very basic things about who you are and your circumstances in life, this is not a high figure. As Seligman suggests, it is great news for people who believe that their circumstances preclude them from being happy.

Instead of the above factors, Seligman's view is that genuine happiness and life satisfaction arise through the slow development of something you may last have heard your grandparents speak of: "character." Character is made up of universal virtues that are found across every culture and in the literature of every age. It includes wisdom and knowledge, courage, love and humanity, justice, temperance, and spirituality, among other things. We achieve these virtues by cultivating and nurturing personal strengths, such as originality, valor, integrity, loyalty, kindness, and fairness.

The idea of character has long fallen out of favor because it is thought to be old-fashioned and unscientific. But Seligman says that character traits or personal strengths are both measurable and acquirable, which makes them suitable for psychological study.

Strengths and happiness

There is a difference between talents, which we are born with and which we are therefore automatically good at, and strengths, which we *choose* to develop. We are more inspired, Seligman notes, by someone who overcomes a great obstacle to achieve something than by someone who does so because of simple natural ability. If will and determination are applied to our talent, we have pride in our accomplishments in the same way that we feel proud if we are complimented on our honesty. Talents alone say something about our genes, but virtues and developed talents (making the most of personal strengths) say something about *us*.

Through the refinement of our "signature strengths" (Seligman provides a questionnaire to identify them) we gain satisfaction in life, and happiness that is genuine. It is a mistake to spend our life trying to correct our weaknesses, Seligman says. Rather, the most success in life and real gratification—authentic happiness—come from developing your strengths.

Does your past determine your future happiness?

For most of the history of psychology, the answer to the above question has been a resounding "yes," from Freud to the "inner child" self-help movement. But the actual research findings point another way. For example, someone under the age of 11 whose mother dies has a slightly higher risk of depression later in life, but the risk is only slight, only if they are female, and even then it shows up in only about half the studies. And parental divorce has only a marginally disruptive effect on late childhood and adolescence, and this wanes in later life.

Adult depression, anxiety, addictions, bad marriage, anger—none of these can be blamed on what happened to us as a child. Seligman's message is a strong one: We are wasting our life if we think our childhood has delivered present misery or if it has made us passive about the future. What matters is the development of personal strengths that do not depend on the quality of our childhood or current circumstances.

Can happiness really be increased?

To some extent, the answer is no. A lot of research suggests that people have set ranges of happiness or unhappiness that are genetically inherited, just like people tend to revert, despite dieting, to a certain body weight. It has been shown that even after a big lottery win, a year later the winner will return to the level of sadness or happiness that was their natural lot before the windfall. Seligman is blunt in his assertion that our level of happiness cannot be lastingly increased, however what *is* possible is to live in the upper reaches of our natural range.

Expression of emotion

The idea of "emotional hydraulics" says we need to ventilate negative emotions, otherwise their repression will cause mental problems. In the West people think that it is healthy to express anger, and unhealthy to bottle it up. But Seligman writes that the reverse is correct. When we dwell on something that has been done to us and how we are going to express it, the feeling gets even worse. Studies of "Type A" (intense, driven) people have shown that it is *expressing* hostility, rather than feeling it, that is the link to having a heart attack. Blood pressure actually goes down when people decide to bottle up their anger or express friendliness. The Eastern way of "Feel the anger, but don't express it" is a key to happiness.

In contrast, the more gratitude you experience for people or things in your life, the better you feel. Seligman's students had a "Gratitude Night" in which they invited someone along they wanted to thank for what they'd done for them, in front of everyone. The people involved were generally on a high for days or weeks afterwards.

Our brain is built so that we can't make ourselves forget things just because we want to. But what we can do is forgive, which "removes and even transforms the sting." Not forgiving doesn't really punish the perpetrator, whereas forgiving can transform ourselves and bring back our life satisfaction.

Final comments

We now live in a world offering endless shortcuts to happiness. We don't have to make much effort to get a positive feeling. But strangely, the easy availability of pleasures tends to leave a yawning hole in many people's lives because it demands zero growth of them as people. A life of pleasures makes us a spectator, not an engager with life. We master nothing and do not use our creativity.

A real life is one where we seek out and respond to constant challenges. Seligman believes that we need a psychology of "rising to the occasion," or what he calls the "Harry Truman effect." When Truman took over from Franklin Delano Roosevelt after FDR died in office, against everyone's expectations he turned out to be one of the great American presidents. The position revealed his character and allowed his long-honed personal strengths to be utilized.

Whether or not we are happy every moment is largely irrelevant. Like Truman, what matters is whether or not we choose to develop what is within us—happiness does not "come along" but involves choices.

One of the best features of *Authentic Happiness* are the tests you can take to determine your levels of optimism, your signature strengths, and so on. Some readers won't like the vignettes of Seligman's personal life that are dropped in throughout the book, such as how he won the presidency of the American Psychological Association, but these do spice the book up and are often amusing. Amazingly, Seligman admits to having spent the first 50 years of his life as a grumpy person, but the mountain of evidence about happiness pushed him into thinking that he should apply it to himself!

We can no longer allow ourselves to believe that happiness is some mystical thing enjoyed only by other people—the paths to it are clearer than ever, and it is up to us to take responsibility for our state of mind.

Martin Seligman

Born in Albany, New York, in 1942, to parents who were both public servants, Seligman attended the Albany Academy for Boys in New York. He graduated summa cum laude in his BA from Princeton University in 1964, and received his PhD in psychology from the University of Pennsylvania in 1967. He has been a professor of psychology at UPenn since 1976.

In 1998 he was elected President of the American Psychological Association, from which he has also received two Distinguished Scientific Contribution awards. Past presidents of the Association include William James, John Dewey, Abraham Maslow, and Harry Harlow.

Seligman has authored 200 academic articles and 20 books, including Helplessness *(1975, 1993),* Abnormal Psychology *(1982, 1995) with David Rosenhan,* Learned Optimism *(1991),* What You Can Change and What You Can't *(1993), and* The Optimistic Child *(1995).*

He is married and has seven children.

1976

Passages

"*We are not unlike a particularly hardy crustacean. The lobster grows by developing and shedding a series of hard, protective shells. Each time it expands from within, the confining shell must be sloughed off. It is left exposed and vulnerable until, in time, a new covering grows to replace the old.*"

"*They had married at 25. And for several years they seemed to be typically eager people enjoying the new experiences of a typical marriage within the professional class. I knew them as friends, but nothing about the quality of threads that bound them as a couple. Except to sense that by now they had their tangles like the rest of us.*"

In a nutshell

What seem like very personal changes are often simply transitions from one season of life to another.

In a similar vein
Erik Erikson *Young Man Luther* (p 84)
Carl Rogers *On Becoming a Person* (p 238)

CHAPTER 46

Gail Sheehy

As a reporter, Gail Sheehy was sent to do a story on the conflict in Northern Ireland and got caught up in the events of Bloody Sunday, a Catholic civil rights march in Derry in which 14 civilians, mostly young, were killed by British forces. The day might have remained simply a bad memory were it not for the fact that right in front of her she witnessed a boy have his face blown away by a bullet.

Returning to America, she took stock of her life. At 35, suddenly her lifestyle of journalistic travel did not seem enough. She felt she had been a "performer" in life, not really participating in it, even though she had had a child and been married and divorced. Her "whole jerry built world," as she describes it, threatened to come apart. She had seen herself as an optimistic, fearless, loving, and ambitious "good" girl, but now she seemed to be looking at the dark side, at what was possibly halfway through her life.

With this terrifying thought, she wondered: What do other people do when this happens to them? Some seemed to push themselves harder with their careers, others began playing dangerous sports, or giving bigger parties, or taking younger people to bed. But she knew none of these things would fill the gaping hole in her psyche.

Passages: Predictable Crises of Adult Life was one of the publishing phenomena of the 1970s. The subject of adult life crises was not obviously hot, but with its distinctive cover, serialization in popular magazines, and Sheehy's talent for publicity, the book became a bestseller. The writing style is what you would expect of a classy magazine feature writer, pulling the reader in from the first page.

It is easy to dismiss *Passages* as dated pop psychology, but many readers are moved to exclaim "That's me!" as they recognize themselves in Sheehy's descriptions of the stages of adult life, and the book has made many feel less alone as they negotiate life's rapids.

Marker events and deeper crises

Sheehy realized that the terrible event she had witnessed was simply a trigger for deeper changes going on within her—some kind of midlife crisis. The experience sparked her interest in other people's turning points, and to her surprise she discovered that these "passages" happened with predictable regularity at roughly the same ages. People tried to blame external events for how they were feeling, but as with herself often the outer events were not the answer.

Dissatisfaction with a life that had seemed fulfilling only a couple of years before indicated that there was something going on at another level.

There was a difference between "marker" events such as graduation, marriage, childbirth, and getting a job—which all obviously have an impact, she noted—and developmental stages that change us from within. We tend to attribute how we are feeling to the marker event itself, when more often the event is simply a catalyst to move us forward into another stage of life. Though uncomfortable and often painful, we should not fear these transition times, as ultimately they mean growth. If we choose to embrace the change, at least we know we are growing.

Sheehy was influenced by psychologist Erik Erikson's idea that at certain turning points we can either move in the direction of personal growth, or stay with the security of what we know. Either way we experience change; the choice is whether we have more control and awareness over the process, or allow it to happen to us.

The stages of childhood and adolescent development have been exhaustively identified, Sheehy notes, but not much attention has been given to *adults*. To write *Passages*, she immersed herself in the literature on life cycles, read a mountain of biographies, and began collecting life stories of people between the ages of 18 and 55. As most of the research related to men, she made sure that the book included the stories of plenty of real women. She also explored life changes within the dynamic of a couple, and the stresses this can place on relationships.

Changing through the decades

To make the life stages easier to grasp, Sheehy's innovation was to break them down into easy-to-understand decades.

The twenties

In our 20s we have to work out our path in life, discovering the ways of being or doing that give us a sense of aliveness and hope. We are likely to go one of two ways: to do what we "should" in terms of family and peer expectations; or to pursue adventure and "find ourselves." We either seek security and commitments, or we avoid commitment altogether.

A man in his 20s feels that he has to do well in his work or be ridiculed. His greatest love is his career. While women may not have the same pressure, if they go the stay-at-home, child-rearing route they may end up with less self-esteem compared to their male partners, who have very clear feedback on how they are doing. Women can begin to feel cut off from the world and valued less for who they are than for their role as a mother. While men in their 20s feel they can do anything, women often lose the confidence they had as adolescents.

Couples in their 20s feel that they will overcome all obstacles, yet behind this bravado is often a level of doubt or insecurity. Women often go for a "stronger one," a man who can replace their family ties to some extent. But in doing this women avoid their own work of development, and may have to face it later; for example, the woman who marries young and changes significantly in her 30s, coming out of her husband's shadow.

When we near the "big Three O," Sheehy notes, normally we feel dissatisfaction with the career or personal choices we have made, as if we have outgrown some of them. We have to chart new directions or make new commitments. We may want to change career, or go back to work, or start having children. If we have been in a relationship since our early 20s, we may get the "seven-year itch."

Generally, Sheehy warns that if we don't have some kind of identity crisis in this "pulling up roots" period of our 20s, we will inevitably have one at a later point when it may take a greater toll.

The thirties

The 30s are the "deadline decade." We suddenly realize, as Sheehy herself did, that there will be an end to our life at some point. "Time starts to squeeze," which refines our priorities. While the 20s are the "anything is possible" decade, the 30s let us know that we may not have all the answers, and this can be a shock. We demand authenticity of ourselves and begin to see that we can't blame anything on anyone else. Women may have bet everything on their marriage and family, but their assertiveness may begin to rise, as they realize that their life is not simply about pleasing others or living up to cultural norms.

Life usually becomes a little more settled. We may tie ourselves to a certain career, and we may buy a house to put down roots. Men may feel that this is their "last chance" decade in which they must become partner in the firm instead of the assistant, or become an established author instead of being "young and promising."

People of both sexes arrive at the conclusion that life is a lot more serious and difficult than they understood it to be in their 20s. The ages between 37 and 42 are peak years of anxiety for most people. In Sheehy's research, the age of 37 in particular came up again and again as a crisis year.

The forties

We feel a sense of stagnation or disequilibrium when we enter midlife. Those who have seemed to climb effortlessly upwards find that life catches up with them. Having intensely pursued a career, we may think, "Was it really worth it? Why don't I have children?" Many a man turning 40 feels underappreciated and burdened, with the sentiment, "Is this all there is?"

The good news is that in the mid-40s a certain equilibrium returns. For those with a renewed purpose these can be the best years, as we see that no one can "do it" for us, and therefore we finally become master of our destiny in a more assured way. The motto of this stage in life, Sheehy suggests, might be "No more bullshit"—we are who we are.

A woman is likely to get more assertive, while a man may want to get more emotionally responsive, having put his emotional needs aside to strive for a career. The opposite sex can begin to lose its magic power over us, since we can now incorporate the opposite of our own sex within our psyches. We feel more independent, less likely to fall in love, but more capable of devotion to another person.

Trying to become ourselves

The search for self-identity is what Jung called "individuation" and Maslow termed "self-actualization." Sheehy's phrase for it is "gaining our authenticity." Whatever we want to call it, this is the aim of the successive life stages.

At each point we have the chance either to define ourselves further, or to succumb to the ideas of the group and its expectations. We have two selves: the one that wants to merge with others and things, and the one that seeks creative independence and freedom. Throughout our lives we may alternate between one and the other, or they compete within us at the same time.

Many of our decisions may simply reflect a desire to get away from or differentiate ourselves from our parents. People often marry for this reason. Intriguingly, of all the couples Sheehy interviewed, none married for love alone. There was always a stronger reason: "My girlfriend expected it," "My family wanted it," "In my culture, it is what you do at my age." For both sexes, a common reason was, "I need someone to take care of me." The problem with this is that we come to judge a spouse on how well they take the place of a parent, rather than on their own merits as a person. This allows us to think, when we are not happy, that "he/she won't let me do it," instead of taking responsibility for ourselves.

To make things more difficult, a couple's development cycles will rarely be in tandem. When the man is growing and enthused, for instance, the woman may be going through a time of doubt and instability, and vice versa. A common result is that we blame each other for what we are experiencing, when the major change is really internal.

Final comments

The chief enjoyment of *Passages* lies in the vignettes of actual people, individuals and couples, whom Sheehy interviewed. Though these are now obviously out of date, there is still a timeless quality about the stories. She includes a quote from novelist Willa Cather: "There are only two or three human stories, and they go on repeating themselves as fiercely as if they had never happened before." Having greater awareness of the stages of our lives does not mean that we are giving up all control; what it does is allow us to see that the problems that seem unique to us have probably been experienced by millions of others, and may have more to do with our time of life than the other people or situations we may be blaming.

Since *Passages* was published, timeframes for the stages of life seem to have changed. In mid-1970s America, the average marrying age was 21 for women and 23 for men. Today, with people settling down much later, it is almost expected that you spend a few years of your 20s and maybe even 30s discovering what you want to do and having minimum commitments. It is also more common for women to delay having children, or not to have them at all. And Sheehy did not consider life much beyond the 40s, an age when—given longer life expectancy—life really begins for many people.

This begs the question: What form will transition points or life crises take when, as scientists predict, people are healthy even beyond the age of 100? Perhaps we will become more willing to see life as a series of inevitable transitions, separated by relatively stable periods. Maybe we will abandon the old distinction between "youth" and "maturity" and instead see ourselves as fluid, continually evolving creations instead of having a fixed identity.

Gail Sheehy

Sheehy is well known for her incisive magazine character profiles, which have included George W. Bush, Mikhail Gorbachev, Newt Gingrich, Margaret Thatcher, and Saddam Hussein. A long-time contributing editor to Vanity Fair, *she has won a number of awards for her journalism.*

Passages *was on the* New York Times *bestseller list for three years and was translated into 28 languages. It was named one of the ten most influential books of our time in a Library of Congress survey.*

Sheehy's other books include Pathfinders *(1981),* The Silent Passage: Menopause *(1992),* Understanding Men's Passages *(1998),* Hillary's Choice, *a profile of Hillary Clinton (1999), and* Sex and the Seasoned Woman *(2006). To take account of changes in culture and society, Sheehy provided an updated version of her work in* New Passages *(1995).*

Beyond Freedom and Dignity

"*Twenty-five hundred years ago it might have been said that man understood himself as well as any other part of his world. Today he is the thing he understands least. Physics and biology have come a long way, but there has been no comparable development of anything like a science of human behavior.*"

"*The nomad on horseback in Outer Mongolia and the astronaut in outer space are different people, but, as far as we know, if they had been exchanged at birth, they would have taken each other's place.*"

"*Although cultures are improved by people whose wisdom and compassion may supply clues to what they do or will do, the ultimate improvement comes from the environment which makes them wise and compassionate.*"

In a nutshell

Like all animals, humans are creatures shaped by their environment—but we also have the ability to adjust or create new environments.

In a similar vein

CHAPTER 47

B. F. Skinner

One of the most controversial figures in the history of psychology, Skinner was famous for seeing humans as no different to animals. Even as a young psychology student he rebelled against what he saw as the romantic idea that human action was the result of inner emotions, thoughts, and drives (the "psyche"). Rather, as Pavlov's work indicated (see p 210), humans should be analyzed as animals interacting with their environment.

Yet in his theory of "operant behavior," Skinner went beyond Pavlov. Humans were not simply reflexive machines, he argued, but also changed their actions according to the *consequences* of their behavior. This philosophical distinction allowed for the incredible variety of human difference, while allowing adhesion to the behaviorist line that humans were basically creatures of their environment.

Skinner became behaviorism's most famous exponent, partly because he was a brilliant experimenter (pigeons were to Skinner as dogs were to Pavlov), but also because he could write. His combination of technical skill and a desire to see the big, philosophical picture was unusual, the result being esteem by his peers *and* the production of bestselling books that made people think.

A technology of behavior?

Beyond Freedom and Dignity was written at a time when issues such as overpopulation and nuclear war seemed a terrible threat. The very survival of the human species appeared to be at stake. What could be done?

While Skinner noted that it was natural to try to solve the world's problems by advances in technology or science, he asserted that real solutions would only emerge when people's *behavior* changed. Having contraceptives was no guarantee that people would use them; access to more advanced agricultural techniques did not ensure their application. *People* caused problems, yet it was not enough to create a better relationship between people and technology, or even to personalize technology. Rather, what was needed was a "technology of behavior."

Skinner noted how little psychology had advanced compared to physics and biology. In ancient Greece, people's understanding of what made them tick was as good as their understanding of how the universe worked. But today, while our knowledge in the hard sciences had moved ahead by leaps and bounds, our understanding of ourselves was no greater.

Creating a new psychology

Skinner believed that the science of psychology looked for the causes of behavior in the wrong place, and was therefore fundamentally in error. We no longer believe that people are possessed by demons, he noted, yet psychology was still based on the view that our behavior is determined by "indwelling agents." In Freudian psychology, for instance, the actions of one human body are driven by the interaction of not one but three of these inner elements (the id, the ego, and the superego). The medieval alchemists attributed to each person a mystical "essence" that shaped behavior, and today we believe in something called "human nature" that is said to move us. The result is that we are told that all the world's problems boil down to changing inner attitudes: overcoming pride, lessening the desire for power or aggression, increasing self-respect, creating a sense of purpose, and so on.

Yet for Skinner, all such conceptions of human beings were "prescientific." Physics and biology long ago gave up the idea that objects or animals are driven by an "inner purpose," yet we still say that a nonphysical feeling "causes" a physical act of aggression. It is a given that states of mind cause behavior. This "mentalism," as Skinner called it, meant that behavior was not studied in its own right.

Psychology of environment, not mind

Skinner noted that if we ask someone why they went to the theater, and they say "I felt like going," we accept this as an explanation. However, it would be more accurate to know what has made them go in the past, what they have read or heard about the play, and any other environmental factors that led to their decision to go. We think of people as "centers from which behavior emanates," when it is more accurate to see people as the end result of the influence of the world on them, and their reactions to the world. We don't need to know about a person's state of mind, feelings, personality, plans, or purposes in order to study behavior. To know why people act as they do, Skinner suggested, all we need to know is what circumstances caused them to act in a certain way.

Our environments are not simply the setting for our self-willed actions, but shape us into what we are. We change the course of our actions according to what we learn is good for us (our survival) or not so good. We believe that we act autonomously, but it is more accurate to observe that we act according to what "reinforces" our actions. Just as a species prospers or withers depending on how it interacts with and adapts to its environment, so the person we are is the result of our interaction and adjustment to the world we are born into.

Better environments, not better people

What is meant by Skinner's title, *Beyond Freedom and Dignity*? He acknowledged that the "literature of freedom" had been successful in the past in inspiring people to rebel against oppressive authorities. These writings naturally linked control and exploitation of humans with evil, and escape from that control as good.

But Skinner found something missing from this simple equation: We have actually designed our societies to involve many different forms of control that are based on aversion or inducement instead of outright force. Most of these more subtle forms of control people are willing to submit to because they ultimately serve their own social or economic ends. For instance, millions of people hate their jobs, yet they stay because of the consequences of not working; they are controlled by aversion rather than force, but controlled nevertheless. Nearly all of us live in communities, and to maintain themselves communities require a certain amount of control. Would it not be better to admit that we are not as free and autonomous as we would like to believe, to be open about choosing the forms of control to which we will submit? Why not get scientific about the forms of control that are most effective? This is the essence of behaviorism.

Punishment, according to Skinner, is a clumsy way of dealing with people who have not understood and reacted properly to society's larger goals. A better way is to change behaviors by reinforcing alternative courses of action. You can't give people a purpose or intention, but you can make some behaviors more attractive and others less so. Given the massive shaping power of the environment, Skinner wrote, it is a much better use of a culture's resources to "proceed to the design of better environments rather than of better men." We can't change a mind. We can only change the environment that may prompt someone to act differently.

Links in a chain

Skinner's point was that we spend a huge amount of energy upholding the ethic of individualism, when as a species we could achieve more by focusing on the type of environmental situations that produce remarkable achievements. He did not deny that there were great people who had made tremendous contributions, but he believed we would produce more such people not through an ethic of triumphant individualism, but through creating more conducive environments.

Skinner put it in these terms: "Although cultures are improved by people whose wisdom and compassion may supply clues to what they do or will do, the ultimate improvement comes from the environment which makes them wise and compassionate." What we consider "traits of character" are really the culmination of a history of environmental reinforcement. In short, Skinner believed that we put human beings on a pedestal. While Hamlet was made to say of man, "How like a god!", Skinner also notes Pavlov's observation of us, "How like a dog!" Skinner felt we were more than a dog, and marveled at the complexity of human beings and their actions—yet he also said we were no different than dogs in being able subjects of scientific analysis. While poets, writers, philosophers, and authors had long celebrated the inner motive that guided the human self, Skinner's clinical definition was: "A self is a repertoire of behavior appropriate to a given set of contingencies."

What about conscience and morality? Skinner had this to say: "Man is not a moral animal in the sense of possessing a special trait or virtue; he has built a kind of social environment which induces him to behave in moral ways."

Although Skinner believed that each person was unique, down to every fiber of their body, he also felt this was missing the point. Each individual was a stage in a process that began a long time before they came into existence, and would continue long after they had gone. Within this larger context, was it not foolish to make a lot of noise about individuality? Surely it was more productive to see ourselves as a link in a long chain, shaped by our genetic history and environment, but also with the capacity to shape that environment in turn.

Final comments

Beyond Freedom and Dignity attracted a great deal of controversy when it was published, as it seemed to undermine the ethic of personal freedom. But were Skinner's ideas really that dangerous?

Freedom is a wonderful concept, but cultures and communities, by their very nature, require a dense apparatus of control to survive. Skinner described the evolution of a culture as "a kind of gigantic exercise in self-control," which was no different to the way that individuals organize their life to ensure their continuing existence and prosperity. Control was therefore a fact of life; his point was that it was possible to create cultures in which there were less aversionary controls such as the threat of punishment, and more positive ones that people freely agreed to. This was the scenario sketched out in his fictional Utopian classic *Walden II*. On the surface this sounds like early communism, but the key difference is that communist ideology was built around a misplaced faith in human nature. In contrast, behaviorism aimed to analyze scientifically how humans really act; any culture deriving from its ideas would not be built on a vain hope but observable facts.

One of Skinner's most fascinating points, which perhaps has relevance for our times, is that cultures that put freedom and dignity above all else, that take the "romantic" view of psychology concerning the freedom of the inner person and so on, risk being surpassed by other cultures that put their survival first. Countries may pride themselves on being "right," but such inflexibility does not always guarantee a future.

If you have always firmly held to an Ayn Rand-like belief in personal responsibility, free will, and the primacy of the individual, Skinner may cause a revolution in your thinking. Did he actually believe that the idea of the individual should be abolished? No, simply that of the "inner person" who is said to heroically manipulate their environment to their ends. We don't change humans by being scientific about them, Skinner remarked, any more than Isaac Newton's analysis of a rainbow lessened its beauty.

While Skinner remains unfashionable, he had a major influence across a range of areas. In time the popular view of him as the cold man of the lab may well change to reflect the reality of someone who knew that there was too much at stake to gamble with ideologies and romantic ideas of humanity. In aiming to find a scientific basis for improving our lot, he was a genuine humanitarian.

B. F. Skinner

Burrhus Frederic ("Fred") Skinner was born in 1904 in Susquehanna, a small railroad town in Pennsylvania, United States. His father was a lawyer and his mother a housewife.

Skinner attended Hamilton College in New York, graduating with a BA in English, and had dreams of becoming a writer. He lived a bohemian life in Greenwich Village in New York for a while, but with no real success in his poetry and short story writing, and having come across writings by Pavlov and John B. Watson, behaviorism's founder, he applied to study psychology at Harvard University.

At Harvard he completed his Master's degree and doctorate, undertook research, and taught. It was at the University of Minnesota (1937–45) and the University of Indiana (1945–8), where he was chairman of the psychology department, that Skinner did much of the experimentation that made him well known. He returned to Harvard in 1947 as William James Lecturer, later becoming Edgar Pierce Professor of Psychology.

Skinner's many honors included the National Medal of Science, awarded in 1968 by President Lyndon B. Johnson. Books include The Behavior of Organisms *(1938),* Walden II *(1948),* Verbal Behavior *(1957, famously criticized by Noam Chomsky),* Science and Human Behavior *(1953), and* About Behaviorism *(1974). His three-part autobiography was published as* Particulars of My Life *(1976),* The Shaping of a Behaviorist *(1979), and* A Matter of Consequences *(1983).*

Skinner died of leukemia in 1990.

Difficult Conversations

"[The] people we've worked with… report less anxiety and greater effectiveness in all of their conversations. They find they are less afraid of what others might say. They have a heightened sense of freedom of action in tough situations, more self-confidence, and a stronger sense of integrity and self-respect. They also learn that, more often than not, dealing constructively with tough topics and awkward situations strengthens a relationship. And that's an opportunity too good to pass up."

In a nutshell

Difficult conversations carry the chance to transform a relationship, but only if you shift your stance from delivering a message to discovering why the other person is acting as they are.

In a similar vein
Robert Bolton *People Skills* (p 32)
Robert Cialdini *Influence* (p 62)
Susan Forward *Emotional Blackmail* (p 94)
Carl Rogers *On Becoming a Person* (p 238)

CHAPTER 48

Douglas Stone, Bruce Patton, & Sheila Heen

L ife is full of difficult conversations, yet we all avoid having them. Is there anything we can do to make them less difficult? *Difficult Conversations: How to Discuss What Matters Most* grew out of 15 years of work at the Harvard Negotiation Project, which also produced the 4 million-selling negotiation title *Getting to YES*. As part of the project, authors Stone, Patton, and Heen had a goal to find out how one-on-one communication could be made vastly more effective. They worked with students and professionals on their toughest conversations and encounters to produce new techniques for understanding conflict and interaction.

Although their backgrounds are in negotiation, mediation, and law, the authors of *Difficult Conversations* based their work on findings in organizational behavior, cognitive therapies, social psychology, and communication theory, particularly as they relate to communication dynamics within families. Psychologists Aaron Beck, David Burns, and Carl Rogers are mentioned among their many influences. The result is a remarkable guide that lets us in on the powerful techniques that have been employed in world troublespots to bring opposing sides together and forge new futures.

What is a difficult conversation?

Defining their subject as "anything you find it difficult to talk about" and try to avoid, Stone, Patton, and Heen note that for most people there are no simple or easy ways to:

❖ Fire someone.
❖ Break up a relationship.
❖ Confront your mother-in-law.
❖ Raise the issue of prejudice.
❖ Ask for a raise.

They liken a difficult message to throwing a hand grenade, which "Coated with sugar, thrown hard or soft is still going to do damage." Throwing it "tactfully" is no answer. Neither is it enough to "be diplomatic." We can't hope that our niceness will ensure that all goes smoothly. So what is the answer? Instead of throwing hand grenades, or "delivering messages" to people, Stone, Patton, and Heen promise to transform our difficult conversations by replacing them with what they call *learning conversations*. While this new way of communicating involves work to master it, it can dramatically reduce the stress of our interactions with other people. Learning conversations increase the confidence of all parties involved because the air of blame disappears, to be replaced by listening. This naturally raises trust and confidence all round. Conflict can be transmuted into understanding.

Three conversations in one

Difficult Conversations is based on the idea that "each difficult conversation is really three conversations." Above and beyond the actual words that are spoken, these other conversations are mostly internal and involve our perception of the encounter and what it means to us.

The "What happened?" conversation

This is when we go through our perceptions of the outcome—who said what, who is to blame, who is right. The problem is, we never question our version of who is right or wrong, and neither do we question that difficult conversations are about "getting the facts right" as opposed to what they *mean*. They are essentially conflicts of perceptions, interpretations, and values.

However, when we shift our attitude from delivering a message to finding out how the other person sees things differently, immediately the conversation becomes less heavy and emotionally barbed. Instead of offering our interpretation of the situation as "the truth," we offer it as our perception.

The feelings conversation

How do I feel about what was said? Were the other person's feelings valid? Are my feelings valid? What should I do if the other person is angry or hurt?

Many strong feelings enter into a difficult conversation, but these are often not expressed. When two people are talking, there is a parallel conversation going on in each of their minds concerning their feelings about the interaction.

Given that feelings cloud judgment and make things uncomfortable, shouldn't we try to steer clear of feelings altogether? Should we just try to stick to "the facts"? While this is a nice idea, Stone, Patton, and Heen note that leaving feelings out of difficult conversations is like having an opera without music: We may get the plot, but we totally miss the point. They point out that "difficult conversations do not just *involve* feelings, they are at their very core *about* feelings."

The identity conversation

Does what we have just said to the other person, or what they have just said to us, shake our sense of who we are? Has the conversation made us suddenly feel we are at heart a bad person, or incompetent, or a traitor? The identity conversation is about self-image or self-esteem.

If we are having a meeting with our boss to request a raise, we get nervous. This is because whether or not we get the raise will involve our boss's—and our own—consideration of our value. It's not just about the money, it's about *us*. Similarly, if we are the boss and have to fire someone, what does this act say about us as a person: that we are a heartless bastard? Firing someone is only partly about them. Just being aware of the "identity conversation" we have with ourselves can have a great effect on our difficult conversations. If we know it's also about our self-image, we are less likely to suddenly lose our balance on an emotional level.

When we understand that difficult conversations are actually three conversations going on at once, and when we are aware of the mistakes we can make in each type, Stone, Patton, and Heen believe that we will shift the focus of our conversations. They become less about right or wrong and more about learning what is at issue. Most difficult conversations involve a strong element of pointing the finger, but all this does is create more conflict, denial, and incorrect judgments. Blame can only ever cloud the matter, preventing us from finding out what went wrong.

The alternative to blame is joint contribution. Instead of trying to find out where the finger should be pointed, we work to ascertain *what contributed* to the problem. This is a subtle shift from the persons to the issues involved. Our stance turns from proving a point or "putting someone in their place" to curiosity and joint problem solving.

Listening to each other's stories

To get from blame to contribution first involves listening. How does the other person see the situation, and what happened to form that perception?

One of the authors' rules is: People never change without first feeling understood. Telling someone to do something makes it less likely that they will, while understanding may just break down their wall of resistance. For instance, Trevor is annoyed that Karen is not handing in her paperwork on time. But for her part, Karen will only consider this important if Trevor stops to understand why she might be doing that. When they do actually sit down to talk about it, Trevor finds out that Karen is not doing it because she is lazy or spiteful, but because she has to put her demanding clients first. She in turn hears from Trevor how nonsubmission of the paperwork causes him all sorts of problems. When they are both understood, they are in a position to work something out—but not before. As Stone, Patton, and Heen put it: "To get anywhere in a disagreement, we need to understand the other person's story well enough to see how their conclusions make sense within it."

Surely, though, there will be times when we know we are right, and the other person is wrong. Aren't we right if we try to stop our daughter from smoking? Perhaps, but in many situations being right is not the issue. Our daughter will know smoking is bad for her as much as we do—the conflict may be more about getting rid of her "good girl" image and becoming more independent. Once the daughter feels that her change in identity is understood, she may have no need to continue smoking.

Don't get emotional—express feelings

Careful expression of feelings is a vital part of making difficult conversations productive. Stone, Patton, and Heen have many wise things to say on this, including:

❖ If we try to suppress feelings, they tend to come out anyway through change of voice tone, body language, and facial expression.

❖ We shouldn't confuse being emotional with the clear expression of emotions, such as "I feel hurt" or "I feel angry." And do not translate feelings into judgments about the other person.

❖ It is very hard for some people to begin a sentence or conversation with the words "I feel," but saying them may make the other person really listen.

❖ We shouldn't disavow the feelings we have—they are real. Be aware "that good people can have bad feelings."

❖ Our feelings are as important as others' feelings. Yet when we deny their validity we can sabotage our relationships. For example, if we bury anger for our spouse, we will not be able to love them properly again until we express it.

The dangers of "all or nothing" thinking

Difficult conversations, the authors note, are a threat to our identity. Their scariness comes not only from us having to face an issue with another person, but facing up to the truth of "the story we tell ourselves about ourselves." Self-image is actually hardwired to our adrenal response, which explains why we may feel a rush of anxiety or anger or a sudden desire to flee the scene.

If, for instance, we go to the boss to ask for a raise, and she says no on the basis that she has questions about our performance this year, our horror at being rejected can make us take either of two attitudes: defiance—we want to defend ourselves and our record; or exaggeration—the boss is right, we don't deserve a raise. Both responses involve "all or nothing" thinking. We are either a saint or the devil, excellent at what we do or incompetent. All or nothing thinking is a weak foundation for our sense of identity and makes us vulnerable to every little criticism. But this debilitating type of thinking, which particularly comes into play in difficult conversations, is not based on reality. Rarely are we one extreme or the other. These reactions oversimplify the world.

The answer is to "complexify" our identity—appreciate that while we may have come up short on some projects this year, on several others we were outstanding, and overall our performance is such that we believe we deserve a raise. Remember that difficult conversations are a fantastic opportunity to get closer to the truth, to become learning experiences without the usual emotional charge. Instead of going in there to deliver our message, "I want a raise," in the context of the interview with our boss we can say, "I wonder if it would make sense if my salary was increased?" It's not a demand, so the boss does not become defensive, and we are not vulnerable to rejection either. We are both exploring, getting information about the situation, so whatever is the outcome neither will feel hijacked and at the very least we will have learnt something.

Final comments

We have only touched on some of the issues and techniques raised in *Difficult Conversations*. It is a book to keep and refer to often whenever you have an important matter to raise with someone. Given that it was written by three people it flows well, and there are plenty of real examples to keep things interesting. One omission is the lack of a bibliography, even though the authors are clearly influenced by many thinkers who have gone before them.

The most refreshing aspect of *Difficult Conversations* is the absence of any manipulative techniques. Its aim is not to teach us how to psychologically trick people into agreeing to what we want, but to change the whole atmosphere of important encounters so that curiosity about each party's needs and desires leads to new appreciation and understanding. As wrong assumptions and blame are taken out of the equation, what is left is the truth.

Douglas Stone, Bruce Patton, Sheila Heen

Stone is a lecturer on law at Harvard Law School and is a partner in Triad, a consulting firm specializing in leadership, negotiation, and communication. He has worked as a mediator in South Africa, Cyprus, Colombia, and Ethiopia, and consulted to the World Health Organization.

Patton is deputy director of the Harvard Negotiation Project and founder of Vantage, a consulting firm. He has also played key roles in international negotiation efforts, including the process leading up to the dismantling of apartheid in South Africa, and talks between the United States and Iran during the 1980 hostage crisis. He co-wrote with Roger Fisher and William Ury the second edition of Getting to Yes: Negotiating Agreement Without Giving In *(1991).*

Heen is a lecturer on law at Harvard Law School and, as well as consulting work with corporate clients, has helped in resolving conflicts between Greek and Turkish Cypriots, and mediated in industrial disputes.

Darkness Visible

"In rereading, for the first time in years, sequences from my novels—passages where my heroines have lurched down the pathways towards doom—I was stunned to perceive how accurately I had created the landscape of depression in the minds of these young women... Thus depression, when it finally came to me, was in fact no stranger, not even a visitor unannounced; it had been tapping at my door for decades."

"Even those for whom any kind of therapy is a futile exercise can look forward to the eventual passing of the storm. If they survive the storm itself, its fury almost always fades and then disappears. Mysterious in its coming, mysterious in its going, the affliction runs its course, and one finds peace."

In a nutshell

Depression can afflict anyone, and its causes are sometimes mysterious.

In a similar vein
David D. Burns *Feeling Good* (p 58)
R. D. Laing *The Divided Self* (p 186)
Robert E. Thayer *The Origin of Everyday Moods* (p 284)

CHAPTER 49

William Styron

t was while visiting Paris in December 1985 that American novelist William Styron finally realized he was suffering from a depressive illness. He was in the city in order to accept a major award, an experience he would normally have found a boost to his ego and enjoyed. But in the mists of his mental darkness, the presentation and gala dinner that followed became an excruciating ordeal. Having to pretend he was normal made it even worse. By the evening, when he had a dinner with his publisher, he could not manage even a forced smile, and could only think of getting back to the United States to see a psychiatrist.

Darkness Visible: A Memoir of Madness is Styron's classic account of his battle with depression. Originally a lecture delivered to The Johns Hopkins University School of Medicine, and then published as an acclaimed essay in *Vanity Fair* magazine, its literary quality makes it stand out from the hundreds of other titles on the subject.

Describing the indescribable

Styron notes that depression is different to other maladies in that, if you have never experienced it, you cannot imagine what it is like—so different to "the blues" or regular doldrums that affect most people in the course of normal life. That it is not describable to others has only increased the mystery and taboo around it, for if everyone could understand what it was like, there would be no shame involved. Sympathy is not really the same as understanding.

Styron's best approximation of the feeling is that of drowning or suffocation, but he admits even that is not quite right. One becomes like a zombie, still able to walk and talk but no longer feeling quite human. Among depression's features Styron identifies:

❖ Intense self-hatred and feelings of worthlessness.
❖ Thoughts or fantasies of suicide.
❖ Insomnia.
❖ Confusion, inability to focus, memory lapses.
❖ Hypochondria—the mind's way of not facing up to its own disintegration, blaming the body.
❖ Loss of libido and appetite.

Styron also notes the idiosyncratic nature of the "black dog." For instance, most sufferers begin the day poorly, often unable to get out of bed, and their mood lightens only as the day goes on. Styron seemed to be the opposite, usually quite "together" in the morning, but by the afternoon dark clouds had gathered and he experienced almost unbearable feelings and thoughts into the evening. Only some time after the evening meal did he again experience some respite. Normally a good sleeper, he had to take a prescription tranquilizer to snatch even two to three hours of slumber. He discovered that depression ebbs or becomes rampant according to the hour of the day because physiologically it involves a disruption of the circadian rhythms, which play a strong part in daily mood cycles.

Styron also reports a "helpless stupor" in which normal thinking and logic disappear. Taken to its extreme, depression literally turns people mad. Stress on the neurotransmitters causes a depletion of the brain chemicals norepinephrine and serotonin and an increase of the hormone cortisol. These chemical and hormonal imbalances create "an organ in convulsion" that makes the person feel stricken. He rues the fact that the word "brainstorm" has already been taken in the English language, because the image of a storm raging inside the brain conveys its violent power—fierce, seemingly unrelenting, clouding everything.

The greatest taboo

Styron writes about his literary inspiration, Albert Camus, whose novels he had discovered relatively late. He had actually arranged to meet Camus when the news came of the novelist's death. Despite never knowing him, Styron felt a great loss. Camus had often battled depression, and many of his novels explore the theme of suicide.

Styron devotes a fair portion of *Darkness Visible* to discussing people he knows who suffered from depression. He wonders how his friend Romain Gary, a distinguished author, former diplomat, *bon vivant*, and womanizer, could become a person who put a bullet to his brain? If someone like this could decide that life was not worth living, could it not happen to anyone?

Families of the dead find it hard to accept that their relative could take their own life. The reason we have a taboo against suicide is that we believe that it indicates cowardice—taking the easy way out—when in fact it is more about an inability to endure the pain of being alive any longer. We forgive people who kill themselves to end physical pain, yet not mental distress.

These days, Styron notes, with greater care and awareness about the condition most people do not end up killing themselves as a result of depression. But if they do, he suggests, "there should be no more reproof attached than to the victims of terminal cancer."

Styron observes that artistic types have a greater susceptibility to depression, hence the long roll call of their suicides, including Hart Crane, Vincent van Gogh, Virginia Woolf, Ernest Hemingway, Diane Arbus, and Marth

Rothko. Vladimir Mayakovsky, a Russian poet, condemned his countryman Sergei Esenin's suicide, only to take his own life a few years later. What message can we take from this? That we should never be judgmental, because those left alive cannot feel or even imagine how people who commit suicide really feel.

Mysterious causes

Part of the reason that depression can be difficult to treat is that it often has no single identifiable cause. Genetics, chemical imbalances, and past experience and behavior may all be important, and to treat one aspect may leave out another. One can attribute a major depression to a particular crisis, but as Styron notes, most people who go through bad things come out remarkably OK and do not descend into a spiral of illness. This suggests that, rather than the event being the cause, it may simply have been a trigger for an underlying depressive potential lying dormant.

This is what Styron believes happened with him: He gave up drinking for health reasons and this allowed his demons, no longer deadened by alcohol, to fly out of their cave. With his shield against a sort of permanent anxiety gone, he had to feel everything he had narcotized into submission. His first sign of depression was a sort of deadness to things normally delightful to him—walking his dogs in the woods or summer on Martha's Vineyard. He turned in on himself, unable to escape a constant barrage of painful thoughts.

It may seem obvious, but Styron points to the one element underpinning all depression: loss, whether fear of abandonment, or of being alone, or of losing loved ones. In Styron's case this seemed correct, as his mother died when he was 13, an early trauma that gave him a deep and early experience of loss. In *Darkness Visible* he comes to the view that his actual event of depression was simply the manifestation of a deeper, lifelong anxiety. He realizes that similar to Camus, depression and suicide had been constant themes in his books, and reflects that his depression, "when it finally came to me, was in fact no stranger, not even a visitor unannounced; it had been tapping at my door for decades."

He mentions that his father, a shipyard engineer, was also a sufferer. Between the genetic heritage, the early death of his mother, and his artistic sensibility, Styron was probably a prime candidate for the disease.

If all else fails, time heals

Psychotherapy does not do much for people in an advanced staged of depression, and Styron found that neither it nor drugs did anything to alleviate his condition. Despite the claims of many doctors, he knew that for serious depression there is no fast-acting remedy. Antidepressants or cognitive therapy, or a combination of them, may do the job of healing the tortured mind, but neither can be fully depended on. Despite many advances in treatment, there is no magic bullet, no quick-acting vaccine. Depression's causes remain somewhat of a mystery.

The dénouement of Styron's depression came only after he admitted himself to hospital. He believes that the anonymous stability of the medical routine saved his life, and he wished he had done it sooner. "For me," he writes, "the real healers were seclusion and time."

What he took from the experience was a knowledge that although depression seems permanent to the sufferer, it is actually like a storm whose fury always dies out; as long as you can just stay alive you will defeat it. He recalls the theme of Camus's *The Myth of Sisyphus* that we still have an obligation to try to survive, even if there is an absence of hope. Easier said than done, yet nearly all who suffer depression come out the other side relatively unscathed. For those who do come through, a uniquely light or joyous feeling awaits.

Final comments

Styron believes that much of the literature around depression is "breezily optimistic." Some patients respond well to certain drugs, or certain forms of therapy, but we are not so far advanced in our knowledge that definite promises can be made. Sufferers are naturally eager to believe in a quick salvation, but it only sets them up for disappointment when there is no speedy alleviation of the misery. Styron was writing over 15 years ago, but the situation has not changed.

When you think that depression is a disease that distorts or brings to the fore issues to do with our very sense of self, surely it is not surprising that cures are not instant. Depression does involve imbalances of brain chemicals and may also result from negative internal conversations, but beyond this it is about the psyche or overall sense of self. Styron, for instance, was only able to make sense of his depressive bouts by reflecting on the entirety of his life. Some of the causes were indeed physical—a withdrawal from alcohol, and an incorrect dosage of tranquilizers—but they went deeper to questions about his identity and past.

Only 84 pages long, *Darkness Visible* will not take you long to read but could be a great teacher. Although so many creative types have succumbed to depression, it is also their responsibility to try to "describe the indescribable," and Styron's attempt is one of the best. Rather than depressing the reader, his essay is strangely uplifting.

William Styron

Born in 1925 in Newport News, Virginia, Styron was able to read at an early age and published many short stories in his school newspaper.

He obtained a BA degree from Duke University, and the following year joined the US Marine Corps, serving as first lieutenant during the last two years of the Second World War. After his discharge he settled in New York, working for the trade division of publisher McGraw-Hill and taking writing classes at the New School for Social Research. He lived in Paris in the early 1950s, where he helped to establish the legendary literary journal Paris Review.

His first novel, Lie Down in Darkness *(1951), which followed the suicidal descent of a young woman, was a literary sensation and was awarded the American Academy's Prix de Rome. Other books include the Pulitzer Prize-winning* The Confessions of Nat Turner *(1967), and the bestseller and American Book Award winner* Sophie's Choice *(1979), made into a film starring Meryl Streep. The award mentioned in* Darkness Visible *was the Prix Mondial Cino del Duca, given annually to an artist or scientist who has made a significant contribution to humanism. Styron died in 2006.*

The Origin of Everyday Moods

"If we think of our moods as emphasizing meaning and enhancing or reducing the pleasure in our lives, we can understand how central they really are. In this respect, they are more important than daily activities, money, status, and even personal relationships because these things are usually filtered through our moods. In many ways, our moods are at the core of our being."

In a nutshell

Given their effect on our quality of life, it is vital that we discover what may cause our moods.

In a similar vein
David D. Burns *Feeling Good* (p 58)
Martin Seligman *Authentic Happiness* (p 254)

CHAPTER 50

Robert E. Thayer

The conventional wisdom is that moods are caused by stress or thoughts, usually our reactions to particular events or pieces of information. A success can put us in a good mood, a failure in a bad mood. While this is true, it is only part of the mood equation.

According to psychologist Robert Thayer, moods are also related to how much sleep we have had, how generally healthy or fit we are, daily cycles or circadian rhythms, what we have eaten, and whether or not we have just exercised.

Thayer has been studying mood since the 1970s and is considered the foremost expert on the subject. Convinced by his students to go beyond his more academic writings and produce a book on the practical applications of his theory, the result was the very readable *The Origin of Everyday Moods: Managing Energy, Tension, and Stress*.

Anatomy of a mood

Thayer defines a mood as "a background feeling that persists over time." Moods can be distinguished from emotions in that, while emotions always have an identifiable cause, moods often do not. They have been so little studied compared to emotions because of their ephemeral and elusive nature—unlike emotions, they can seem to come and go like the wind, seemingly without any trigger. Why is this so?

While emotions are generally phenomena tied to what goes on in the brain, moods result from processes going on in both mind *and* body, with each affecting the other in complex ways. Thayer likens a mood to a thermometer that takes a reading of our current psychological and physiological condition. It exists for a biological purpose—to tell us when we are in danger or should lie low and regroup, or when we are in a comfort zone and ready for action.

Thayer's research led him to the conclusion that most of our moods emerge out of two basic dimensions: energy and tension. A depressed mood is characterized by low energy and high tension (with accompanying feelings of hopelessness), while an optimistic mood involves high energy and low tension (we feel we can accomplish much and are enthusiastic). In short, we can't separate how our body feels from how our mind feels. If we are physically tired we are also likely to feel edgy, distracted, or "brain dead." Similarly, if we are depressed, we will not feel like energizing ourselves through exercise.

The four basic moods

Thayer argues that all moods can be understood according to four basic states along the energy–tension spectrum.

- ❖ *Calm-energy*—a feel-good state, confident, energetic, optimistic. The ideal state for working; most people have their greatest supply of calm-energy in the morning. High energy, low tension.
- ❖ *Calm-tiredness*—the feeling we have just before going to bed: not stressed, but not energetic either. Low energy, low tension.
- ❖ *Tense-energy*—the feeling we have when racing to a deadline. A sense of urgency is expressed in raised heart rate, thanks to the release of adrenalin, and skeletal-muscular tightness. In an evolutionary biology sense, the body's "fight or flight" mode. High energy, high tension.
- ❖ *Tense-tiredness*—"when you feel all used up," as Thayer puts it. Physical tiredness combines with nervous anxiety or tension, negative thoughts. Low energy, high tension. For most people, experienced in the afternoon. A natural low point often exacerbated by lack of sleep the night before, junk food, and use of stimulants like caffeine.

Daily rhythms

The circadian rhythm is the daily ebb and flow of our natural physical and mental energies. Our energy rises during the morning and reaches a peak around noon or 1 p.m., declines during the afternoon, rises again as a mini-peak in the early evening, then declines again until bedtime. While most of us are "morning people," within the basic circadian rhythm there are many individual variations: Some people get more energetic as the day goes on, and this is more true of extraverts than introverts. However, for the average person the peak of tense-tiredness comes around 4 p.m., and between 9 and 11 p.m. a decrease in natural energy leads to a rise in tension, the tense-tired state, which results in negative feelings (a low or bad mood).

When people are trying to stop smoking, after a few days it is rarely the actual withdrawal from the nicotine that prompts a relapse, it is the daily feelings of stress that spark the psychological need to reduce the stress and tension. Relapse to addictions, plus the binging and purging of bulimics, tends to happen in the afternoons when people's energy is low and they need relief from tension (4.34 p.m. is the average weak point). Awareness of the times when we are most likely to relapse can obviously help us build exercise or some other healthy mood regulator into our daily routine.

Regulating our moods

When feeling a bit down or low in energy, we may:

❖ Seek social interaction or withdraw from people (depending on whether we are an introvert or extravert).
❖ Try to control our thoughts (e.g., positive thinking).
❖ Engage in a pleasant activity such as a hobby or shopping, or lighten the feeling with humor.
❖ Read a book or magazine.
❖ Drink alcohol.
❖ Have a cigarette.
❖ Eat a chocolate bar or cake.
❖ Drink coffee.
❖ Watch television.

Exercise, the data shows, is the best mood regulator. A brisk walk of 5–15 minutes when we are feeling tired paradoxically restores our spirits and can energize us for up to two hours.

Another excellent, healthy mood regulator is social interaction. Phoning or talking to a friend can lower stress significantly. Another is listening to music, which ranks high on surveys for reducing tension and increasing energy.

Food

The effects of what we eat on our mood are difficult to measure scientifically. However, Thayer published a study demonstrating the paradoxical effects of eating sugary snacks: They improve mood in the short term, but also give us a "letdown" an hour or two later, both in terms of a reduction in energy and a rise in tension.

Mood is connected to overeating and dieting, and Thayer suggests that people who consume a lot of sugar get into further bad eating patterns, because the drops in energy they create lead to the need for more snacks.

Health

Healthy people generally have high energy levels. Ill people have low energy. Research shows that on days when people rate themselves as in a generally negative mood, their immune system response is not as effective as on days when they are in a positive frame of mind.

Sleep

Mood is significantly affected by how much sleep we have had, to the extent that sleep deprivation over several nights can lead to depression.

Other mood affecters include:

❖ Nicotine—generates calm-energy on a temporary basis, which is perhaps why it is so addictive. Makes us enthused but also relaxed—briefly.

❖ Alcohol—a depressant, but at first provides more energy (parties show this dynamic).

❖ Caffeine—produces tense-energy, but people seem to desire this. Thayer hypothesizes that while calm-energy is the most desirable state, the tense-energy effect that coffee or cola produces is a good alternative.

❖ Weather—SAD (seasonal affective disorder) or winter depression, which can be alleviated by bright light or melatonin.

Why are moods so important?

Thayer did an experiment with people who all had a significant personal problem. He asked them to rate how they saw the problem at five different times in the day. Intriguingly, after a 10-day rating period it emerged that the same problem was perceived as less serious in the morning than in the afternoon. And whenever a person was in a state of tense-tiredness, the problem loomed larger.

Therefore, if at all possible, it is best not to consider your problems in times of tense-tiredness, as they will seem worse than they actually are. At the same time, our thoughts in a period of high energy may make us more optimistic than the reality calls for. Current energy levels do not simply affect our mood, but also what we feel we will be capable of in the future—so we need to be aware of how our energy levels influence our ability to make judgments.

Thayer's remarkable point is that moods are in fact "more important than daily activities, money, status, and even personal relationships," because we experience all of these through the filter of whatever mood we are in. If we are in a dark mood, none of our achievements or our wealth matter to us; in a positive mood, even the worst circumstances seem manageable.

Final comments

The Origin of Everyday Moods provides practical pointers on how to be more self-aware about your moods and vulnerable points of tense-tiredness, and with that knowledge it can help you to choose healthier ways of mood regulation. You may learn that it is best not to make major life decisions at 3 in the morning, a time when notoriously dark thoughts are to be had, or to hold off that confrontation with a co-worker at 4 in the afternoon, when your energy level has dropped and feelings of tension have risen.

More than the actual tips on the danger times for tense-tiredness, the value of Thayer's book is in showing us just how much mood is like an invisible bubble that surrounds us. While on the surface moods are of no great import, Thayer shows how they are in fact basic to our whole being. Other psychological theories may help us to consider our lives as a whole, but the study of mood is arguably more useful, since it concerns how we are feeling on an hour-by-hour basis—and life, after all, is lived in the present.

Robert E. Thayer

Robert Thayer has been a professor of psychology at California State University, Long Beach, since 1973. He received a BA at the University of Redlands, and his PhD from the University of Rochester.

In addition to many frequently cited academic articles, he is the author of The Biopsychology of Mood and Arousal *(1989) and* Calm Energy: How People Regulate Mood with Food and Exercise *(2001).*

50 More Classics

1 **Gordon Allport** *The Nature of Prejudice* (1954)
Standard work on the roots of discrimination that inspired Martin Luther King and Malcom X.

2 **Virginia Axline** *Dibs in Search of Self* (1964)
Bestselling classic of child therapy about a withdrawn boy's slow journey toward normal relations with the world.

3 **Albert Bandura** *Self-Efficacy: The Exercise of Control* (1997)
How expectations of what we can achieve influence what we actually do achieve, by a leading contemporary psychologist.

4 **Aaron T. Beck** *Cognitive Therapy and the Emotional Disorders* (1979)
Landmark work on how erroneous thinking can lead to depression, from the founder of cognitive therapy.

5 **Ernest Becker** *The Denial of Death* (1973)
Pulitzer Prize-winning discussion of the lengths that people go to to deny their own mortality. Very Freudian but still a superb read.

6 **Bruno Bettelheim** *The Uses of Enchantment: The Meaning and Importance of Fairy Tales* (1976)
Popular and insightful work into the psychology of fairy tales.

7 **Alfred Binet & Theodore Simon** *The Development of Intelligence in Children* (1916)
Key work from the pioneers of intelligence testing.

8 **John Bradshaw** *Homecoming: Reclaiming and Championing Your Inner Child* (1990)
Practical application of Erikson's stages of human development, showing how adult hang-ups have their roots in earlier turning points not being properly brought to a conclusion. By reclaiming your "inner child," you can move on as an adult.

9 **John Bowlby** *Attachment* (1969)
The first in a trilogy exploring the mother–child relationship that established "attachment behavior" as an area of psychology.

10 **Joseph Breuer & Sigmund Freud** *Studies on Hysteria* (1895)
A book of case studies that was a precursor to psychoanalysis. Its theory that bizarre hysterical symptoms often result from suppressed painful memories was later disowned by Freud.

11 **Jerome Bruner** *Acts of Meaning: Four Lectures on Mind and Culture* (1990)
A founder of cognitive psychology argues for a model of the mind based on the creation of meaning rather than computational processing.

12 **Mary Whiton Calkins** *An Introduction to Psychology* (1901)
Worked with William James and was the first female president of the American Psychological Association (1905), yet was denied a PhD by Harvard University. Considered psychology to be the "science of the self."

13 **Antonio Damasio** *Descartes' Error: Emotion, Reason, and the Human Brain* (1994)
Prominent brain researcher's theory that debunks the separation of mind and body and shows how emotions form a vital part of rational judgment and decision making.

14 **Hermann Ebbinghaus** *Memory: A Contribution to Experimental Psychology* (1885)
Account of first ever experimental lab work into learning and memory, setting a high standard for future research.

15 **Leon Festinger** *Theory of Cognitive Dissonance* (1957)
Famous theory of how people try to maintain consistency in their beliefs, even when what they believe has been shown to be wrong.

16 **Eric Fromm** *Escape from Freedom* (1941)
Influential study on people's willingness to submit to fascist regimes, written before the full horror of Nazism became apparent.

17 **William Glasser** *Reality Therapy: A New Approach to Psychiatry* (1965)
Alternative approach to mental illness, resting on the idea that mental health means an acceptance of responsibility for one's life.

18 **Dennis Greenberger & Christine Padesky** *Mind Over Mood: Change How You Feel by Changing the Way You Think* (1995)
Popular work of powerful cognitive therapy techniques, not just for depressives.

19 **Robert D. Hare** *Without Conscience: The Disturbing World of the Psychopaths Among Us* (1993)
By the world's foremost sociopathic researcher, showing how sociopaths are aware of the difference between right and wrong yet have no guilt or remorse.

20 **Richard Herrnstein & Charles Murray** *The Bell Curve: Intelligence and Class Structure in American Life* (1994)
Caused storm of controversy in its contention that IQ differs according to race. Was wrapped within a broader theory that intelligence, rather than class background, has become the new predictor of economic success.

21 **Eric Kandel** *In Search of Memory: The Emergence of a New Science of Mind* (2006)
Nobel Prize-winning neuroscientist's compelling account of his 30 years' work to discover how nerve cells in the brain store memories. Interwoven with personal memories of Vienna under the Nazis and his family's escape to America.

22 **David Keirsey & Marilyn Bates** *Please Understand Me: Character and Temperament Types* (1978)
Bestselling personality typing work in the Jung/Briggs Myers tradition, which includes a "temperament sorter" to determine your type.

23 **Joseph Le Doux** *The Emotional Brain: The Mysterious Underpinnings of Emotional Life* (1996)
Leading neuroscientist's overview of how the emotional centers and circuits in the brain evolved to ensure our survival.

24 **Harriet Lerner** *The Dance of Anger: A Woman's Guide to Changing the Patterns of Intimate Relationships* (1985)
Popular work from an expert in female psychology that addresses the taboo of women's anger, its real sources, and its role in relationships.

25 **Daniel J. Levinson** *The Season's of a Man's Life* (1978)
In its day, groundbreaking work on the male adult life cycle that further developed Erik Erikson's theories. Levinson was a strong influence on Gail Sheehy (see p 260).

26 **Kurt Lewin** *Field Theory in Social Science* (1951)
Known as the father of social psychology, Lewin's field theory held that human behavior was the result of a combination between interactions with others (group dynamics) and inner characteristics.

27 **Elizabeth Loftus** *Eyewitness Testimony* (1979)
Forensic psychologist's attack on the reliability of eyewitness accounts in criminal trials. Also well known for her challenge to the validity of repressed memory syndrome.

28 **Konrad Lorenz** *On Aggression* (1963)
Nobel Prize winner's famous study of the "killer instinct" in humans, and the devastating results of our combination of irrationality and intelligence.

29 **Rollo May** *Love and Will* (1969)
Existential psychologist's powerful bestseller on the idea that love (or "Eros") and sex are two different drives. Love motivates our highest achievements, and the opposite of love is not hate but apathy.

30 **Douglas McGregor** *The Human Side of Enterprise* (1960)
Psychologist McGregor became a business guru through his categories of management styles into "Theory X" (directive control by bosses) and "Theory Y" (employees left to motivate themselves). Inspired by Abraham Maslow's humanistic psychology.

31 **Hugo Munsterberg** *Psychology and Crime* (1908)
German-born founder of experimental psychology invited to work at
Harvard with William James. Was a pioneer in industrial psychology (the
behavior of people in the work environment), criminal behavior, and film
theory.

32 **Richard Nesbitt** *The Geography of Thought: How Asians and Westerners
Think Differently... and Why* (2003)
Leading psychologist's surprising contention that Asian and Western people
think differently, challenging assumptions of universal behavior.

33 **Sylvia Plath** *The Bell Jar* (1963)
Plath's brilliant fictional (and autobiographical) account of a young
woman's mental breakdown remains compelling reading.

34 **Otto Rank** *The Trauma of Birth* (1924)
By one of Freud's original inner circle, describes the separation anxiety felt
after birth and how people spend their life trying to recreate the original
maternal connection.

35 **Wilhelm Reich** *Character Analysis* (1933)
Controversial Austrian psychoanalyst's theory that a person's overall character could be analyzed as opposed to specific neuroses, dreams, or mental
associations. Also contended that repressed psychosexual energy could take
on physical expression in the muscles and organs ("body armor").

36 **Flora Rheta Schreiber** *Sybil* (1973)
Compelling true story of a woman with 16 personalities and her fight to
become an integrated person. Sold millions of copies and scored a mention
on television show *Frasier*.

37 **Hermann Rorschach** *Psychodiagnostics: A Diagnostic Text Based on
Perception* (1921)
Presents the results of the Swiss psychiatrist's psychoanalysis of 400 mental
patients and normal subjects, based on his famous ink blot test.

38 **Thomas Szasz** *The Myth of Mental Illness* (1960)
Famous critique of psychiatry, suggesting that mental illness is in fact usu-
ally "problems in living." Linking modern psychiatric diagnoses to the
Inquisition, Szasz argued against any type of coercive treatment.

39 **Virginia Satir** *Peoplemaking* (1972)
Family systems therapist's influential exploration of family dynamics.

40 **Andrew Solomon** *The Noonday Demon: An Atlas of Depression* (2001)
Award-winning journey into all facets of depressive illness. Suggests depression will never be eradicated but rather is part of the human condition.

41 **Harry Stack Sullivan** *Interpersonal Theory of Psychiatry* (1953)
Maverick American psychiatrist's explanation of how the "self-system" or
personality is formed by our interpersonal relationships, as opposed to the
Freudian inner self.

42 **Deborah Tannen** *You Just Don't Understand: Women and Men in Conversation* (1990)
No. 1 bestseller by a linguistics professor on why communication can be so difficult between the genders. The first book to bring the subject to a wide audience.

43 **Lewis Terman** *The Measurement of Intelligence* (1916)
Pioneering cognitive psychologist and inventor of the Stanford-Binet IQ Test (an adaptation of the Binet-Simon test), who believed intelligence was inherited. Also did early work on gifted children.

44 **Edward Lee Thorndike** *Animal Intelligence* (1911)
American psychological pioneer who demonstrated how all animals learn, using his famous cats in puzzle boxes.

45 **Edward B. Titchener** *Experimental Psychology* (four volumes, 1901–05)
Major work of a student of Wilhelm Wundt who helped found the first psychology laboratory in America, at Cornell University.

46 **John B. Watson** *Behaviorism* (1924)
A readable book that established the behaviorist school of psychology.

47 **Max Wertheimer** *Productive Thinking* (1945)
German-American Gestalt psychologist's contribution to the art of thinking; specifically, seeing the underlying structure of the problem and taking account of anomalies.

48 **Robert Wright** *The Moral Animal: Why We Are the Way We Are* (1995)
Influential work of evolutionary psychology that reveals the genetic strategies behind human behaviors, including monogamy, altruism, sibling rivalry, and office politics.

49 **Wilhelm Wundt** *Principles of Physiological Psychology* (1873–74)
The book that made Wundt the dominant figure in the new science of psychology. Translated into English by Edward Titchener in 1904.

50 **Irvin D Yalom** *Love's Executioner: and Other Tales of Psychotherapy* (1989)
Frank exploration of the relationship between psychotherapist and patient, with fascinating case histories.

Chronological list of titles

William James *The Principles of Psychology* (1890)
Sigmund Freud *The Interpretation of Dreams* (1900)
Jean Piaget *The Language and Thought of the Child* (1923)
Alfred Adler *Understanding Human Nature* (1927)
Ivan Pavlov *Conditioned Reflexes: An Investigation of the Physiological Activity of the Cerebral Cortex* (1927)
Anna Freud *The Ego and the Mechanisms of Defence* (1936)
Karen Horney *Our Inner Conflicts: A Constructive Theory of Neurosis* (1945)
Hans Eysenck *Dimensions of Personality* (1947)
Eric Hoffer *The True Believer: Thoughts on the Nature of Mass Movements* (1951)
Fritz Perls *Gestalt Therapy: Excitement and Growth in the Human Personality* (1951)
Alfred Kinsey *Sexual Behavior in the Human Female* (1953)
Melanie Klein *Envy and Gratitude* (1957)
Erik Erikson *Young Man Luther: A Study in Psychoanalysis and History* (1958)
Harry Harlow *The Nature of Love* (1958)
R. D. Laing *The Divided Self: A Study of Sanity and Madness* (1960)
Albert Ellis & Robert A. Harper *A Guide to Rational Living* (1961)
Carl Rogers *On Becoming a Person: A Therapist's View of Psychotherapy* (1961)
Eric Berne *Games People Play: The Psychology of Human Relationships* (1964)
Thomas A. Harris *I'm OK — You're OK* (1967)
Carl Jung *The Archetypes and the Collective Unconscious* (1968)
Nathaniel Branden *The Psychology of Self-Esteem* (1969)
Viktor Frankl *The Will to Meaning: Foundations and Applications of Logotherapy* (1969)
Edward de Bono *Lateral Thinking: Creativity Step by Step* (1970)
Oliver Sacks *The Man Who Mistook His Wife for a Hat: And Other Clinical Tales* (1970)
Abraham Maslow *The Farther Reaches of Human Nature* (1971)
B. F. Skinner *Beyond Freedom and Dignity* (1971)
Gail Sheehy *Passages: Predictable Crises of Adult Life* (1974)
Stanley Milgram *Obedience to Authority: An Experimental View* (1976)
Robert Bolton *People Skills: How to Assert Yourself, Listen to Others, and Resolve Conflicts* (1979)
Isabel Briggs Myers *Gifts Differing: Understanding Personality Type* (1980)
David D. Burns *Feeling Good: The New Mood Therapy* (1980)

Milton Erickson (by Sidney Rosen) *My Voice Will Go With You: The Teaching Tales of Milton H. Erickson, M.D.* (1982)

Howard Gardner *Frames of Mind: The Theory of Multiple Intelligences* (1983)

Robert Cialdini *Influence: The Psychology of Persuasion* (1984)

Anne Moir & David Jessel *Brainsex: The Real Difference Between Men and Women* (1989)

William Styron *Darkness Visible: A Memoir of Madness* (1990)

Mihaly Csikszentmihalyi *Creativity: Flow and the Psychology of Discovery and Invention* (1996)

Robert E. Thayer *The Origin of Everyday Moods: Managing Energy, Tension, and Stress* (1996)

Gavin de Becker *The Gift of Fear: Survival Signals that Protect Us from Violence* (1997)

Susan Forward *Emotional Blackmail: When the People in Your Life Use Fear, Obligation, and Guilt to Manipulate You* (1997)

Daniel Goleman *Working with Emotional Intelligence* (1998)

V. S. Ramachandran *Phantoms in the Brain: Probing the Mysteries of the Human Mind* (1998)

John M. Gottman *The Seven Principles for Making Marriage Work* (1999)

Douglas Stone, Bruce Patton, & Sheila Heen *Difficult Conversations: How to Discuss What Matters Most* (1999)

Steven Pinker *The Blank Slate: The Modern Denial of Human Nature* (2002)

Martin Seligman *Authentic Happiness: Using the New Positive Psychology to Realize Your Potential for Lasting Fulfilment* (2002)

Barry Schwartz *The Paradox of Choice: Why More Is Less* (2004)

Malcolm Gladwell *Blink: The Power of Thinking Without Thinking* (2005)

Louann Brizendine *The Female Brain* (2006)

Daniel Gilbert *Stumbling on Happiness* (2006)

Credits

The editions below were those used in researching the book. Original publication dates are stated in each of the 50 commentaries.

Adler, A. (1992) *Understanding Human Nature*, Oxford: Oneworld.
de Becker, G. (1997) *The Gift of Fear: Survival Signals that Protect Us from Violence*, New York: Random House.
Berne, E. (1964) *Games People Play: The Psychology of Human Relationships*, London: Penguin.
Bolton, R. (1986) *People Skills: How to Assert Yourself, Listen to Others, and Resolve Conflicts*, New York: Prentice Hall.
de Bono, E. (1970) *Lateral Thinking*, London: Penguin.
Branden, N. (2001) *The Psychology of Self-Esteem*, New York: Wiley.
Briggs Myers, I. with Myers, P. (1995) *Gifts Differing: Understanding Personality Type*, Palo Alto, CA: Davies-Black.
Brizendine, L. (2006) *The Female Brain*, New York: Morgan Road.
Burns, D. (1980) *Feeling Good: The New Mood Therapy*, New York: William Morrow.
Cialdini, R. (1993) *Influence: The Psychology of Persuasion*, New York: William Morrow.
Csikszentmihalyi, M. (1996) *Creativity: Flow and the Psychology of Discovery and Invention*, New York: HarperCollins.
Ellis, A. & Harper, R. (1974) *A Guide to Rational Living*, Los Angeles: Wilshire Book Company.
Erikson, E. (1958) *Young Man Luther: A Study in Psychoanalysis and History*, London: Faber and Faber.
Eysenck, H.J. (1966) *Dimensions of Personality*, London: Routledge & Kegan Paul.
Forward, S. (1997) *Emotional Blackmail: When the People in Your Life Use Fear, Obligation and Guilt to Manipulate You*, London: Transworld.
Frankl, V. (1969) *The Will to Meaning: Foundations and Applications of Logotherapy*, London: Meridian.
Freud, A. (1948) *The Ego and the Mechanisms of Defence*, London: The Hogarth Press.
Freud, S. (trans. Joyce Crick) (1990) *The Interpretation of Dreams*, Oxford: Oxford University Press.
Gardner, H. (1983) *Frames of Mind: The Theory of Multiple Intelligences*, New York: Basic Books.

Gilbert, D. (2006) *Stumbling on Happiness*, London: HarperCollins.

Gladwell, M. (2005) *Blink: The Power of Thinking Without Thinking*, London: Penguin.

Goleman, D. (1998) *Working with Emotional Intelligence*, London: Bloomsbury.

Gottman, J. & Silver, N. (1999) *The Seven Principles for Making Marriage Work*, London: Orion.

Harlow, H. (1958) "The Nature of Love," *American Psychologist*, 13: 573–685. Also at http://psychclassics.yorku.ca/Harlow/love.htm.

Harris, T.A. (1973) *I'm OK—You're OK*, New York: Arrow.

Hoffer, E. (1980) *The True Believer: Thoughts on the Nature of Mass Movements*, Chicago: Time-Life Books.

Horney, K (1957) *Our Inner Conflicts*, London: Routledge & Kegan Paul.

James, W. (1950) *The Principles of Psychology, Vols I & II*, Mineola, NY: Dover.

Jung, C. G. (1968) (trans. R. F. C. Hull) *The Archetypes and the Collective Unconscious*, Princeton University Press.

Kinsey, A. (1953) *Sexual Behavior in the Human Female*, Philadelphia: Saunders.

Klein, M. (1975) *Envy and Gratitude: And Other Works 1946–1963*, London: Vintage.

Laing, R. D. (1960) *The Divided Self: An Existential Study in Sanity and Madness*, London: Penguin.

Maslow, A. (1976) *The Farther Reaches of Human Nature*, London: Penguin.

Milgram, S. (1974) *Obedience to Authority*, New York: HarperCollins.

Moir, A. & Jessel, D. (1989) *Brainsex: The Real Difference Between Men and Women*, London: Mandarin.

Pavlov, I. (2003) *Conditioned Reflexes*, Mineola, NY: Dover.

Perls, F., Hefferline, R., & Goodman, P. (1951) *Gestalt Therapy: Excitement and Growth in the Human Personality*, London: Souvenir.

Piaget, J. (1959) *The Language and Thought of the Child*, London: Routledge & Kegan Paul.

Pinker, S. (2003) *The Blank Slate: The Modern Denial of Human Nature*, London: Penguin.

Ramachandran, V. S., & Blakeslee, S. (1998) *Phantoms in the Brain: Probing the Mysteries of the Human Mind*, New York: HarperCollins.

Rogers, C. (1961) *On Becoming a Person*, Boston: Houghton Mifflin.

Rosen, S. (ed.) (1982) *My Voice Will Go With You: The Teaching Tales of Milton H. Erickson*, New York: WW Norton.

Sacks, O. (1985) *The Man Who Mistook His Wife for a Hat: And Other Clinical Tales*, London: Pan Macmillan.

Schwartz, B. (2004) *The Paradox of Choice: Why More Is Less*, New York: HarperCollins.

Seligman, M. (2003) *Authentic Happiness*, London: Nicholas Brealey/New York: Free Press.

Sheehy, G. (1976) *Passages: Predictable Crises of Adult Life*, New York: Bantam.

Skinner, B.F. (1971) *Beyond Freedom and Dignity*, Indianapolis: Hackett.

Stone, D., Patton, B., & Heen, S. (1999) *Difficult Conversations: How to Discuss What Matters Most*, New York: Viking.

Styron, W. (1990) *Darkness Visible: A Memoir of Madness*, New York: Vintage.

Thayer, R. (1996) *The Origin of Everyday Moods*, Oxford: Oxford University Press.

THE BESTSELLING "50 CLASSICS" SERIES BY TOM BUTLER-BOWDON

50 Prosperity Classics
Attract It, Create It, Manage It, Share It
Wisdom from the best books on wealth creation and abundance

"A terrific compendium of the best ever books written on the sources of prosperity, from famous classics to off-beat unknowns, distilled to the point of joyous clarity."
—Richard Koch, author of *The 80/20 Principle*

Discover how to make money and make it work for you—and find out how creating wealth can lead to fulfilling your personal potential and gaining peace of mind. *50 Prosperity Classics* provides a unique overview of the landmark titles on wealth creation and abundance.

Understand what prosperity is and discover how to:

◆ ATTRACT IT with the power of Rhonda Byrne's *The Secret*, Charles Fillmore's *Prosperity* and Napoleon Hill's *The Master-Key to Riches*

◆ CREATE IT with the strategies of Richard Branson, Bill Gates, Conrad Hilton, Anita Roddick and Donald Trump

◆ MANAGE IT with insights from Benjamin Graham's *The Intelligent Investor*, Suze Orman's *Women and Money*, Dave Ramsey's *Financial Peace Revisited* and Peter Lynch's *One Up on Wall Street*

◆ SHARE IT with inspiration from Andrew Carnegie's *The Gospel of Wealth*, Paul Hawken's *Natural Capitalism* and Lynne Twist's *The Soul of Money*

£12.99 UK/$19.95 US PB Original 320pp ISBN 978-1-85788-504-0

For details, discount information or to request a free catalogue, please visit www.nicholasbrealey.com